After John Jumped

Eileen Bellew

AFTER JOHN JUMPED

Eileen Bellew

Published 2026 by True Blue Press, Pearl River, NY
ISBN: 979-8-9949335-0-3 (Hardcover)
ISBN: 979-8-9949335-1-0 (Paperback)
ISBN: 979-8-9949335-2-7 (eBook)
Library of Congress: 2026904548

Cover design: Lisa Lucca, Eileen Bellew, and the Bellew Family
Interior design and cover production: JohnEdgar.design
Photographs provided by Eileen Bellew

Dedication

For Brielle, Jack, Katreana, and Kieran,

to whom I wrote this book,

in hopes you will understand how we got here.

And for John… until we meet again.

Table of Contents

Dedication V

Vocabulary Terms IX

Foreword XIII

Prologue XV

Part I
Before John Jumped

Chapter 1 Meeting John 3

Chapter 2 Before John Jumped 12

Chapter 3 Chance Meeting...................................... 18

Chapter 4 Raising Children..................................... 24

Chapter 5 The Day My World Ended........................ 45

Part II
After John Jumped

Chapter 6 Last Goodbye 53

Chapter 7 Waiting Room... 64

Chapter 8 The Memory Of Their Faces 71

Chapter 9 Funeral 80

Chapter 10 Meeting With Claire 99

Chapter 11 FDNY Support.. 107

Chapter 12 Competition Of Grief 115

Chapter 13 We're Not The Suing Type.................... 126

Chapter 14 Inner Demons.. 130

Chapter 15 Anti-Anxiety Medications 137

Chapter 16 Our New Relationship With John.......... 146

Chapter 17 The New Normal 155

Chapter 18 It Takes A Village… 165

Chapter 19 Christmas 173

Chapter 20 Plaque Dedication 180

Chapter 21 The Timeline Of Grief 188

Chapter 22 Living With An Anxietyholic 196

Part III
After After John Jumped

Chapter 23 Criminal Trial 213

Chapter 24 Dating 234

Chapter 25 Hawaiian Wedding 245

Chapter 26 Civil Trial 265

Chapter 27 Second Marriage 275

Chapter 28 Eileen 2.0 283

Chapter 29 Psychology Of Grief 287

Chapter 30 Positivity Of Tragedy 295

Epilogue When I Get To Heaven 304

Afterword 308

Gratitudes 310

About the Author 315

Vocabulary Terms
In The Fire Department

(CHRONOLOGICAL)

Turnout Gear - the firefighter's uniform, also called bunker gear. Helps to protect them from high heat

"The List" - refers to the numerical list created after a fire department entrance exam is taken. It gives a number to those eligible to be hired or promoted

24-hour Mutual Partner - the person in the firehouse who is in the opposite group number as you. He/She is the person you would be paired up with to create a 24-hour shift

Probie - newest member serving probation period

Truckie - firefighter who works in the Ladder or Truck side of the firehouse; they are responsible for ventilation, entry, and search

Engine - firefighters who are responsible for EMS calls, to stretch and operate the hose line, and put out the fires

Ladder - another name for Truck (see above)

Across The Floor - when a firefighter is detailed to the adjoining company for a shift

Onion Skin - someone who has an unofficial transfer pending an official transfer order

Brothers - how firefighters refer to their colleagues

First Due/Second Due - refers to which engine or truck will arrive first at a fire; this will determine the specific task they will perform at the fire

Hostage - a firefighter is ordered to work

Quarters, or The House - the firehouse they are working in

Chauffeur - the firefighter who drives the ladder truck to the fire and operates the aerial ladder

Personal Safety System (ropes) - ropes which enable safe ascent/descent for firefighters working at heights or in hazardous spaces

Means Of Egress - path to exit the room, apartment, or house

Mask Up - the order firefighters are given when they are entering a dangerous situation and need to put on the breathing apparatus

Rescue - specialized firehouse that only reports to working fires. They are trained to do technical skill work when needed

Slight Extension - fire has extended beyond the original fire area to a minor degree

Vibra Alert - mechanism in the breathing apparatus that warns firefighters they are running low on air

Burst Length - something causes a rupture in the hose line

Charged Line or Hose - a hose that has been supplied with water

Can - pressurized fire extinguisher

Flashover - condition where the contents of a room are heated to their ignition temperature causing a sudden, nearly simultaneous ignition

Mayday - critical radio call, signaling a firefighter is in immediate, life-threatening trouble, lost, trapped, injured, running out of air, requiring urgent rescue

Foreword

To you, "After John Jumped" may sound shocking and harsh. My kids didn't want me to use the phrase in my writing because it sounds like John died by suicide. I understand why they don't like it. Why would they want to remember the horrific events that took place on January 23, 2005? Why would they want to think about the horrors of an apartment fire that forced John to jump out of a fourth-story window? And why would they want me to continuously reference the event that killed their dad?

I tried for a long time not to use that language. But I have to. Those words invoke so much emotion in me. Those words define me and my life. Though I held his hand as twenty machines briefly kept him alive, the moment he jumped was when I lost John. I hope that, as he jumped into the cold air, his soul left his body before he landed, and he did not feel the impact of the fall. That is why "the jump" must be when we lost him. To consider anything else is unimaginable. There will always be life before the jump and life after the jump.

It represents where I feel the dividing line in my life is. I could sugarcoat it and write "when John died" or "when John passed away," but it won't help you understand the anguish and pain that physically sits in my chest when I think about that day. It won't help you understand John's agony and the torment my mind goes through thinking about it. There is no day I don't think about John and his jumping. I understand why he had to do it, but I am haunted daily, wondering what happened seconds before he jumped. I only know what happened after. So when I write "After John Jumped," understand that I am referencing my new beginning—a beginning I did not choose.

<h1 style="text-align:center">Prologue</h1>

The dread starts right after Christmas. As I turn the calendar, the day stares back at me: January 23rd. *Black Sunday.* I think back to the days leading up to that bitterly cold morning in 2005, reminding myself of every second I had with John, as if I could have changed the outcome. I can still recall every minute of that day, the physical and mental impact it had on my body and mind.

As the morning's moments unfolded, my body started taking on blows like a fighter in the ring right before a knock-out—first, the gut, then a stab straight into my heart. The saying "suffered from a broken heart" started to reel itself right there in my living room. Heart cells that loved so deeply, felt so much for one man, a genuine soul mate, were slowly destroyed by every minute of that morning. I'm sure it took years off my life. Not only did my heart get destroyed, but my brain started re-wiring itself, so I was physically not the same person as I was before. My brain's neurons went from a grid of pathways that moved in an organized manner to a chaotic traffic jam, like cars driving at eighty miles an hour on black ice.

My cortisol levels shifted from exhibiting peaks and valleys to a constant state of fight-or-flight. My ability to sleep through the night ended, and though I had bouts of anxiety in the past, I never truly understood the tremendous toll anxiety could have on one's health.

Who knew that one day, one minute, could change everything?

When your husband decides to do the courageous profession of firefighting, they do not hand out a guide to their family on how to handle a line-of-duty death. So I sat in my home with our four young children, ages six, three, two, and five months, and let panic fill my chest. I love the brotherhood of the FDNY, but on that day, the day I needed them the most, the higher-ups failed me.

I wanted an FDNY car to come get me, I wanted the person knocking on my door to say, "I'm sorry, Mrs. Bellew, there has been a fire, and your husband is in the hospital. Can you find someone to watch the kids and come with me now?" I wanted them to bring me to see John. I wanted to have immediate knowledge and communication about my husband's status as he lay in a hospital fighting for his life.

I wanted the opportunity to reassure my four small children that "Daddy is fine, Mommy has to go with these nice firemen to see him," even though that was the furthest from the truth. Could their trauma journey have been paved more smoothly if the day's events had been presented to me more like today?

But none of the above events happened twenty years ago. This description is the opposite of my reality. So many things went wrong that day that they referred to it as "a perfect storm." Every year I have to relive the story by attending a memorial Mass at the firehouse.

I have a love-hate relationship with these memorial Masses held every January. As an FDNY widow, you feel an obligation. An obligation to honor your husband, to show your children that their father is a hero, and that he is remembered. At first, the obligation serves you; it keeps you connected to a firehouse family that you also lost. It keeps your kids connected to their dad.

My kids dreaded the annual mass. Katreana would often have panic attacks when we got to the firehouse, so I would have someone walk around with her on the streets of the Bronx until the Mass was over. On the one hand, it was a beautiful tribute for them to see on behalf of their father, and the firefighters were so gracious and kind, cleaning, cooking, and preparing for it. On the other hand, the day was sad and had the potential to regress any progress in healing from the trauma that my children had built up over the previous year. *If the day made me uncomfortable, why would it be good for the mental health of my kids?*

Over the years, school and activities prevented them from attending, and I think they were thrilled when a conflict occurred. I was jealous that they had somewhere else to go. I was thankful to have at least one of them with me as my crutch. There are plenty of moments during the day when you feel lonely in the firehouse—seeing John's plaque on the wall and his turnout gear. You feel his presence, but he is not there, and the reality is that you are at his memorial Mass once again. Another year without him, another year further away from our last conversation. My kids have the right idea. Why are we not just memorializing him in our way, talking about the moments we had with him, instead of the last moments of hell he experienced?

But the feeling of obligation haunts me. And I am not the only person affected by Black Sunday. Other families lost loved ones that day. John's family attends Mass, so I think I have to be there. So, I'm dreading every minute of it as an FDNY car pulls up to my house to take me to the 20th Anniversary Memorial Mass, going down the same road I drove twenty years earlier.

Katreana and I walk into the firehouse, and panic rears its ugly head. I put on my best face, but the faces looking back don't feel welcoming. We sit down in the front row, "Reserved for the Bellew Family." I look around and no longer recognize many of the firefighters in the house, as they were not here two decades ago. The music begins, and my palms start sweating; the friendly confines of the firehouse seem to have changed.

When you are a widow of one of New York's Bravest, they forget to tell you that *you and your children* are actually becoming one of New York's Bravest. Partners and children of firefighters have to be strong every time they say goodbye to their loved ones. But a different kind of bravery evolves in them when there is a line-of-duty death. It is as if the hero leaves behind their bravery and instills it in their loved ones who remain.

I'm not sure when this reincarnation happened. Maybe when the dignitaries handed me the American flag or when we watched the flyover as the casket was raised on top of the firetruck to be driven through our town while 10,000 firefighters saluted him, but at some point, John's bravery entered our souls. We became the silent heroes, ones who never signed on to be heroes and would give back all the courage if we could just have John back.

PART I

Before John Jumped

Life was simple and sweet . . . until it wasn't.

CHAPTER 1

Meeting John

It was 1993. Oprah was playing in the background, talking to a woman who had been through an unthinkable tragedy but somehow rose from the ashes to recreate herself.

I stared at the clock and had an inner debate with myself: *How long should I give this guy to call before I decide he's uninterested? Why am I letting him control this situation? I should go out, go for a run, or go shopping. If he calls, my mom will write it on the kitchen chalkboard, as she always does.*

If a guy wanted to ask me out, he had to call my landline. If I wanted to talk to him, I had to be home and near the phone. I hated waiting by the phone and wondering if he was thinking of me. *I'm better than this... and him!*

My sister was packing to go to the Jersey Shore, where she had rented a house for the summer. "Come with me for the weekend," she said.

I gave one last look at the clock, then the phone. "Screw it. I'm in!" I threw a bunch of clothes in a bag and headed out to the beach with her. Oprah would have wanted me to "seize the day." Plus, waiting for a guy to call was not worth sacrificing a weekend at the shore.

That night, we went to the Brielle Yacht Club, where mutual friends had organized a $20 all-you-can-drink open bar. I wasn't a drinker, so I might've been the only person losing out on the deal. I loved the energy in the room, even though I only knew a handful of people.

Nothing is better than being at a social event with new faces, stories, and opportunities to meet people. I have never had trouble talking to people. I could talk to a wall if it spoke back. People are so intriguing to me, even the odd ones. It's fun analyzing them and figuring out why they are who they are.

As I talked to a guy who was clearly a smoker, my sister yelled, "Eileen, come here, what did Oprah say today?" I turned around, thankful for the distraction, and ... that was it. A 180-degree turn was the most significant movement in my life. John was standing in front of me, wearing a hunter-green Ralph Lauren polo shirt and khaki shorts. He was tall, well-built, and had the prettiest icy blue eyes I had ever seen. Little did I know that meeting this handsome guy would be life-changing.

"So you are a big Oprah fan?" John said, grinning as his eyes locked with mine.

"I have been known to watch it. How about you? You seem like a guy who wouldn't mind learning a thing or two from Oprah?" John laughs. I could see he is getting my sarcasm and is intrigued.

"Unfortunately, I'm working when Oprah is on, so I don't get the opportunity to be educated by her." There it is, this half smirk that would win me over for years to come and get him out of a few arguments.

"I work. Are you insinuating I don't?"

"No, not at all, what would your employment be?"

"I'm a science teacher."

"Oh, very interesting, cool, what is your favorite science? I am more of a history guy."

"Actually, biology would be my favorite type of science, but I currently teach Earth Science."

"OK, so teach me something about biology."

"OK, you are a man, you have light blue eyes, which makes it harder for you to see in the sun, it appears you had braces because your teeth are very straight, you are health conscious because you look as if you work out, and your parents must be tall because your genes are telling me this."

"Wow, you got all that in the five minutes we have spoken? Well, you know your biology except I never had braces; I was just born with great teeth."

"Your turn, tell me something about history."

"OK, well, if I am reading you correctly, which I hope I am, you and I are going to have a long history together."

I never felt this at ease before. Given our similar backgrounds, we compared our parents, childhoods, and upbringings. Like me, he was the youngest of five. He grew up in an Irish Catholic background, and both our fathers worked for Con Edison. It was as if he had researched my life and had inside information before we talked. I hung on to every word he said. He was so confident, cute, and engaging. His friend kept refilling his drink. The drink was clear, with ice and a lime. *I thought, this is amazing—a guy who is confident in social settings and doesn't need alcohol. He can drink seltzer and be engaged, just like me.* I found out later that those refill seltzers were actually gin and tonics.

We decided to walk home from the yacht club and continue our first conversation well into the early morning. Only because the sun was rising, and we knew we should get some sleep, did we part for the night. I crawled onto a linoleum floor covered with sand and made a makeshift bed with a pillow and blanket I brought from home. Even though it was 6 a.m., I couldn't fall asleep. Once I finally dozed off, dreams of the night and my future were dancing in my head. I knew this guy was different. I would not have to wait for any more phone calls… Oprah would have been proud.

The following two weeks were the whirlwind everyone dreams of, marked by five-hour phone calls that flew by. I never wanted them to end. We saw each other the next two weekends, and the time spent together grew more passionate and exciting. I couldn't believe there was a person on this Earth who was this perfect for me. I was so blessed to find my match; the man I wanted to spend the rest of my life with.

Three weeks after our first meeting, we sat on the beach watching the waves roll in. I wore a fluorescent pink bikini and didn't have a care in the world. Riptides, sandbars, and the depth of the water never crossed my mind. Focused on looking my desirable best, I dove into the waves uninhibited by all fears of the ocean, showing off my fit, tan body, when a monstrous wave hit me and sent me tumbling. My bathing suit fell down for all the world to see, and my bottoms took in two pounds of sand. I composed myself and my bathing suit while John hysterically laughed at me.

"I thought you were a big, strong lifeguard in Rockaway! Some lifeguard you are; you let me drown!" I stood up, releasing the sharp grains of sand from my bottom while continuing to watch John laugh.

"You told me you could swim. I was enjoying the show." After drying off and watching the day turn into night, John looked at me with those icy blue eyes.

"What are you doing two years from now?" he asked.

"Nothing."

"Would you want to marry me?"

"Yes! Of course!" I said, immediately.

We kept our future commitment to ourselves. People thought I was being impulsive, and that my feet and senses would eventually settle back down to Earth, but I knew my heart was telling me the truth: John was my soulmate. I was twenty-three, and my heart overruled any logic. He was put here on Earth to be with me. The world was our oyster. We would live out our lives free to love each other and grow a beautiful story we would tell our grandchildren.

John understood that though we loved each other, our families would have issues with the swiftness of our decision. So, I spent the next two years driving two hours, fighting traffic, and waiting in toll booth lines to cross over two bridges just to get to his house to spend a few hours with him in Howard Beach, Queens. He would take the train up from Wall Street after work so we could spend a couple of hours together. He would then sleep on our uncomfortable sofa bed that my mom would make up for John in the living room, while I retreated to my bedroom upstairs (which he was not allowed in).

My mom would happily wake him in the morning, hand him a cup of instant coffee, and I would drive him to the train station for his morning commute. This was life before texting and FaceTime. So if we wanted to see each other, it required work. John jokingly referred to me as Geographically Undesirable, but told me, "You are an exception to my rule." We managed the miles between us, made weekly plans and somehow the distance was never an issue.

One night, I drove a treacherous four hours on black ice to get home from his place. I didn't feel danger or think about the consequences that could arise from my reckless desire to see John. I was carefree, and nothing would stop me.

When we met, John worked for Brown Brothers Harriman. It was a Wall Street company that traded bonds. That was all I knew about his job; it involved moving money from one place to another. I also knew that he did not find his job inspiring. John graduated from Manhattan College with a degree in finance. I knew very little about this world, so I figured he would find another job that interested him, maybe in a different area of finance.

One day, he called with unexpected news, "I have something to tell you, I got called off the FDNY list."

"Okay, what does that mean?"

"I have been on "The List" for the New York City Fire Department for years; my number has finally been called."

"Okay… what does that mean?" I wasn't trying to be difficult, but I legitimately had no idea what this meant. It was the first time I had ever heard anything about him wanting to become a firefighter.

"I never mentioned it before because I didn't think I would be called; I thought "The List" would expire before my number came up."

It was like he was speaking another language. All this lingo he was saying was so foreign to me. My naivety and ignorance shone through, "Oh, I see, of course you will turn it down, right? You could get hurt or worse, killed. I don't want to be a fire widow. I don't want to be on the front page of the Daily News or the Post where they plaster photos of widows crying."

Immediate panic hit me, and the thought of him running into a burning building while everyone else was running out scared the hell out of me. "I don't want anything bad to happen to you. Why can't you stay at your safe job on Wall Street, where if there is a fire, you would be running out of the building, not running into it?"

John laughed at me, "Don't worry, that would never happen. You will never be a fire widow. I am going to be a great firefighter. Nothing is ever going to happen to me. You know my job is unfulfilling, I have always wanted to do something more admirable, something that means more than moving money around."

We went back and forth about why he wanted to leave his safe office job, where, for the most part, no one would get burned or face death. He considered my feelings, worries, and anxiety. He postponed his appointment, giving me three months to get used to the idea of being married to a fireman. Firefighting is a calling. Some say it's in your DNA. I now know that only extraordinary people take on this calling. You must have an inner desire to help people, to make a difference at your job, and at all costs, to make a difference in the community you are serving.

At twenty-four, I was being egocentric while simultaneously not understanding the bigger picture. John had seen this profession firsthand with his brother and cousins. He understood that he could choose a job more noble than trading bonds. So when the next class came around, John accepted the appointment and entered the Fire Academy. *Godspeed, John,* I thought.

When he entered the academy, my new world of understanding the fire culture and vocabulary began. I also began to see a new man emerge, one who was happy and fulfilled.

In June of 1994, John officially proposed to me, a year after we started dating. He nervously got down on one knee, "I have known since the first night I met you, will you do me the honor and be my wife? Will you marry me?"

I couldn't believe it. Even though I knew it was coming at some point, I was still shocked. "YES! Oh my God, YES!" That night, John splurged on a bottle of Dom Pérignon, and it tasted like liquid gold. It cost us $100, well beyond our budget.

After a year of planning and saving, on July 7, 1995, we were ready to make the commitment to ourselves and God at our local church. Almost two years exactly to the day when John asked, "What are you doing two years from now?" we exchanged our vows and said our "I do's" in front of family, friends and even some of my students. Our happily ever after began.

John and I at his Fire Academy Graduation

CHAPTER 2
Before John Jumped

Everyone has a plan until they get punched in the mouth.
~Mike Tyson

We all make life choices, and mine were clear-cut. Before I met John, I chose to get my undergraduate degree in Elementary Education with a specialization in natural sciences. I then got my extended certification in biology so I could also teach seventh through twelfth grade. I loved science and teaching, so I was over the moon when I landed a sixth-grade teaching position in my hometown.

My students made me laugh, challenged me, and gave me great purpose. I tried to connect with each child, as I taught up to 120 students in one year. Primarily, I taught through storytelling, sharing personal stories while infusing the science curriculum. Telling stories about what I was like in middle school, making fun of myself while connecting concepts, helped them socially while also helping them understand science. Middle school is, developmentally, the worst time in most kids' lives; I just wanted to connect with them and show them that all they were going through would be funny one day. This teaching style created a safe space for my students to open up, and they shared parts of their lives with me.

Whenever I ran into one of my students, they never mentioned a science lesson I taught them, but a story I shared with them and how I made them feel. This always made me very proud. I taught for a few years before getting my masters in Curriculum Development. My goal was always to make science interesting and fun for my students. My creativity was a strong point in my teaching style because I loved creating lessons where kids learn by doing rather than just hearing about concepts.

By the time we got married, John and I both had secure jobs. I continued my education to earn additional credit and help maximize our combined income. We found the perfect house to raise our children in, and the owners were the parents of one of my past students. We had to basically rob Peter to pay Paul to pull together a down payment, but we did it.

We had the perfect plan. Our jobs would never make us rich but would fulfill our innate desire to help people and make a difference. We would be rich in memories and relationships with people we touched. We would have kids, love them, and give them extraordinary lives. I would take as much time off as we could afford financially after each child, but the plan was always for me to return to work. We would eventually retire with well-earned pensions after years of dedicated careers. This was our American dream.

At first, the plan seemed golden. My mom would provide child-care after my maternity leave ended. John would fix his schedule to maximize our children's caretaking, making it his priority. Our schedule was unpredictable and scattered at times, but my mom was so flexible and adjusted her life around ours.

On mornings when John was working, I would wake up at 6:00 a.m. and get the kids and myself ready to go to my mom's house. I usually packed the car the night before with clothes, diapers, food, toys, breast milk, an Exersaucer, and anything else essential to make the day run smoothly. I dropped them off around 7:00 a.m. and was at work by 7:20 a.m. Since I worked close to my mom's, I would have lunch at her house to check in with them.

When I was breastfeeding, I would pump during my breaks and sometimes during meetings with fellow teachers. My colleagues were all very supportive of me, including one meeting when a male teacher kept his back to me while I pumped and we discussed the curriculum. I'd pack and refrigerate the milk for the next day's feedings and go back to teaching.

At the firehouse, John was paired with a 24-hour mutual partner. Each firefighter is assigned a twelve-hour shift. They matched up with someone in the house to combine two shifts into one longer shift. They worked out their schedules to best suit both of their needs. This system helped maximize our children's ability to have one of us at home, limiting our need for childcare. Sometimes it meant John and I did not get to see each other much on weekends, as John would choose those shifts since I was off. We couldn't have done it without the help of my flexible, fantastic mom, who took on the quintessential grandma role and did it flawlessly. It was like a well-oiled machine.

Eventually, I became familiar with firefighter language. Words like probie, truckie, across the floor, and onion skin all became common vocabulary in our house.

John did everything: every library program, Tiny Tots Soccer, Mommy (Daddy) and Me, and the co-op preschool program, where he worked in the classroom twice a month. He was Mr. Mom. I would sneak away during lunch or a break in my schedule to catch some time here or there, but John happily loved being a dad. The mommy guilt was eased knowing that John was at these events and would give me a play-by-play of everything our children did.

John was also well known to my classroom students. Before schools were in lockdown and security guards kept everyone out, John could come into my classroom without being fingerprinted or frisked. He was a well-known figure in the school hallways. The kids would make small talk with him.

John would drop off a Starbucks coffee, and we would exchange keys when we had to swap out our cars because we only owned one minivan with car seats. Then he'd head to my mom's house to pick up the kids. On days when John went in for a night shift, we often visited Starbucks together just to sit and talk outside the house. We would share our day's events or discuss future ones. We would bring toys to keep the kids entertained. Sometimes we could get in a 20-minute conversation, and other times a 5-minute one before we needed to move on to avoid disturbing the whole store.

"So what does the schedule look like this coming week?"

"I am up and down on Friday into Saturday and then back in on Sunday night." I handed Brielle an old magazine to turn the pages and rip out a page at a time. She looked at the photo and then threw it on the floor. I didn't mind cleaning it all up if it gave us ten minutes of adult conversation.

Years earlier, as a new teacher in 1994, I sat in the faculty room eating lunch with my principal and mentioned my life's plan. "I am going to get married and have three kids, and two will be a set of twins, so I will only have to be pregnant twice." I knew I sounded young and naive, but my principal sat quietly eating his lunch, listening to me, and laughing. He was a very wise man and a fantastic boss.

He looked up, smiled at me, and said, "Life is what happens to us while we are making other plans."

I smiled back and thought, *Yeah, but this is how it will happen.*

John and I on our wedding day, 1995

CHAPTER 3

Chance Meeting

One thing you can always count on is that when one firefighter meets another firefighter, they can talk for hours. They always know a mutual friend or have worked in the same battalion. They share stories and a secret language, forming a bond within their strong community. So when John would come across a fellow firefighter, I would leave him alone and let them have their debriefing without me, knowing they were part of a unique and close-knit family.

In early 1997, we had Science Fair Night at the Pearl River Middle School, where I worked. My students presented their science projects to their families and community in the gymnasium. It was the culmination of the hard work the kids put in on their projects. My job was to meet as many parents as possible and discuss the different projects the kids created. John came to support me and see the work I had discussed for the last two months. I knew it might be a boring night for John while I spoke with students and parents, so when I saw a dad I knew was a fireman, I introduced John to him immediately.

Predictably John spent the rest of the night talking to my student's dad. As another successful Science Fair wrapped up, we got into the car, and I thanked him for coming.

"Do you know who that was?" he asked.

"Yes, a boy in my class's dad."

"Yes, but he's also a Chief, who serves as the Assistant to the Fire Commissioner." This position meant nothing to me, but apparently it was a big deal.

Right out of "Probie School" in 1996, John had first been assigned to 10 Truck. It was located at the base of the World Trade Center. He loved his firehouse in Manhattan but was looking to move to the Bronx. I was against the move because it would mean a busier firehouse and more fires, which, to me, meant greater danger.

"You should want me to go to a busier firehouse," John explained, "So I can get more experience and become a better fireman. Then I will know what I am doing and never get hurt."

I was unsure of his rationale but understood that he would prefer to fight fires rather than answer false-alarm and broken-down-elevator calls at the World Trade Center. Apparently, the fireman John met at my school function had the power to move John's house, and the next day, he was in the Bronx.

In March of 1997, John's new home would be The Cross Bronx Expressway, Ladder 27 in the South Bronx. He couldn't have been more thrilled about it. John would come home and tell me, "These guys are legendary, they fought fires when The Bronx was burning, and they are teaching me so much." He truly loved this house and the guys he worked with. I sometimes thought he'd rather go to work than stay home with four crazy kids. He ate better at the firehouse than at home, considering they were located next to Arthur Avenue, which had all the Italian delicacies to feast on. I know John wasn't considered one of the better cooks in the firehouse, but I sure benefited from him learning from the best. He enjoyed cooking for us. He would joke that he would lose weight while on vacation away from the firehouse because he ate so well there.

Four years later, on September 11, 2001, we walked into my sister's beach house at the Jersey Shore for a week-long vacation. We turned the TV on and heard, "A plane has struck the World Trade Center." At that moment, all the lives of all Americans stopped. At first, I didn't put it together, but John did. He immediately understood that his brothers were in danger. He also understood that the First Due at the World Trade Center was 10 Truck, his old firehouse. So John's brothers were running up the stairs to help people, and it easily could have been him, too. We didn't unpack anything; we just turned back around and headed home. By the time we were in the car, both towers had fallen, and John was heartbroken knowing that he would know many who had just lost their lives.

Later that day, the bridges reopened for first responders, and John was allowed to cross over the George Washington Bridge. He left to help. He was hopeful he would find many survivors. Sadly, he did not. Those times were so uncertain, and I was so afraid to let John go.

He lost many friends and 343 brothers on 9/11. Everyone felt the impact of that tragic day, and it was a stark reminder of the preciousness of life.

A few months after the World Trade Center attacks, I felt compelled to write the dad a note. I wanted to thank him for moving John. If he hadn't made the move, there was a good chance John would have been in those buildings. I wanted to tell him how much I appreciated what he did for our family. Thinking it was the right thing to do, I never considered the other side. A couple of weeks after I sent the letter, I ran into his wife at the local supermarket. I greeted her with a smile and said, "Oh, funny, I would run into you; I just sent your husband a thank-you note."

She smiled and said, "Oh yes, he got it."

I felt like my intentions weren't well received, so I repeated, "I really wanted to thank him for moving John."

Her response was chilling. "Yes, I understand, but he is struggling right now, with all the moves he made that ultimately protected some men, he moved others into harm's way, and we lost some of those men."

I felt horrible. *How could I have only seen one side of his gesture?* What a weight to carry if you were him. I was writing on my and John's behalf, but it turns out this was a selfish act of kindness. I thought I was acknowledging his kind gesture when I was actually pointing out the horror of another family. It's a lesson I will never forget. Now, I try to consider all sides before acting, because something could be good for one and deadly for another. How important it is to consider all perspectives, even when expressing gratitude. I thought my appreciation would brighten his day, but I possibly sent him further into despair.

The irony is that I was the one who introduced John to the Chief, who ultimately moved him to the Bronx house. If I had never connected them, then maybe he wouldn't have been lost on Black Sunday, but perhaps he would have died on 9/11 or not at all. Katreana and Kieran might not even be in this world without that chance encounter.

I can't live my life contemplating all the "what ifs." We all make decisions every day that ultimately change our destiny. That chance meeting at a science fair greatly impacted my life. I didn't know it at the time, but maybe destiny did.

John on a training run at work

CHAPTER 4
Raising Children

John and I had thoughts of a big family right from the beginning. Since both of us were the youngest of five and came from large extended families, we knew the benefits of having many siblings. There was a feeling of love, connection, and belonging when you grew up in a chaotic household. There are endless life lessons when five siblings live under the same roof. I loved being part of a big family, and we wanted that for our children.

I did not have much growing up, but I did not know anything different, so it never really bothered me. Since I was the youngest, I got all the hand-me-downs. However, because I was much taller than my siblings, my dresses and pants were often a bit higher off the ground than what was considered fashionable. I remember my Communion dress was very short on me, so my mom had me practice bending my knees if I needed to pick something up, or else I would have given a show. I also remember lying to friends when they mentioned all the new clothes they got for Back-to-School. We never went on shopping sprees like that, so I would make up lies to fit into the conversation.

We all had to watch the same TV show on one black-and-white television set. It was not too difficult since there were only six channels back then. One night, after two of my siblings got the chickenpox, my mom put us all in one room to watch *Eight is Enough*. She told us, "Don't come out until you all have chickenpox; you might as well all get it now since I have to take care of two of you." Sure enough, two days later, we all had it.

There were many fights and arguments, some even getting physical but life in a big family taught you how to be tough, how to live without material things, how to compromise, how to manipulate a situation to fit you best, how to be manipulated, how to be blamed for things you did not do, how to blame others for things they did not do. You learn how to know when to ignore a sister who is crying and how to know when to step in and give a hug, how to alter a game depending on which siblings were home, how to know when to run faster than your parents' heavy hand came calling after you did something wrong and when to lie low until things cool off. All of these lessons can't be taught in the real world, but having siblings teaches you amazing skills that you can use to survive in the real world.

John and I wanted all of this for our kids. We wanted them to have a similar loving experience to ours. We also knew we couldn't financially provide them with everything, but we had love, guidance, and happiness to spread and nourish.

The day I discovered I was pregnant for the first time, I was in complete shock. We weren't actively trying, but we weren't actively avoiding it either. John was off on a ski trip with his friends, and I was going to my annual gynecologist appointment. I was hoping to squeeze it in before my period, because somehow my period always seemed to coincide with the appointment I had made a year earlier. As I sat in the waiting room, I was relieved to check it off my list and get the dreaded yearly gyno visit over with.

After weighing, I gave my urine sample, then sat patiently on the white, crinkly paper, staring at the stirrups, knowing my feet were heading there soon. The doctor walked in and said, "Congratulations on your pregnancy!"

I was sure she had the wrong room. "Not me. I'm here for my annual."

"No, it's you. Your urinalysis shows you are pregnant."

What? I'm not prepared to share my food with my child.

I don't know why that was my first thought, but that's how I saw motherhood—the mom would cut off a piece of her food and share it with her child. *I don't want to share my food. I enjoy the whole serving to myself.* Suddenly, the white, crinkly paper was soaked. I was sweating like crazy. Despite the initial shock, a wave of unexpected joy and hope washed over me. I was both scared and excited about the new journey I was about to embark on.

The doctor explained the schedule of visits I would now have to attend. I went from dreading my yearly appointment to having a series of monthly appointments. I wasn't ready for this new step at twenty-eight, after only being married three years. I dragged my butt off the table and went to the reception desk, where they all congratulated me. The reality of motherhood was sinking in, and I was filled with anxiety and uncertainty.

In the parking lot, I sat in my Ford Escort and stared at my stomach. I had just run the New York City Marathon in November and planned on rocking a bikini that summer. Only now I would be four months pregnant. Looking at my back seat, I was unsure if I could fit a car seat in there. Thoughts of minivans popped into my head, and the sweating started all over again.

I wasn't ready for *that*. In a split second, I went from rocking a bikini to driving a minivan.

John returned from his ski trip out West a few days later. He was excited to see me and picked me up by my flat, skinny waist, twirling me around. *How much longer could he do this without throwing his back out?* I had a small bag waiting for him on the kitchen counter. He read my face and saw my apprehension.

"What is wrong? What is this?"

My palms began to sweat again. "Just open it! You'll see." He opened it while all along watching my body language, and I'm sure I went stark white. *Were we really doing this? Did we actually create a new life? I still consider myself my mom's baby and call her for comfort and cuddling every once in a while. We are way too young.*

John screamed, "You are kidding me? Oh my God! This is amazing!" The gift was a Yankee onesie along with the positive pregnancy test.

"Is it? Are we really ready for this? I just called my mom because I have a cold and wanted to know what I should take."

"What is the matter? Why are you not jumping up and down?" He hugged me and kissed me and twirled me around some more. His reaction helped to calm my terrified body. His return brought a sense of relief and happiness, and his smile lit up the room, reassuring me that I was not alone on this journey.

"I'm scared, John. Babies require a lot. I will have to grow up, I'll have to feed another human, I'll have to learn how to change a baby and make sure they learn how to read and write. And what if they vomit? I can't handle seeing myself vomit. You know I don't like sharing my food. I see mom's cutting up from their plate and sharing their chicken fingers and french fries, I want all of my chicken and fries and don't get me started about my dessert."

"I promise we will order multiple dishes, and you will not have to share any of your food. And I will be right there next to you, always. We will do this together. Now and forever. There is nothing to worry about."

Our baby was a week overdue when my water broke early one morning. I felt a little cramping, thinking that would be how painful this process would be. Twenty hours later, the pain was like nothing anyone could accurately describe. My pregnancy plan of going natural and letting my body work to deliver a beautiful, healthy baby with minimal intervention of any sort was blown up when the first real contraction happened twelve hours into labor. I agreed to medication and anything else that would get this child out of my uterus. John witnessed a new me, one capable of ripping his head off if he even looked at me wrong. He read the room and took all my abuse like a champ.

Brielle, named after the yacht club where we met, arrived on Thanksgiving Day, November 27, 1998, at 2:35 a.m., weighing 9lbs., 12oz. We never found out the sex before the birth of any of our kids. When the doctor yelled, "It's a girl!," we were shocked. All along, everyone said I was having a boy. I thought so, too. We had fun guessing what it would be based on how I carried. I gained seventy-five pounds with my first pregnancy, so I'm sure everyone assumed I was having a football player. Even twenty-four hours after giving birth, I walked into the nursery, convinced I was picking up a boy. Never again would I look like I did the day I found out about my pregnancy. There was no need for me to buy another bikini; those days were done.

At twenty-eight, when I delivered Brielle, I still felt like my mom's child and was shocked that the hospital staff even allowed us to take this tiny person home. It's the craziest concept: people are interviewed and given home visits to foster a dog, but you can walk into a hospital and walk out with a human being, one that's yours to keep. I remember when the nurse came in and said to John, "You're ready to go. Why don't you bring the car around?"

"To go home with her?" I said. The nurse laughed. I nervously laughed back, but said to myself: *Now what?*

A couple of weeks into motherhood, I called my sister, Patricia, and said, "I want to leave, I need to get away."

My concerned sister asked, "Where do you want to go?"

"I don't know, I just feel like I need to leave, maybe head to Albany." Now, nothing against Albany, NY, but there are not too many people in their right mind who choose Albany to escape to. Not that I actually left; I didn't. But I was not in my right mind; the feeling of forever came crashing down on me. I would be responsible for this human being *forever*. It was the first time I was on someone else's schedule; I couldn't sleep when I wanted to sleep, I couldn't shower when I wanted to shower, I couldn't eat when I wanted to eat, and my body was responsible for feeding another human. I had to maintain proper nutrition and protect this human with every cell in my body. No pressure or anxiety at all, right?

The baby blues hit me hard, and I found myself crying for no apparent reason, feeling overwhelmed, and questioning my ability to be a good mother. Patricia recognized my desperation and often came over. Thank God for John, Patricia, my mom, and my family, who reassured me that I was not alone on this new, terrifying journey.

A week after I stopped breastfeeding her, at a year old, Brielle got very sick. Sick enough that the doctors put her into the hospital. She was having trouble breathing.

A group of doctors came into her room and asked, "Are either one of you an asthmatic or did you have asthma growing up?"

I quickly responded, "No," for both of us.

John said, "Yes, I was an asthmatic when I was younger."

I gasped and quickly looked his way, "You never told me that before?" I had no experience with asthma, and just that word scared me to death.

John turned to me and said, "Well, it never came up before; it is not something people mention while dating. Would it have changed anything?" The obvious answer was "no," but in the moment, when your child is sick, you become so protective of them. *Yes, from now on, I want a family tree listing every possible disease and DNA samples from all blood relatives over the past 500 years. I don't want any surprises, so I can best protect her and any future Bellew children. I should have known this. What kind of mommy am I? I know nothing about asthma, and it is now affecting my daughter.*

From that moment on, Brielle had a difficult road, health wise. We had many sleepless nights while holding the nebulizer machine up to her tiny nose and mouth while she slept. We had many hospital visits for oxygen. She had more sleepless nights of coughing than any child should ever endure. If I weren't treating her, I would be staring at her chest to make sure she was still breathing. It was crushing to watch Brielle suffer during days-long asthma attacks. She is one tough kid; never complained and just dealt with it. For me, it was a mix of fear, uncertainty, and a deep sense of responsibility.

One of my biggest fears when first finding out I was pregnant was the possibility of having to clean up vomit. I convinced myself that maybe I wouldn't have kids who were big vomiters, but that couldn't have been further from the truth. I learned quickly that asthmatics innately learn to vomit to help open their airways. So when Brielle would start a coughing episode, I knew vomit was coming soon after, and I was forced to get over my fear quickly. My fears did not come close to her suffering, so I learned how to handle it with many plastic bags and holding my breath. Mommies somehow tackle their fears to better care for their loves.

Thank God I had John in the early days of learning about asthma. It was helpful to have two parents to deal with nebulizers and medications. When I had to get up for work, he would take the nighttime nebulizers, and during his twenty-four-hour shifts, I was on my own. I had many sleepless nights before heading into work. John hated being away for such long shifts during those illnesses and hospital stays, but it was part of his job. Little did I know the foreshadowing these absentee nights represented.

There were many days early on when I didn't feel prepared to raise a child. I'm not sure if anyone ever feels ready. But somehow, John and I went back for more. This time, my pregnancy story was different. We actively tried and became pregnant quickly. This pregnancy felt so different from the first one. My morning sickness was less, my leg hair grew like crazy, and I had insomnia for most of the third trimester. Back in 2001, there was not much on TV at 3 a.m., so I often watched porn and spent the time trying to figure out the storyline and meaning of the show. People looked at me strangely when I referenced episodes in conversation, as this is what my life became—no sleep, weight gain, and porn.

With all these new pregnancy symptoms, we were guessing this one might be a boy. Other than gaining too much weight again, not having the ability to nap because I had Brielle, and the popping out of an umbilical hernia, the pregnancy was fine. But then my due date came and went with no baby. I was twelve days overdue when they sent me for a sonogram, which I failed. The baby had no leg or arm movement, so they sent me in to be induced. I cried leaving Brielle. I felt so guilty about changing her status from Only Child to Big Sister. *How could I do this? I couldn't possibly love someone as much as I love her.* I was so wrong; a sibling is the best gift I could have given her.

Once labor began, the delivery was much quicker than Brielle's. Jack flew into the world four hours after induction. It was so fast that John almost missed it. I'm not sure what he was thinking, but I heard him say, "Can I get anyone something from the cafeteria, coffee, sandwich, or bagel?" The nurse and the doctor looked at him strangely.

The doctor said, "Where do you think you are going? She is ready to push. You are going to miss the delivery." He was thinking we had another eighteen hours like Brielle's experience.

He gasped, "Oh shoot, I didn't realize." He moved into position at the top of the bed, and Jack screamed into this world on April 5, 2001, at 12:46 pm, at 9lbs., 6oz. My hunch was right; he was a boy! A whole new set of worries rushed in as the epidural wore off. *Will I be able to be a boy mommy with all the new body parts, different wiring, and a whole lot of energy?* One thing was certain: I loved this boy with every cell of my body, and my heart just doubled in size.

John stood stunned! He fumbled with his phone to let everyone know. "I have a son. I can't believe I have a son!" I'll never forget his excitement and giddiness after each kid was delivered. He was so thrilled to have a son and to experience something new. Oh, what a challenge our son would be. Just when we thought we had this parenting thing down, Jack entered our world.

Jack was not an easy baby; he cried all the time. I mean all the time. He wasn't colicky; he was healthy and ate all the time, but he refused to settle down and wanted to be held every minute of every day. Brielle walked around the house, plugging her ears. Jack spent the first eight months of his life in a Baby Björn carrier. I always thought maybe this was payback since they induced me, and he wasn't ready to come out. *Maybe he was just pissed, so he made us pay the price by never wanting to be separated from me again.* The crying was so bad that strangers would come up to me at our town pool and offer to walk him around so I could get a break. I ended up developing carpal tunnel syndrome because of the constant motion of rocking him to settle him down, and I had to wear a brace for three months. He was exhausting but thank God he was so damn cute; it saved him.

Unlike our experience with Brielle, there were many breakdowns, tantrums, and meltdowns. If I ran out to do an errand, I would come home, and it was guaranteed that John would be doing laps around the kitchen, living room, and the rest of the house with him. Jack was our disgruntled family member, but we loved him to pieces.

Jack was such a boy. He quickly became John's best friend, and John loved to show his son how to fix things while Jack wore his tool belt with plastic tools hanging from it. Ironically, once we got past his first year, he became a chill, fun, energetic boy who rarely cried. He grew out of his irate phase and became a rambunctious family member. Jack used Brielle's Barbie dolls as weapons, turning them into soldiers and creating war scenes. He often dove off couches, usually onto Brielle while she walked by in her plastic high heels, tutus, and boa wraps. She would scream at him, and he would continue to act out his war scene.

We had to shift our parenting approach to accommodate Jack's innate desire to play rough. John took him outside to run, kick, swim, hit, throw, scream, and get as dirty as possible so we could find peace in the living room. There were many mornings that we started our day with a wrestling match between John and Jack on our bed. John understood the wiring of a little boy and his desire to move. We often split household chores. John's job was entertainment, getting them outside to get dirty and exercise. While I read, fed, and bathed them. It all worked.

The months following 9/11 were a blur. I wanted to be selfish and have John stay home, but there was no way I could stop him. He was either at the pile or attending funerals. He was rarely home. But apparently, he was home one night because I found out I was pregnant somehow, on my birthday, December 1, 2001. Jack was only eight months old.

I was still breastfeeding and had not gotten my period yet when I started feeling ill. John came home from another funeral, a regular occurrence during that time.

"Hon, these funerals are really tough. I feel so bad for the families," he said, looking exhausted. "Promise me if anything happens to me, Giuliani or some other dignitary won't speak at my funeral."

"We are not having this conversation; you promised it would never happen."

"I know, and it won't, I'm just saying, it is tough for me to listen to Giuliani and Von Nessen speak about these guys whom they don't really know."

"Enough of that."

He looked at me with concern in his eyes. "Are you feeling okay? You look a little gray."

"Well, I'm not sure if the word is gray. How about I look a little pregnant?"

"What! Seriously! How? When? I haven't even been home."

"You tell me, I don't even know how far along I am… I could be just pregnant or two months pregnant. I never got my period back after Jack."

"This is amazing, what a beautiful gift we are getting after all the sadness." I hadn't thought of it that way. He was right, so many lives were taken away from us, and now a bundle of hope was being blessed upon us. Once again, John had the right perspective.

"Not sure when this happened, but how lucky are we!" And we were.

Soon after we learned of our third pregnancy, John received a fantastic opportunity. The pharmaceutical company GlaxoSmithKline had some sort of connection to John's firehouse and asked if they could bring two firemen to Scotland to honor their efforts after the 9/11 attacks. At first, John struggled to accept any accolades, as he was not at the site when the towers fell. But the liaison between Scotland, GlaxoSmithKline, and John's firehouse insisted that John and another fireman go on this trip and represent the 343 lives lost that day. As difficult as it was to let him go while I had two toddlers and was in my second trimester, I knew it was an opportunity of a lifetime.

He was treated like royalty. They gifted them handmade kilts, took them on a tour of St Andrew's golf course, he drank a hundred-year-old whisky, and was honored at a banquet with the nicest people in the world.

"People were referring to us as heroes and asking for our autographs," he said. "I kept reminding them that the real heroes were the brothers we lost that day, but they just kept giving us more mementos and shaking our hands."

"But you represent the heroes they are seeing on the TV," I reminded him, "It's not like you do not do heroic things every day when you show up for work. You are still a firefighter who runs into buildings when everyone is running out. Take the praise, you deserve it."

Four months later, I walked around the town pool dilated by six centimeters. Katreana was also overdue, but I would not dare induce her. My midwife could not believe I was not in labor. I made sure the other two kids were getting tired out so they would be easy for my mom later if I went into labor. Finally, around 8 p.m., contractions started, and I knew it would be quick since I was more than halfway there.

We arrived at the hospital around 10 p.m., checked in, and I announced, "Ready for my epidural!"

They checked me and told me, "You are too far along and probably too late for an epidural."

"Probably?? How about we do it anyway!" The anesthesiologist gave me something for the pain, but I remember yelling,

"You are lying, you didn't give me anything, I'm feeling everything!" And just like that, I was pushing by midnight.

At one point, I stopped pushing because it hurt so much, and the hospital staff yelled, "This is it, you need to push, come on, Eileen, start pushing!"

And I was like "NOOOO! Would you touch a hot stove? If I push it, it's going to kill me!" I boycotted for a minute until I had no choice, and I let the whole maternity ward know that I was pushing out my daughter under protest. The screaming that comes out of your body during labor is like no octave that you could reach on any other day of your life, along with the profanity and harsh words you scream at your husband.

Our quiet, inquisitive Katreana arrived on August 18th at 1:41 a.m., 2002. From the moment her 8lbs., 8oz. brilliance entered this life, she sat back calmly and took in the world around her. Kat was the easiest baby ever created. Some would say the opposite of her brother. She was dragged around everywhere. I don't think she was ever put in her crib for a nap; she slept on the road and was fed in malls, parks, and beaches. She never cried and required little attention. Her entertainment was her two siblings, who ran around and included her in their busy day of playing.

John carried her around everywhere; it was easier than putting her down while keeping an eye on the other two. She sat on his hip, absorbing the world as he read, ate, cooked, and played with Brielle and Jack. He would read her the New York Times out loud, and she would take in the happenings of the Middle East, the weather, or the latest economic crisis, all while sitting on his lap. I'm convinced it is why she is a gifted writer to this day.

Katreana was a late talker, but everyone could see she was watching and analyzing everything, taking it all in. I never worried about her because it was clear she had figured this life out on her own. When Katreana eventually did speak, at fourteen months old, she spoke in perfectly articulated sentences, not words. One day, she was in the kitchen, pulled my leg, and said, "Can I have a drink?" I looked down, stunned. She didn't need to waste her time on words; she communicated in sentences from now on.

Kat was so easy that we could leave her in her car seat at the top of a hill while sledding with the other kids. She wouldn't make a peep and watched everything going on around her. I often forgot I had three kids because Kat didn't require anything. Katreana was not a fan of exercise and playing outside, so when we were in the yard, she would sit on the stoop and play with her Polly Pockets. I fed her what the others were eating; she played what they were playing; she watched what they watched. I put her in the tub with the others for bathtime, and when Kat didn't want to do what they were doing, she sat and entertained herself. Unfortunately for Brielle, that meant she remained Jack's target because Katreana never gave anyone the time of day.

Jack tried to play with Katreana, but nothing moved her or bothered her, so when Jack was in the mood to aggravate a sibling, she was not the one to go to. One morning, Katreana was watching TV when Jack tried to lift her by her knees while she was sitting on them. She probably didn't even look up while he attempted. He, of course, was not strong enough to do this, and she fell back, breaking her elbow. She screamed and cried so loudly that I ran because I didn't recognize the child screeching. I was shocked to see it was Kat. I knew something was wrong because she wasn't one to cry wolf. Even after the initial cry,

Katreana let the doctor set the bone, and she was excited to pick out the color of her cast. She was one of those kids; if they all came out that way, you would have a hundred.

John and I discussed having a fourth child for about five minutes before we decided it was a perfect idea.

"I know you have to carry the child, but don't you think this is the perfect time to have a fourth?"

"How do you see that?"

"Well, if we have a boy, he would only be three years younger than Jack, and they would be close in age to go to the bars together."

"And if we have a girl?"

"Then Jack will have to be big and strong so he can fight off the future boyfriends of his three sisters. We have to get two connecting hotel rooms with three kids anyway, so there would be room for four with two queen beds in the next room."

"I'm not sure of your reasoning, but I am all in."

The truth is, we loved having the kids so close in age, and if we were to have a fourth, now would be a good time. John used his rationales to justify his desire for a large family full of chaos and love. He hoped Jack would have a brother because he knew the special bond of having three brothers of his own. John wanted Jack to have an automatic best friend and to experience their lives together.

My 2004 pregnancy with Kieran was an experience. I started showing after two months. Once we started sharing our news, I immediately got asked, "How many are you having? Twins? Triplets?" I even thought, *maybe there are more in there than just one?* Later on, I would get the comment, "You must be due any day, right?" while I was only six months pregnant. They sent me in for a sonogram at thirty-two weeks, and I measured thirty-eight weeks in size, but the baby, though large, was gestationally thirty-two weeks. My due date was late August, so I had to find a maternity bathing suit that could hold this child. I had a friend who told me, "Every time I see you, my uterus hurts."

I went in for my thirty-eight-and-a-half-week check-up, and while the doctor was checking me, she blurted out, "Ooops, I broke your water!" I was so annoyed because I was a big advocate of having the child decide when they were entering the world, not a doctor.

So, John and I headed to the hospital. I wasn't really in labor yet, so John thought he should stop for a Starbucks in case it was an all-nighter. While waiting for him in the car, the labor pains started really kicking up. John strolled slowly back to the car, and Labor Eileen emerged, and he got an earful.

"Glad we can stop to make sure you got your coffee while I sat in the car in labor! Are you aware of what my uterus is doing right now? It's contracting so it can push this large child that you implanted in me out of my vagina." My labor personality came shining through. John did not dare to answer those rhetorical questions, placed his Venti coffee in the cup holder, buckled his seatbelt, and drove off quickly. Those outbursts created by Labor Eileen are never my finest, but I guess it's one of the few times you get a pass in life.

The hospital was aware we were coming, and the room was ready for us. When the nurses hear that it's your fourth child, you get treated differently. I guess they know you can do this, so you barely see them. We were not going to have a repeat performance like Katreana, so I immediately requested an epidural. We knew this baby would be big; we just didn't know how big.

My pushing coincided with Michael Phelps competing for his fifth gold medal at the 2004 Summer Olympics. The whole room was joking and discussing the Olympics, talking about whether Phelps would accomplish this remarkable feat. No one was focusing on me as I pushed this massive baby out of me until the shit hit the fan. The doctor turned away from the TV and looked at me and said, "Holy crap. We need to move." The doctor directed the nurses to move John and my sister away from me. I realized they were worried about the size of his head.

Things went from talking about Michael Phelps to chaos. I looked up, and a nurse was sitting on top of my stomach and screaming at me, "You listen to me, you are going to push this baby out now! You bear down, and you give everything you have on the next contraction. Here it comes, no holding back, bear down and push!" She was serious, borderline mean, but completely essential. She had a Jamaican accent and wore some sort of head dress. She pushed on my stomach as I propelled Kieran out. We don't know where the nurse came from. We say she is the ringer they bring in when a mom has to push out a large baby.

We asked the other nurses about her afterward, and they had no idea who we were talking about. I described her and mentioned I wanted to thank her, but their response was, "I have no idea who you are talking about; there is no one with that description who works on this floor." We still wonder whether she was real or my guardian angel helping me deliver. In the end, I was able to push Kieran out at 8:41 p.m. on August 16, 2004; he weighed 11 lbs., 2 oz., and was 24 inches long. Kieran was literally a two-foot human in my uterus. Congratulations to Michael Phelps; even amid all the chaos, he won the gold.

John was ecstatic about having another son. He was so proud of him and loved bragging about his size. He wanted to go with the nurses while they cleaned him up so he could find out his measurements. Moments later, John came running back into the room, elated. "We had a toddler!"

I had to remind him that "I had the toddler!" not him.

"The nurses had to go to the pediatric floor to get the next size diapers because the newborn size didn't fit Kieran," John told me. He was so proud, beaming like he was with all his children.

I thought having one boy in the house was a lot, but then there were two. The boys were best friends, but I'm sure it didn't look that way to the outside world. I guess "playing" meant tackling, wrestling, jumping off the couch, taking each other to the floor, grappling, and boxing. Our small living room often became a boxing ring or obstacle course where every toy was in play as a weapon or prop for their made-up game. Barbie dolls were frequently used as swords, feather boas served as ropes to tie one another up, and American Girl dolls served as fellow army soldiers. Kieran brought much excitement into Jack's life.

When Kieran got a little older, they shared a room and woke each other up with a morning hug. They talked about a game they wanted to play or make up for the day. Within half an hour, it all went wrong, and they chased each other, hoping to hurt the other. They would make up fifteen minutes later, and the routine started all over again. By the end of the day, they hugged each other goodnight and went to sleep as best friends. This daily routine taught my boys more life lessons than anything I could ever have taught them.

It was not always easy, but John and I somehow knew that these years, with four young children, would be the toughest yet the best of times. We knew the days would be long, but the years would go fast. During those early days, I dreaded John leaving for a twenty-four-hour shift. He would leave at 3 p.m. and not return until 7 p.m. the next night. Those long days were tough, taking care of four kids all by myself. I loved hearing the front door open, knowing I no longer had to care for all of them alone. I felt relieved that I was not the only one there.

Bringing children into this world is daunting, but what helped was knowing I was doing it with John. During my uncertainty, I knew I was not alone, and that made me come off the ledge. We would learn together, fail together, but most importantly, laugh together. Even on days when John did twenty-four-hour shifts, I knew he would eventually come through the door. When I heard his car pull into our driveway, a feeling of relief came over me. I took mental notes on everything I wanted to tell him throughout the day. We loved talking about our kids; of course, we thought everything they did was special.

With every additional child, we grew better at handling new worries and didn't sweat the small stuff. Like a leaky bucket, we would plug one hole, and another started dripping. But at the end of the day, we could always laugh and know we had each other's backs. We would do this life together.

Pregnant with Kieran, July 2004

John, the kids, and Lamby (who is still with Brielle), July 2004

CHAPTER 5

The Day My World Ended

On January 22nd, 2005, John woke up early to relieve a firefighter who had covered for him at his Bronx firehouse on another day. A blizzard was expected, so he wanted to beat the snow. When John kissed me goodbye, he said, "Remember, I bought the kids that Dr. Seuss tape for them to watch today." It would be something good to put on after an exhausting day in the snow.

I heard the door close and then reopen soon after. "I forgot the donuts for the guys, don't want them to give me hell for forgetting breakfast and showing up empty-handed." He did a quick about-face, "Actually, I just wanted one more kiss from you."

"You intentionally forgot so you could squeeze one more kiss from me, huh?" I said, after his lips met mine over Kieran's head as I nursed him.

"Yep, that was exactly my master plan." He gave me his signature smile with the ice-blue twinkle in his eye.

Then he walked out the door for the last time.

In the afternoon, John called to tell me he would most likely be held hostage for a second shift. John was expected home at 6 p.m. on January 22nd, but with the blizzard, other firefighters would not be able to get in safely.

We spoke on the phone again around 10 p.m. "You would be very proud of me."

"Why is that?" I asked.

"I skipped dessert tonight; I'm trying to stick to my New Year's Resolution."

"Nice job! Any chance you will have to stay for the day shift tomorrow?"

"No, I plan to get out of here right away so I can take the kids sledding tomorrow."

"Great, I'm looking forward to it, love ya."

"Love ya more."

We hung up, and that would be the last time I heard his voice.

The morning of January 23rd, I woke up to the wind outside howling, an unrelenting reminder of the previous night's blizzard. I woke up to a day that should have been simple, sweet, kind, and complete, not knowing it would become one of confusion, sadness, depression, and anxiety. As I did many mornings before, I turned on the TV with a trusting core that life is beautiful and that I was blessed.

"Breaking News," the newscaster said, "There's a huge fire currently taking place in the Bronx."

Those fourteen words blew up my life, my dreams, and my happiness ever after. Time stopped, and there was no sound, no air, and no feeling as I listened and took a deep breath. *It can't be. John is fine. He's strong. He is a great fireman. He knows what he's doing. He is fine.*

I listened intently as the news reported that two firefighters had fallen from the roof. I started making calls. First, I called John's cell phone—no answer. Then I called the firehouse, but no one answered. I continued trying until someone finally picked up the phone. "Hi, this is Eileen Bellew, wife of John Bellew. Can you tell me if they are at the fire?" There was a long pause.

"Yes, they are." *Ok, that's it. Tell me everything is okay, tell me John is fine, tell me they are heading back to quarters, and that he will call me when he gets there.* Instead, I begged and pleaded for more information.

"Can you tell me if a chauffeur would be on the roof? John was chauffeuring. Can you tell me if it was John who fell?"

His response left me lost, "We are relocated to 27, I don't have any information. Call back in a few minutes, we will have more information then."

Does no one want to give me an answer? Does no one want to be the one to break it to me?

I called back five minutes later, and no one picked up. With every ring, my heart pounded harder and harder. *Why are you not picking up! I need answers! Pick up! Is it John?*

I remembered that John once told me that someone from the fire department would come and get me if anything ever happened to him. I looked out the window every five minutes to see if a car was pulling up. I told myself, *That's great news. It must not be him. He must be busy at the fire. He is fine, strong, a great fireman, and he knows what he is doing.* Two hours passed. *No car showed up. No phone calls came. He must be fine.* I kept calling the firehouse and his cell phone, but no one answered.

While all this was taking place, I was putting on an award-winning performance for my kids so they didn't suspect something was wrong. I fed them, clothed them, read to them, and changed diapers, all on autopilot, with a half-smile and constant thoughts of John.

My mind started wandering in brutal agony. *Why has there been no contact from him? Is he okay, or is he just fighting the fire? Maybe he will be hurt, but I can take care of him. He is young, only thirty-seven, so it will be a challenge, but we can do it. This fire is just a bump in our road, but it will bring us closer. He is strong, and I am strong too. I can take on anything as long as he is by my side. It will make the kids stronger, too. Love can conquer all as long as he is fine.*

No car showed up. No phone calls came. *He must be fine.*

Family in the hospital right after Kieran was born

PART II

After John Jumped

This day forever divided my life into "Before" and "After," like a fault line through my core. All the photos I looked at would now have a tag in my head: *Oh, this is life when I was happy—when John was alive, or is this from my new life, the one I didn't ask for and didn't plan to live?*

CHAPTER 6

Last Goodbye

After two and a half hours passed, it finally dawned on me that I should call one of his friends from the firehouse. *His friend will think I'm silly because a Fire Chief would've come to get me if something were truly wrong. No one has even called me, so why should I be overreacting? He'll tell me I was crazy to worry and that John is probably just heading home. His cell phone's battery ran out, and he didn't have a car charger. He just wanted to get out of the firehouse, and he would tell me all about it when he got home.*

But when I called John's friend, I got his wife instead. Her voice came through the phone, and her tone changed when she realized it was me. *She knows something. How could she know something? John isn't her husband.*

"Oh, Eileen, how is John?" *Why does she sound sorry for me? He's fine, right? He's strong, young, and brave.*

"What do you mean...how is John? Why are you asking me that?"

With a quick flip of her voice, she replied, "I'll get Joe, hold on."

Why is she quickly rushing off the phone and handing it to her husband? Where is the small talk we're supposed to have, the jokes about me overreacting? Where is our good laugh? Why do I have a funny feeling that laughter will soon turn into tears?

Joe came to the phone and asked if someone had come to get me. "What? Why? Why would someone need to come and get me?" I screamed.

"Do you want me to come get you?"

Panic started to set in. "Where are we going? Why would you need to get me?"

Finally, he told me what I already knew. "It was John. He's one of the firemen they're talking about on TV."

He's the story the news is running. *Why am I the last to know?* But maybe I did know all along. When the news reporter spoke about the fire, my inner cells knew John was in danger. It was a gut feeling, almost as if my heart began to break before I got any official confirmation. It was like the angels were preparing me for the inevitable. Maybe John's soul was taken then, even though his heart continued to beat for a few more hours.

I waited to be picked up and looked out the door, still expecting someone from the fire department to come and get me, as John had told me they would. *John must not be that bad, as I'm not worthy enough for a ride to the hospital. They only keep those rides for the wives who will be getting bad news.* I watched as a car drove down my street. *Is this my death ride?* But, no, it was my mom coming to watch my four kids.

"Mommy has to go with Joe and Aunt Patricia for a little while. I'll be back soon." I tried explaining to my kids.

Brielle said, "Is Daddy coming home soon? He is taking us sledding."

I smiled. "He will be back as soon as he can."

Joe pulled up in his four-wheel drive at the same time as my sister. Everyone was trying to make light of the situation, pretending that my later fate might not play out.

As I was leaving the house, I started to feel sick. I kissed my precious loves goodbye, knowing that I might not return as the same mom they knew. I was walking out the front door of a home where four (maybe five, someday) children would be raised by two parents, with two value systems, two morals, and two life experiences from which we could teach the kids life lessons. I was leaving my household, which had a partner with whom I had signed up to be a co-parent. As crazy as the world could be with four kids under six, we were prepared to do it together. I was walking out as a "we," knowing very well that I could be walking back in as only "me."

I looked up the street, searching for the car that should have come to get me if something was really wrong. *This is unbelievable! Why am I driving with Joe in a blizzard? Who drives in a blizzard?* The roads were a mess, and we could barely see two feet in front of us. We made small talk about how much fun the kids would have if John needed crutches or a wheelchair for a short time. However, phone calls kept coming in, and Joe took them on his cell phone. I listened between nervous laughs with my sister, but I couldn't hear what was being said.

Finally, I stopped being polite and just asked, "What are all those calls about?" He told me there wasn't much news yet. But I knew something was up. *Why are there so many phone calls?*

We reached the George Washington Bridge, and I got an eerie feeling. We made the turn off the ramp onto the bridge, and in front of us were two cop cars with their lights on.

"Joe, watch out for those cop cars." Joe is on the phone describing the car we were driving. "Why are you describing our car? What is going on?"

"We are getting a police escort from the bridge to the hospital."

"WHAT?! WAIT A MINUTE! I DON'T WANT A POLICE ESCORT!" *Is this my death ride? Is this my promised drive to the hospital if something is really wrong? STOP! STOP THE CAR! I WANT TO GET OUT!*

I looked at my sister; her face said it all. A cross between desperation and reassurance that everything will be okay, someday.

The ride was surreal. The two police cars with lights and sirens were ahead of us, and one car was behind us. People were looking into our car, trying to figure out my story. It was the first time of many when my mind and body went someplace else, almost like when no one remembers the pain of a car accident. My mind lifted above me. The air grew heavy; I could no longer hear what was said. I tried to understand what was happening to me, but my mind would not let me go there as a defense mechanism. I became robotic, moving automatically but not intentionally. The only two things I could feel were my heart beating quickly and my lungs trying to breathe enough air to continue living.

I don't want to be the story. I want to return to my house with my four kids and wait for my husband to come home. He promised the kids he would take them sledding today. Why aren't I making hot chocolate and putting their wet clothes in front of the fireplace? Instead, I'm in a car with screaming sirens announcing my arrival.

We pulled up to the St. Barnabas Hospital parking lot and were greeted by four camera crews. My first thought was that something big must have been happening, maybe a celebrity had been admitted. But I quickly realized they were interested in *our* car—they wanted *my* photo! I rushed to the front door through the flickering flashes. The scene was bizarre. No one had ever wanted my photo before. *Just stop!*

The emergency doors automatically opened, and a wave of eyeballs fell on me. It had to be serious. There were between 300 and 400 firefighters waiting in the hallways. Some were in their turnout coats, some in their uniforms, and many in their regular clothes. I recognized quite a few of them and noted that they all lived farther north than I did. *How did they get here before I did?* It would mean they passed my exit on the way to the hospital. I didn't understand how they didn't stop to pick me up or call. *Shouldn't I have taken precedence in communication?* I was too worried to be angry then. The anger came later.

I was greeted by the senior firefighter in John's firehouse. I walked up to him and blatantly asked, "Is he dead?" I thought that by asking such an extreme question, he would calm my fears, allowing me to tackle whatever the real challenge was. But he didn't calm my fears; he only made them grow. Instead of responding, I was escorted through a maze of firefighters to a waiting room for family members awaiting news.

The room was packed with firefighters, so they ushered me to a small office with chairs. I sat in a folding chair next to my sister, facing a woman typing at her computer. The woman quickly realized the severity of the moment and excused herself. An older man and woman came in and sat next to us. I would later find out they were the Cawleys, parents of Brendan, another injured firefighter.

The first doctor came in and sat next to me. He began to talk, and seeing his serious nature, the Cawleys got up and left. Only my sister remained with me. I had started my walk from the car with media and cameras flashing and was greeted by hundreds of firefighters. Then, I was directed to a room with a secretary and other family members. Finally, it was just me, my sister, and a doctor. It's incredible how your community dwindles so significantly as the seriousness of your event escalates. It surely reflects the cruel irony of life: though many people can surround you, when the real shit goes down, you're the only one standing, waiting to take the blow. Thank God my sister was willing to take it with me.

The doctor began to explain the gravity of John's condition. "Mr. Bellew is very, very sick, and we are going to do everything we possibly can to help him." At first, I thought that this was an odd way of saying it. *If he's sick, then you can give him medication, and he will get better.* My brain wasn't understanding. I also thought: *Well, of course, you are going to do everything you can to help him. Why wouldn't you?*

What the doctor should have said was, "Mr. Bellew is very, very broken, and we will try everything to put him back together again." Essentially, that's what was wrong with John. The fall had broken his body into many pieces, and they had to first deal with the trauma placed on his brain before they could fix anything else.

"Mr. Bellew has already coded twice but has been brought back to life. He must know you are in the hospital and wants to see you." *What are you saying? John died twice, but was still fighting? What are we waiting for? I want to see John now!*

The doctor warned me about his appearance. I disregarded his warnings. I needed to see him. They were bringing him to the

ICU to stabilize him. They took me up in the elevator to another waiting room filled with many other families. It was cramped and hot, and at that point, I realized just how many families this deadly fire was affecting. I heard that one fireman had lost his life in the emergency room.

I waited until they were ready for me, then entered the ICU, filled with machines buzzing and nurses and doctors running around. It was exactly like the trauma wards you see on TV. I entered John's room, and his captain stood guard at the foot of his bed. When a firefighter is injured, another firefighter is assigned to watch over them at all times. I expected John to be unrecognizable, but he was the same old John: the dominant cowlick in his hairline, his rosacea complexion, the scar on his right cheek from a ski accident years before, his collar bone that stuck out because of the same accident, the hole in his ear from an earring he wore in the 80s, and his freckled skin that he insisted got tan, but I knew it was just millions of freckles mushed together. The only thing I couldn't see were the icy blue eyes I fell in love with. Instead, they were swollen shut, and all I could do was pray I would see them again.

It's surreal to be talking to your husband in such a dire condition. You feel like you're in the movies playing a role and waiting for the director to say, "Cut, let's do it again," but reality quickly sets in. This is really happening.

I walked over to his bed and could tell his right leg was shattered, so I pensively sat on the side of the bed so as not to cause him any additional pain. I could see his ears were burned, along with some of his face, but those were the least of his injuries. Machine after machine was attached to every part of his body. Nurses monitoring his every breath, his every heartbeat. It did not take long for me to see that John was not in a good way.

John looked very tired but had a smirk on his face. One could even argue it was a smile. There were so many machines beeping and screaming that I couldn't even begin to ask, "So this one is monitoring what? Do we want him in a certain range?" I felt so helpless; even if I knew what to ask, I'm pretty sure I wouldn't have wanted to know the answers.

"Hi, love, we are in a tough spot here. It's going to be okay. We're going to fight this. We will figure this out together. It'll take time, but you are strong, and we'll do it together. Don't leave me, John. I don't want to live this life without you; the kids need you, so keep fighting. The kids need their dad. I need you. Fight like hell." *That's what I'm supposed to say, right?* I spoke to John the way I saw people do on TV on *ER*. Once I said it, he would squeeze my hand, open his eyes, and give me a hopeful look. But as I continued to speak, that didn't happen, and my heart slowly broke.

"We need to make sure those burns don't leave a scar on that handsome face of yours, Mr. Bellew," the nurse said, while she pushed his hair back and put ointment on his burns. I will forever be grateful to her for treating John like a king. She wiped away the blood flowing out of his nose so I couldn't see. But I soon figured out that he was bleeding to death. The blood was coming out of every opening. She fixed his blanket fifty times while I was talking to him, knowing he was dying, but making sure he was going to go out with dignity.

For the hour I spent with John, this reality hovered between us and was hard to ignore, but she and I did our jobs the best we could. For my sake, she nursed a dying man as if he were going to live. For John's sake, I lived as a hopeful wife pretending not to be dying inside.

But we both knew.

I held four photos while talking to him. The nurse got me a plastic bag to put the pictures in and put them beside his head as she plumped up his pillow. As I continued to give John a pep talk, my tone changed. I realized this wasn't the movies, and John was dying. It was selfish of me to ask him to fight. It was selfish of me to ask him to stay. It was selfish of me to ask him to endure a life that would not be John; it would have been a shell of him. His life would not have been anything close to what he knew if he had survived. It would have been hell to watch him be inside his body and not be able to talk, read, communicate, laugh, and contribute to this world the way he wanted.

I quickly realized the cruelest thing I could have done was beg him to stay. So, I gave him permission to go. I had a gut feeling that was what he was waiting for.

"You know what, John, I can see that you're tired, and I completely understand if you don't want to fight. We will be OK. I promise you, the kids and I will be okay. You know how much we love you and want you with us, but we don't want you to suffer. If you have to go, I understand, but make sure you watch over them and help me from heaven. I love you more than life itself, so if you have to leave, I understand; just be the first to meet me when I get there."

At that point, the neurosurgeon came into the room. "We will need you to leave so I can evaluate Mr. Bellew for surgery. We need to try to relieve the swelling in his brain." I was trying to read his demeanor and see if he looked hopeful. My look must have been one of desperation, because he followed with: "I promise, after my evaluation, I will come get you, and you can come back in."

In a small way, I was relieved; it was a lot to sit at the side of the bed watching John fight for his life. I wanted him to go into surgery and be fixed, but I had a feeling that this might be my last time seeing him alive. I kissed John, touched his hand, trying to take a mental picture of him to keep in my memory bank.

"Can I have one of those?" I asked the nurse, pointing to one of the gauze pads she had covered in his blood. I'm not sure why I wanted it. I guess it was something I could hold that was part of him. She put it in a plastic bag for me, and I left the four pictures of our kids right next to his head on the pillow.

They again promised I could come back in once the doctor finished his evaluation. I went to the waiting room, and that promise would never come true. John would leave this world with the photos of his four kids on his pillow.

John with Brielle

CHAPTER 7

Waiting Room

I felt like a rock star, with people clawing to get to me... patting me on the back or giving me endless hugs and words of encouragement, until the doctor walked into the waiting room. All the people who wanted to be around me no longer wanted to be. He was the plague no one wanted to be near. I might as well have had the disease, too.

The doctor looked around, glaring at the person whose heart he would break. I looked up at him, but I was next to three other families waiting for news of their loved ones. The expression on his face told the story. I knew he was John's doctor, but maybe he was the other firefighter's doctor, too. *Please don't let it be John.* I prayed to God really, really hard that the doctor would be telling another family that their loved one had passed, not me. I know wishing death upon another family isn't moral, but I was desperate. I didn't want anyone else to die that day, but I wanted even less for it to be my husband. *Please, please, God, I can't do this life without that man, please, please have the doctor tell another family.*

I remember staring at this one tile on the floor: the lines made a distorted heart; it was my focal point, so I didn't have to watch everyone else staring at me. The doctor walked toward me. I looked away and stared at my heart. The room became quiet, and my world was silent. My world went deafeningly silent. Although I felt him walk toward me, I hoped he would keep walking past me toward the other families. *Keep walking. Please, keep walking. Don't stop.* I promised God that I would be supportive of those poor families who lost their loved ones.

But instead, the doctor stopped. He actually stomped on my heart. He stood on my tile heart, and then his words stomped all over my heart: my dreams, my life, my kids' lives, and our future.

How can this be? Maybe he thinks I'm someone else. Yes, that's what's happening. He thinks I'm the wife of one of the other firefighters. It makes no sense. John is strong, fit, and built like a brick shithouse. He has legs like tree trunks and a wingspan that lets him carry all his kids at once, with room to spare. He works out every day. He can survive one fall. Okay, some broken bones make sense. I already considered the rehab ahead of us, but we would tackle it together. *The kids will have fun playing with his wheelchair and his crutches.* All these thoughts passed through my mind as the doctor approached me during his 10-step trek to reach me.

"Mrs. Bellew, I'm sorry. We tried everything; his injuries were too traumatic and difficult for him to overcome."

WAIT, WAIT, WAIT! STOP TALKING! STOP TALKING! WHY ARE YOU TALKING TO ME? After that, I heard nothing; the air grew heavy, and everything slowed to a crawl. It took every ounce of energy I had to lift my head to look at the doctor, and when I did, there it was: the loneliness. No one except the doctor, my sister, and a chaplain was in the room. I was the rock star two minutes earlier, and everyone wanted to be around me. Then, I was alone.

Stunned, I rocked back and forth, almost in a fetal position. *What should I do next? Our kids... How do I tell our kids? Who will teach the boys how to shave? Who is going to walk the girls down the aisle at their wedding?* I looked for the chaplain. I needed guidance. I needed help. My faith was shaken. *He had to have taken a course on this? A course that gives them a speech they hand off to the widow to tell their children after their parent dies. How could God take him from me?*

God just took my whole world from me, so, as you might imagine, I wasn't a big fan of God at that moment. *How could you take him? He was my world; he was the world of our kids. And how am I supposed to move on? How am I supposed to be enough for those kids?* I was standoffish when the chaplain sat next to me. Representing God, he also represented my disappointment in God. He didn't give me much insight. He didn't deliver a magical speech that would help soften the blow for my kids. He was kind and comforting, but what words could change what just happened?

And then the obligations started.

The Mayor of New York, Michael Bloomberg, appeared out of nowhere to give me his sympathies and his obligatory speech that all FDNY widows must get.

"I'm so sorry for your loss, Mrs. Bellew. And may I speak for the people of New York City to express how indebted we are to Mr. Bellew's supreme sacrifice, and for dedicating his life to keeping us safe. The City of New York appreciates your husband's service. He is one of the bravest, running into the building when all else ran out... Thank you for your service and your children's service..."

The Mayor of New York is standing in front of me! What do I do? Curtsy? Talk politics? Make small talk? I just stared at him. In my head, he was saying, "Blah, blah, blah."

I sat there, stunned. "Thank you." *Why am I thanking him?* The City of New York just took my life, took my future, took my kid's dad, and I said thank you.

I heard a doctor offer my sister Xanax to help me deal with this trauma and get through the following week. My sister told the doctor I was breastfeeding, and the doctor said, "Oh, sorry, then she can't take anything." What a fantastic way to add salt to my wound; I couldn't even benefit from any mind-numbing drugs. I think I would have liked to have been in a different dimension that first week. Though between my broken heart and scrambled brain, my body put me in a numb state naturally. I was numb all over.

The other families eventually returned to the waiting area and gave me sympathetic looks. I hated them all. Of course, I didn't really, but their loved ones were still alive, and mine was not. I was supposed to be giving them awkward, sympathetic words, but I had to hear theirs instead. I wanted to scream, "You know what you can do with your supportive, sympathetic gestures? You can shove them where the sun doesn't shine." Thank God I had some sense and kept it all inside, but I don't blame anyone who lashes out in similar situations.

After all the formalities of the waiting room had passed, John's body was ready to be driven down to the morgue. His friend Bobby, a fellow firefighter at his house, would stay with John for the ride. A firefighter was assigned to stay with John's body twenty-four hours a day until he was handed off to the funeral parlor. And as I would quickly learn, a firefighter would be parked outside my house to provide standing guard and protection for our family.

I walked behind John's body, draped in white on a gurney. Hundreds of firefighters lined the halls, forming a pathway and saluting the body as we walked past. Despite the crowd, as I stared at the floor, the silence enveloped me, pierced only by the stifled cries from New York's strongest, bravest, burliest men ever created. This solemn walk out of the hospital felt like an out-of-body experience, almost like something you would watch on TV. I was walking my lifeless husband out to the ambulance, where we would part ways. I would drive back to our home to tell his loves that he was dead while the morgue prepared for his heroic departure.

My body turned into a sack of bones as I could barely walk out of the emergency room. I was aware of all the stares and how some firefighters looked away because seeing me reminded them that this could be their wife. I represented what could go wrong by choosing this profession and what could happen to their families if their nightly prayers went unanswered. The walk through the lobby seemed longer than when I had arrived. I appreciated some of John's friends breaking the tension with a sympathetic hug. Yet, every face looked the same. I couldn't remember anyone's name or even muster up a thank you. Somehow, I got into a car, but not before I heard cameras taking photos of me in my worst hour of grief. *Does that make the media happy? A woman in the worst hours of her life?*

John and I parted at the emergency room doors. They would analyze his broken heart that could not keep up with his injuries and then prepare him to be honored by thousands. I would drive home with my broken heart and go break his children's little hearts.

John got a police escort to the morgue, where they performed an autopsy that no one asked if I wanted him to have, but I guess it was protocol. I hated the thought that every part of his body would be cut open, examined, measured, and put back together. Wasn't it obvious why he died? John jumped. Still, as my brilliant husband's beautiful, strong body lay on a cold gurney, a doctor made notes about his insides as he took out his organs, weighed them, evaluated them, and created a story of John's last minutes on Earth.

Twenty-four hours earlier, my love was capable of benching 240lbs., running a mile, and making me laugh.

John and I running the NYC marathon

Katreana's 2nd Birthday - 5 months before John jumped

CHAPTER 8

The Memory Of Their Faces

There are a few things ingrained in my mind, playing on repeat. One of them was my six-year-old daughter's face when I told her that her dad would never come home again. I see it as vividly as if it just happened. If I allow myself to return to that moment, I lose my breath, even though twenty years have passed.

I drove home from the hospital in a fireman's car. I didn't want the ride to end. As each mile passed and I was getting closer to my house, my stomach became physically ill. *What was I supposed to do with this information?* I was about to ruin four kids' lives. The lives they were supposed to have will vanish in a split second once the words leave my mouth. A thought crossed my mind… *What if I don't tell them? What if I tell them their dad is at work? How long will it last before they know I'm hiding something?* The idea was ridiculous, but I knew 100% of people in the world wouldn't want to take on this task.

I could hear my kids playing upstairs with my sister, Kathleen, when I entered my house. They were jumping up and down on the beds and laughing hysterically. *This is the last laugh they will have with two parents.*

My house was crammed with people. My breasts were filled with milk and ready to feed my five-month-old. I had to take care of that before I could do anything else. Even in the worst moments of my life, I still had to be a good mommy and feed my son.

My family sat in our small Cape Cod living room, with toys scattered everywhere, and no one was crying. I come from an Irish Catholic family where it seems tragedy happens often, and we are expected to deal with it. Crying is a weakness; you have to deal with what is handed to you, pull up your bootstraps, and handle it. My mom is the strongest person in the world. She had been given a tough life, and she dealt with it. At that moment, though, and many moments after, I didn't want to fit that mold. I didn't want to deal with it. I wanted to scream, I wanted to cry, I wanted to throw a tantrum. I didn't want to be Irish. I wanted to be whatever ethnicity where you can scream and cry and not hold it together.

My family looked at me; I don't even remember being hugged. They must've told me they were sorry, but that was it. When life is too sad, we don't discuss it. Such is life as an Irish Catholic. But in that moment, I struggled with the expectations placed on me by my upbringing and my own need to express my grief.

I finished breastfeeding and put Kieran in a mechanical swing to rock him back and forth before I went to my room to lie alone on John's side of the bed. I half tried to suffocate myself while screaming into his pillow, crying as I had never cried before. My new reality hit me hard. John's sneakers, sitting under the bed, would never be worn again. *Do I fold his clothes in the laundry basket next to me?* This is a defining moment of my life, a defining moment in my kids' lives, the very moment I will tell them that their lives have changed for good. I took a deep breath and asked for Brielle to be sent to my room.

Even now, while writing this twenty years later, my stomach feels sick, and my palms sweat. Even after all we have tackled and accomplished, I can't think about this moment from my past, the worst moment of my life. I'm having a panic attack as I type. I'm sweating, and it feels like a 1000 lbs. weight is on my chest. I have tried writing this many times before, and I physically can't. I usually move on to other things to write to avoid this entry...

Brielle walked into my bedroom with a huge smile and jumped into my arms, yelling, "Mommy, you're home!" I squeezed her hard, and the tears flooded my eyes. I felt like I had to rip the Band-Aid off immediately. I couldn't wait any longer. Brielle was only six, but intuitive and could sense something was wrong.

"Did Daddy come home? Are we going sledding?"

"There was a fire. Daddy was searching for a baby when the fire got out of control. Daddy couldn't get out and got hurt badly. He went to the hospital, but the doctors couldn't save him."

Her brow curled, and her gaze stared into my eyes. "Why are you saying that? Why are you being so mean? Don't say that about Daddy! Don't be so mean. Why are you being mean to Daddy? He's coming home."

And then I had to convince my baby that no, her dad was never coming home, even though we told her that he would always come home.

How stupid were we? Why did we promise that? There was always a chance John could have gotten hurt; why would we promise his safety? We did what every other fire family does when their loved one leaves for a 24-hour shift.

Brielle was furious at me. "How could you be so mean and say such horrible things about Daddy?"

"Daddy was doing his job, and he was told that a baby was in the building. He got caught in the fire. The doctors did everything they could, but Daddy didn't make it and is now in heaven." It broke my heart to keep telling her I wasn't trying to be mean, but was just telling the truth.

"Why are you saying that? Why would you say something so mean about Daddy? Stop saying that."

"I'm so sorry, sweetie, I wish it weren't true." And just like that, I crushed her world.

Firefighters have different jobs from other parents. They must explain to their kids that they will miss holidays, birthdays, and family events due to their job. They have to explain that they are protecting their community every minute of the day, not just from 9 a.m. to 5 p.m. They risk their lives for others. We explain this to our children early on. Children understand the heroic profession their parents chose for the betterment of society, but no parent wants to expose their children to the real dangers of firefighting. Why choose to create anxiety when 99% of firefighters go home safely? We didn't explain the risks before John jumped, so it was difficult for my children to understand what happened to him.

I hate when people say, "Oh, they were young; they won't remember." Young children live in a protected bubble where bad things don't happen to them. When your dad jumps out of a burning building and plummets to his death, that bubble pops. Bad things happen, and when kids are young, it takes more effort to explain that to them because they haven't yet experienced sadness. I wouldn't tell my kids full details until years later, but the story behind the words, "Daddy isn't coming home. He went to heaven," doesn't need details. Unfortunately, I had to tell them repeatedly until they understood, because children know only happily ever after. And our story had a different ending.

I told each child individually so I could personalize what each might need to hear. Jack went second. He came barreling into the room like always, jumping on the bed. I experienced a sudden shift from extreme joy to sadness in thirty seconds.

"Where's Daddy? Are we going sledding?" Jack was only three, and your dad is your best friend at three. Jack had spent most of his life with John.

"There was a fire, and Daddy went to it, and he got hurt. Daddy went to the hospital, and the doctors tried hard, but Daddy didn't make it, and he won't be coming home."

I couldn't use the word "died."

"So when is Daddy coming home?" Jack asked.

"He isn't sweetheart."

"So I'll see him tomorrow." Jack smiles at me and gives me a hopeful look. Another piece of my heart is broken.

"Daddy went to heaven with all the other angels."

"Can I call him in heaven?" Jack asked.

"You can always talk to Daddy, but he won't be able to answer." My shattered heart continued breaking as I tried to help my boy understand. "Daddy loves you, he'll always love you, and I love you so much."

"Can I go back and play?" he says.

I hugged him so hard and just said, "Yes."

Kat walked into the room and ran to me for a hug. By this time, my eyes were beyond swollen from crying, and I'm sure my face looked like a wrecking ball had hit it. She wasn't able to jump up on the bed like her brother, and I pulled her up into my arms. Katreana squeezed me hard and then looked at me with her curious stare. Even at two, she knew something was wrong.

"What's a matter, Mommy? Why are you sad?"

"There was a fire, and your daddy got hurt, and the doctors tried everything, but he did not make it." I'm unsure if she fully got it, but she started crying. She understood this was a heavy moment, a sad moment. I'm just not sure if she understood it was a life-changing moment.

"Jack pushed me off the bed." Her little face looked confused. She asked, "Daddy isn't coming home tonight?"

"Right, not tomorrow either; he's in heaven." I couldn't say "or never," but that was the truth… Never again.

Kieran was the last one to tell. You may wonder, *Why did you tell a five-month-old?* I don't know why it was important for me to tell him, but it was. I didn't want him growing up with no one ever telling him that his father died. I went to the mechanical swing he was swaying in, and as I approached, the most miraculous sight appeared, signaling our future connection to John. A beautiful rainbow shot across Kieran's sweet face. I was stunned. *Where is this rainbow coming from?* The swing was not near a window, and we were in the dead of winter during a blizzard.

I picked him up and brought him to my room, as I had with the other three. I told him the same thing as I did with the others, but I used the word "died" this time. I think that was for me. I needed to say the words, "Your dad died," after watching my language carefully for the others. I was freer to spit it out with Kieran. Of course, he just looked at me, but I squeezed him as hard as I could, knowing that his life just became so very different.

Kieran would have a life without a dad, coach, teacher, or anyone to teach him how to tie a tie, shave, or treat a lady. I felt terrible for my kids; they were stuck with only me. Fifty percent of what they deserved, and now that I was broken, I couldn't even guarantee fifty percent. They deserved more. A life without John's guidance, love, support, and help was an unbearable thought and even worse, they were left with just me, broken and feeling like I was incapable of being enough for them.

To this day, I look at every picture taken, and I figure out my kid's ages to decide if this was taken before or after sadness. Is Kieran younger than five months old, Katreana younger than two, Jack younger than three, and Brielle younger than six years old? If it's close, I look for evidence in the photo for the time of year. I don't know why I still do this, but I need to know where our headspace was when the photo or video was taken. *Is the smile tainted? Am I faking it for the photo op? Do my kids think that someone is missing from this event?* From an outsider's perspective, our photos depict a happy family that celebrates every birthday and holiday with loved ones around them. Still, the reality is that there is always someone missing.

It took me fifteen years to watch John on a video. To me, video is much sadder than still photos. I didn't want to see him moving or talking because it filled my day with too much sorrow. I got all our home videos put onto DVDs (now antiquated), and it took me years to gather the nerve to watch them. My kids haven't watched them either; I'm not sure why not. They are old enough to make their own decisions, but I'm still trying to protect them. Maybe I feel like it will open up wounds that have been scarred over for a while. Why show them what they missed? He was an awesome dad and a fantastic husband. If I show the videos, they will see what they missed and be reminded of a life before. But I also know they carry a part of him within them, keeping me going.

When I finally got the nerve to look at my wedding videos fifteen years after John jumped, some crazy things became clear. The power of genetics was screaming through the screen. John's mannerisms, his walk, the way he cocked his head, the way he half smiled, the way you can tell John is deep in thought, even though he is not talking. These were all the things I was trying to avoid seeing because, as much as I wanted to remember everything about him, I tried to remember nothing. But as I watched the video, I realized that everything I tried to avoid was happening in my kitchen every day.

My two sons have all of John's mannerisms, his smirk, his personality traits, everything I was trying not to see. You can't fight genetics. I was scared to see John alive on video, but who was I kidding? He is alive in his kids. Though they did not physically see him as they grew up, they somehow have all his looks, style, sense of humor, and thank God, the trait of being a good human being. I watch the videos now, but they still make me sad. Though I love visiting the happy times, I now watch them and calculate how much time has passed since After.

Even while I write about telling my kids their dad died, I try to think of anything else to write about so I can avoid it. I go off on a tangent to avoid the feelings. Twenty years later, I still don't want to remember it.

Christmas - One month before John jumped

CHAPTER 9
Funeral

When the death of your husband is a public story, you lose some intimacy in the events following it. Within the first twenty-four hours of John's death, the FDNY took over my house and took charge of all the pageantry. Part of me was thankful, because, at thirty-five years old, I could honestly say we never had a serious conversation about his funeral arrangements, life insurance, or where or how I would lay my husband to rest. I thought we had plenty of time to discuss it after our children had children and we retired to a warm place. At that point, I would be able to say how John would like to be laid to rest and what his wishes around his burial were. Of course, by then, we would have our finances set up so neither of us would have had to worry about the future. But none of that took place. *Oh my God, our finances! How am I going to pay for this house, food, and car payment?* All of a sudden, person after person entered my small house that was cluttered with toys and breakfast dishes to discuss the grandiose ceremony they would call my husband's funeral.

There is no course for the wives called Just in Case… when your loved one enters the Fire Academy. Instead, when tragedy strikes, you are blindsided, and every waking moment becomes a blur. The firefighters who come into your house are a part of the Ceremonial Unit; unfortunately, they have done this before. They understand the plans that must be made, the arrangements, the phone calls, and the decisions, and they have a checklist to get through. Each task has to be completed in a particular order, and then they move on to the next. The first question: What funeral parlor do you use? It was as if the question were as simple as: which pizza parlor do you order from?

"Wait, stop! How am I paying for this? Do I still have health insurance? I think my mortgage payment is due in a few days."

"I apologize, financially, you will be okay. The FDNY will pay for the funeral services; you will continue to receive John's salary, and you will also receive Social Security Benefits for your children. We thought someone explained that to you." *Why would I know that? John died less than twenty-four hours ago.* I took a deep breath and tried to focus on the questions they asked me.

"No, I don't have a funeral parlor that I use."

Then came a barrage of other questions, some personal and some related to Fire Department protocol. Everything was moving so fast, and I had no time to think about what I was answering. John's life, our life, and my kids' dad's life were wrapped up in a few questions. I quickly started having trouble breathing; it was becoming too real and too much.

I needed my world to slow down, but there was a funeral to plan, and they had to make arrangements for another firefighter as well. I wondered whether that widow felt the same way. *Was she struggling as much as I was? Was she having trouble breathing? Was she better prepared?* I love firefighters; they are the most extraordinary people in the world, but they are trained to save lives physically, not mentally. The Ceremonial Unit went through their checklist, asking crazy questions like how many limos I wanted, what kind of flower arrangements would be on John's casket, and who would be his pallbearers. They needed to know the eight firefighters he was closest to in the firehouse. *Oh God! Why didn't I listen better? I only knew their nicknames: Digger, Smackey, Rooster, Chachi, Tonto, Spunky, Wojo, Ski, Lomack, Bapo, Vomitbag, and The Hoot? What if I pick someone John hated?* The pressure to do everything right to honor John was piling up on me.

"Ummm, who is the one with two kids, his wife is pretty with auburn long hair, and he works for the Teamsters as his side job?"

They looked at me, shocked, "Oh, that would be Bobby."

Yes, that is his real name. How could I forget that? I was happy I got one name down. They start mentioning other names, "Oh no, not that one, John couldn't stand him."

Again, with the surprised looks. "I guess John shared a lot with you."

They discussed the dignitaries that would speak, and something inside me yelled, "Stop!" I found my voice deep beneath the grief and began to take some control back when it hit me: John died as a fireman, but that wasn't all he was. I couldn't let his life be defined by just one facet. That made his life feel so small, even though he was so much bigger than that. I appreciate the FDNY, but we must not forget that John was a son, brother, uncle, friend, father, husband, and a great fireman. My job was to push the brakes and allow all aspects of John's life to be celebrated. John had never met the Fire Commissioner or the Mayor of New York, so why would John want them to speak on his behalf? I didn't want a dignitary to read a speech crafted by a staff member who had researched John's life over the past twenty-four hours and had written it in the limo on the drive up to the church. "He was a hero for New York, a family man, and he made the supreme sacrifice by running into the building while everyone else ran out." They did not know John or the man he really was. They only knew the profession he chose.

"I don't want any dignitaries to speak on his behalf," I told the Ceremonial Unit.

Chaos erupted in my small house, and this time it had nothing to do with my children. Two of the firemen got on their cell phones and excused themselves to the bitter temperatures of my backyard.

"The Mayor and Commissioner want to speak. They usually speak in these circumstances," one of the others said. There were more side conversations, more phone calls, but I didn't care. This decision was non-negotiable. I didn't care what they thought of my decision.

The two from the yard returned, "If you make this decision, there is a good chance the dignitaries would not attend John's funeral."

"OK, no problem. The truth is, if John died in a car accident, they wouldn't be at his funeral. The church is small anyway, so it will leave more seating for others." Little did they know that the decision had been made long before this conversation.

After 9/11, John and I had a very morbid conversation about eulogies. He was adamant about not allowing Giuliani (or whoever the Mayor of New York was) to speak at his funeral. John was disappointed by how his administration treated firefighters. He was also disappointed that Giuliani, a fellow Jasper, and alumnus of Manhattan College, could disrespect firefighters the way he did. So, long before the Ceremonial Unit showed up at my house, John had decided that no dignitaries would speak on his behalf. At the time, that conversation was not real to us; it was just another one of our discussions about the day's events. There were no real discussions about John ever really dying in a fire because he always convinced me it would never happen.

On the day of the funeral, my sisters dressed my kids in expensive clothes that they had brought for them. My sister Terry bought my girls American Girl Doll coats because I'm sure their current coats were dirty, ill-fitting, and not funeral-ready. Terry also bought my boys outerwear so they wouldn't have to wear their current Rescue Heroes multi-color puffy jacket. My friend Marie bought me clothes and arranged for someone to come and blow-dry my hair.

I can't express just how invaluable those tasks were. I was in no position to get my kids or myself what I called "funeral ready." Not only did we not have proper clothes for the church, but I was well aware that my children would be in front of TV cameras, and though most people would be sympathetic, I didn't want my kids to represent their father looking disheveled and dressed in rags. It is an added pressure and obligation to present "funeral ready" to the world that has a lens into your saddest moments. I didn't want to let the world in, but obligation told me otherwise.

We were on a tight schedule and already running late, since it takes a long time to get four kids TV-ready. I say that in jest, as there was extra pressure to make sure the kids were bathed, with their hair combed, in nice clothes, and fancy winter gear. My sister ensured the kids looked presentable, which took the added stress off. We couldn't show up at their dad's funeral as we would have shown up on any other day.

Typically, I would let my kids wear whatever they wanted, but I knew these photos would follow them for eternity. If I allowed Brielle to pick out her outfit, she would have worn a pink boa, Dorothy's Wizard of Oz red, sparkly flats, and a tiara. Jack would have worn his alligator rain boots with his Rescue Heroes winter jacket, Katreana would have worn comfy leggings, and there was no chance her hair would have been combed. But I thought of the TV cameras and photographers circling the church.

The limousine picked us up at our house. My kids ran to the door, "Are we driving in that! Mom, this is soooo cool!" I just smiled at their innocence, *yes, very cool to be driving in a limousine to your father's funeral.*

We met the Ceremonial Unit at the funeral parlor, where I had my kids go in after John's casket was closed. Two lines of firefighters were lined up from the casket to the front door, making a pathway for us. There were more flower arrangements than you could ever imagine. One massive arrangement caught my eye as the kids barreled in. I looked at the card, and it read: *Brave to the End - With Sympathy, GlaxoSmithKline Pharmaceutical.* The rush of happier times flooded back to when John was honored in Scotland by the pharmaceutical company with a fellow fireman. Ironically, John represented the sacrifice of life that firefighters risk when leaving for work each shift. Four and a half years later, John, too, made the same sacrifice that the people of Scotland celebrated him for.

Now he is one of the Bravest he represented. *What a perfect sentiment to put on John's gravestone,* I thought.

I directed the kids along the path as the firefighters saluted them. Jack decided it would be fun to run around the funeral parlor. I couldn't get angry. He had no idea the gravity of the situation, and being three years old, he was always looking for an opportunity to play. I thought it was important for the kids to pray and see the closed casket, but I wasn't sure that was the right thing to do. Having them at the funeral home could have been the worst, most jarring thing I did for their development and grieving process, but no one was telling me what the right thing to do was.

I'd asked the chaplain in the ICU waiting room what I was supposed to do. He didn't have any answers. I asked many people what they would do, but no one had answers for how to help children grapple with sudden grief. No one wants to be responsible for giving the wrong advice. It could screw the kids up for life, so I did what I thought was right at the time. If I could go back in time, maybe I wouldn't bring them to the funeral parlor.

The kids were interested in returning to the limousine, so I sent them with my sister and asked if I could say goodbye to John alone. The FDNY always has two firefighters standing guard next to the casket, so I had to ask them to step away from their post. I appreciated the pageantry but needed time to say goodbye alone. Once the kids were back in the limousine, I had the funeral parlor director open the casket so I could talk to John and see him one last time. This conversation was an impossible one. *What do I say?* He knows I love him more than anything, I'll miss him more than words could ever explain, and what I really need is impossible.

I needed answers. I needed John to talk to me. I didn't need to speak. I needed him to tell me what to do next. "How am I going to live this life without you? We had a plan. The plan didn't involve you jumping and leaving me to raise our children alone. I know it wasn't your plan either, but now what am I supposed to do?" I touched his hair for one last time. I wanted to hug him.

What about all the parenting issues that are going to come up? I didn't even know what most of them were yet. Since Brielle was only six years old, I had a feeling that what we'd faced so far were easy parenting issues.

"How am I supposed to navigate the years ahead without your help?" My thoughts spiraled. *I don't know what I don't know, which was scary enough when I did it with him.*

"How about all the boy questions that I have no experience with?" *Are the kids going to be scarred forever by this? Did their destinies just take a left turn down a path of sadness and destruction?*

Even while sitting in front of John at the funeral parlor, I knew I wouldn't portray him only as an angelic hero to them because that's not real. It would have been easy to do that. Everyone else was doing it, but my job was to make their dad real to them. He had flaws. We all have flaws. They would see all of their mom's flaws firsthand, so I needed to point out their father's flaws, too. *I know I'll tell them about his crazy, double-jointed big toe, how he was color blind or how he still struggled with acne in his thirties. Will I tell them that if you pissed him off, he wouldn't back down, or that he often forgot to check in with me to let me know he would be late?*

Their dad needed to be authentic. The kids will ask questions about John as a person, but would I know the answers? I certainly didn't have his life history memorized. Will I make things up?

"Who is going to be my best friend now? Who am I going to grow old with? I can't have one of our epic debates by myself.

You made me a better person and a better mom; now I'm alone."
I had never felt more alone than in that funeral parlor. My whole
life lay in front of me, without John talking back.

I felt the time ticking. I knew everyone was waiting for me
to return to the limousine. Kneeling on the pulpit, I felt 500 lbs.
heavy. I didn't want to stand up. After this talk, I would have to
live without seeing John's face ever again. *Will I remember it? I
think I will, but I know that over time, things will fade. I can't
remember the sound of my dad's voice anymore. Memories are
increasingly clouded, and I don't want them to be. I wanted to
stay there forever.

The funeral director came behind me and put his hand
on my shoulder. *DON'T TOUCH ME!* I wanted to yell. *Let's do
the funeral tomorrow.* I knew he was doing his job, but he didn't
know me. John knows me. He would know not to touch me
during a tough time like this. There would be no one else who
knows me as John did. *I have to stand up, return to the limousine,
and be stronger than I have ever been in my whole life while the
rest of the world looks at me and judges me.*

"I'm okay." I returned to the lively limousine, with the kids
jumping from seat to seat, playing with the electric windows and
the divider separating them from the driver, while the driver
played peek-a-boo with them. Then we began the six-mile trek
to St. Margaret's Church behind the firetruck carrying John's
casket. Traffic was shut down for our procession so all the lim-
ousines could clear the traffic lights. At one of the intersections
leading to the church, an older man stepped out of his car as
we passed, even though the temperature was in the single digits.
While he stood on the street, he saluted the hearse as we passed
him by. It brought me to tears. The man has no idea what impact
this had on me. A stranger, standing in the frigid temperatures,

gave John a respectful goodbye. It was a beautiful tribute for his kids to see and remember. Thank you, stranger! It proves that one person's act of kindness can make a lifetime of difference.

The kids didn't want the ride to end, nor did I. There were cars parked along the highway for miles. It was something I had never seen before. The town was filled with a sea of blue uniforms.

We pulled up to our church, situated on a hilltop, overlooking our town. My young kids had no idea of the gravity of the situation and were just interested in raising and lowering the windows to watch the zoo outside the car. The quarter-mile hill was filled with firefighters all dressed in their heaviest department overcoats. An estimated 10,000 firefighters from all over the United States, and even other countries, came to show John respect for his sacrifice. I have been told it remains the coldest funeral ever attended by the FDNY Bravest. The support should have given me a sense of pride and honor, but it brought me nothing but a sense of reality.

Is this really happening? I read all of these stories on the front covers of the Daily News and New York Post, but I never really thought it would be my story, our story. John promised I would never be one of those women walking out of the church, being handed a folded-up flag with the flyover of helicopters.

Scaffolding was built across the street from the church to hold numerous TV reporters, satellite dishes, and lots of clicking cameras. They were all there to capture the tragic family that no longer had a father. My children were thrown into the spotlight, and I quickly realized they were being used as a photo opportunity. The moment was not lost on me; I knew we were today's news and maybe tomorrow's, but that was it. We would soon be distant memories, and all these caring faces would go home to their lives, while I am left to raise four children by myself.

Katreana and Brielle continued to play with the limo's windows. I wondered what they were thinking. *Why are all these people looking at us? Why are there so many cameras flashing photos of me?* Jack was interested in the firetruck in front of the limo. Jack only saw the truck and not his father's coffin lying on top of it. Kieran was getting antsy as it was time for his nap. I was hoping he would sleep right through the funeral.

We stepped outside, and all you could hear was the shutter of cameras one after another. The bagpipers played. The music I used to enjoy would no longer bring me joy, but remind me of this unbelievably cold funeral, my husband's funeral. I looked down the hill of Central Avenue and saw a sea of firefighters. *John's funeral is really happening.*

The Ceremonial Unit lowered John's body from the firetruck, and we watched as the eyes watched us. I walked into our church behind my husband's coffin on that freezing day in January. Every firefighter's partner will see this on TV at some point and pray to God they are never in this situation. I felt lifted out of my body, as if I were watching this happen to someone else.

It was so cold that for a minute, I could only focus on whether each child had enough clothing to protect their hands and face. My sisters helped me get the kids up the stairs and into the church, jammed with people I had never seen before. The adjoining auditorium and gym were simulcasting the service so others could see. A choir recruited from a Broadway cast sang from a loft the most beautiful, sad songs anyone would ever hear. I slowly walked in behind the coffin and couldn't look up because all the faces looking at me were sobbing. I hated the pity, and I knew it was kindness they were showing me, but I didn't want pity. Mostly, I didn't want to be there.

Many "important" dignitaries were there, but I didn't care. All I could think was *I am attending my husband's funeral.* However, I appreciated the send-off from Archbishop Egan from St. Patrick Cathedral in New York City and the other high-ranking priests. Standing in the front row were Mayor Bloomberg, the New York City Fire Commissioner Scoppetta, Governor Pataki, the Chief of Department, Peter Hayden, and several dignitaries and firefighters. It felt impersonal. *How many of these people would be here if he had died in a car accident? I just hope John's friends and family get into the church.*

The Mass was beautiful, the singing was amazing, and it went by all too quickly. Kieran was not happy to be sitting in my arms, and as time passed, my breasts began to fill with milk. Wouldn't that be a great story? The widow pulled out her breast in the middle of the funeral to feed her son. As Kieran fussed more and more, I could feel myself letting milk flow. A woman came down the aisle and asked if I wanted her to take him.

I wanted to say, "No, this is his father's funeral. Is he bothering everyone's experience? I'm sorry if I am making everyone uncomfortable, but you will all have to listen to him getting fussy because he has more of a right to be here than any of you." Instead, I politely declined. He eventually settled down.

At the end of the Mass, the eulogies followed. No dignitaries spoke on John's behalf. The captain from John's firehouse spoke instead. Chief Sullivan did a great job of personalizing John as a person and a fireman. Afterward, his best friend, Tom Moran, spoke and described John as True Blue. This reference would be used many times moving forward, and later, his memorial shirt, made by the FDNY for its fallen heroes, said "True

Bellew" along the back. Tom described John as a loyal friend, brother, husband, and father. John would always help anyone in need, and you could always count on him. He was honest, trustworthy, and constant. He was true blue.

John's brothers spoke, giving an insight into their upbringing. John was what Irish families call a "change of life baby." Just when you think you are done having kids, God decides you need one more. There was a significant age gap between John and his brothers and sister. He was the youngest of five, so they all treated him like their baby. He enjoyed the benefits of being spoiled by four siblings who didn't mind taking him everywhere and giving him the advantages they didn't have growing up.

Then it was my turn. It was important to me to speak on John's behalf. I thought it was a good idea a couple of days earlier, so my sister's husband, Bill, helped me put something together. However, I wasn't sure if I could speak once I reached the pulpit. The air in the church was so heavy. The smell of incense and the heat of hundreds of bodies jammed into one place made it hard to breathe. I handed Kieran off for someone to hold and unsteadily walked along the marble floors with shoes that were way too tight and high for the moment. I made sure not to look up at the crowd, knowing it might knock me off my game. I had my speech typed out on paper, now drenched with sweat. I just wanted to do a good job for John, my kids, and his parents. And then the numbness took over, and I left my body. Somehow, I delivered it. My eulogy was a letter to God.

"Dear God..."

My voice cracked. *If I am going to do this, I want everyone to hear it.* I stepped closer to the microphone and belted out the best I could.

"I am writing to let you know a little bit about the newest angel to join your legion. As you are aware, and as the circumstances of his death prove, John Bellew was a strong, kind, and courageous man."

Just saying his name melted my heart.

"He died bravely, choosing to ignore the basic instinct of fleeing from danger in favor of the truly generous response of helping those in need. I know that he was not scared as he ran into that burning building, but rather, he was excited and determined to help others who, at that time, were unable to help themselves.

"While I know he loved being a fireman, his true love and his true gift was being a dad. He was truly the greatest dad a child could have.

"I first became aware of this gift, and his boundless love of kids, as I watched the nurses give him ice chips and ask if he was okay while I gave birth to our first child, Brielle."

I prayed the audience would laugh. Luckily, I could hear the crowd chuckle. *OK, they are with me, we're going to do this. They understand my mission, to express my deepest love for him with sentiment and humor, just as John did for me daily.*

"He quickly took on the role of Mr. Mom and somehow trained Brielle to sleep in the nook of his arm until 10 a.m. every morning. Don't get the wrong idea, though, God. He did this trick simply so that he did not have to wake up early.

"He also proved to be a good teacher, as the first thing he taught Brielle was how to load and run his coffee machine."

The church was with me, listening to my every word. Sometimes you don't have to look up to know you have their attention.

"When Jack was born two and a half years later, John made sure that he was "all boy." The snuggle-loving father of a little girl gave way to the rough-and-tumble dad of a tough little boy. They played karate in the living room, and they gave each other head butts instead of kisses. John made sure that Jack would be ready for the world and insisted that Jack help out with projects around the house instead of just holding the flashlight while Dad did the work. A few weeks ago, we took Jack to the firehouse, and I could see the gleam in Jack's eyes as he gazed in amazement at the sight of the trucks. We knew at that moment that Jack had just decided what he wanted to be when he grew up.

"The soft side of John showed up again, however, after the birth of our third child, Katreana. After enduring the pain and sorrow that resulted from 9/11, John was determined to make sure that sweetness and love would be the rule in our house. John and Katreana would play with Polly Pockets for hours, pretending they were together in her little dream world. The sweetness in her voice, which he could imitate so well, was exactly what he had in mind when we decided to bring her into this world.

"Kieran was born just over five months ago and was the burly football player who joined the Bellew team. "Jumbo" as John called him, was big and strong from the moment he entered the world. Someone mentioned that the Jets received word of this boy's size, and Herm Edwards himself called to try to sign him. John decided that he would wait for an offer from the Giants."

I got some laughs and jeers with that comment. This reaction helped me keep going.

"Our family became the entire world to John, and he spent his time planning and dreaming of ways to make our family's life better. And in the end, maybe this job was too big to do from here and perhaps the best way to take care of his kids was to do it from heaven.

"It is said that the true measure of a man's strength is shown in how he rises to master the moment when he is tested. John proved his strength as a fireman on Sunday when he and his brothers ran into that burning building, and he proved his strength as a father every day of his life as he showed his children what it means to be a father, a husband, and a best friend."

At this point, I knew my job was almost done, but a rush of sadness came over me. I so wanted to honor John, but the moment was now complete. I didn't want the moment to end; it also meant another task was finished, closer to saying goodbye to John. I finished fighting back tears with the final statement, and my voice began to waver.

> "God, you get back a wonderful man today. Thank you for letting us have him for a while. And when you see him, please buy him a cup of Starbucks coffee and thank him for giving me the four greatest gifts in the world."

The church stood and gave me a standing ovation, and the relief of having represented John to the best of my ability fell from my shoulders as I walked off the pulpit and past John's casket.

When I reread the eulogy today, I am amazed that I delivered this. I remember going up to the pulpit, but I can't recall actually reading it. I knew I was in the church and that people were appropriately reacting to what I was saying, but it still felt like an out-of-body experience.

The last time I read John's eulogy was twenty years ago. So much has changed since I wrote it that I even forgot John used to imitate Katreana's voice. The speech offered a snapshot of our young life together, and so much time has passed between then and now. The saddest part of that snapshot is that it is where John's story ends. There are no added stories to mention, and there is no more growth as a father, brother, husband, or friend. His story ended with this eulogy, and my kids' lives continued.

When I read that twenty years ago, I had no idea the saddest part of that eulogy was marking the end of the examples and stories. It seems surreal that he does not have a place in our family memories, just the aura of what he was. I'm also surprised at how few examples and stories I shared in the eulogy. Maybe I was trying to keep it short, or did we have such little time with John that there weren't more stories to tell? Time is precious, but lost time is even more precious.

Recently, I delivered my mom's eulogy, and while I was reading it, I felt myself floating above my body, looking down, and watching myself read. It was the strangest feeling; I could hear myself speaking and even see myself standing there, yet it wasn't me doing it. Maybe it was my body's way of getting me through an extremely difficult situation. I obviously read both eulogies in reality, but I stopped feeling for some time and just spoke. It's almost like when people don't remember an accident and the pain you initially go through. I think my mind spared me the pain, which allowed me to give the eulogy. My mom's and John's eulogies were important to me; I wouldn't have been able to get through delivering them unless my brain dulled the emotions.

John's funeral in Pearl River

John's funeral in Pearl River

CHAPTER 10

Meeting With Claire

Two weeks after John jumped, I met my therapist for the first time. The FDNY Family Assistance Unit sent Claire to talk with me, and I'll admit I had a chip on my shoulder. Two weeks earlier, I didn't need a therapist. For the first thirty-five years of my life, I was good. I was stable; I didn't need help with my mental health.

We met down in my basement while four kids ran through the house as if it were the Kentucky Derby. My mom came for an hour so I could talk with Claire without interruption. I think there were at least three or four interruptions because someone was "bleeding to death" as Brielle put it, and a few other things that only I could answer. But Claire overcame the chaos, and somehow, we completed our first session.

I found it odd that Claire first asked me to tell her about my childhood. *Didn't she know what just happened to me? I just lost my husband, a father of four young children, and was left to navigate life on my own.* Despite my resistance, I mustered the courage to share a brief synopsis of my childhood with her.

I told her I grew up in an Irish Catholic household, the youngest of five in a great town called Pearl River, a mile from where we lived now. My parents, Diane and Austin McCarthy, worked hard to raise us, gave us what we needed, and for the most part, we had a very loving, normal childhood. My dad unexpectedly died of a heart attack at age fifty, leaving my mom alone to keep our family afloat both financially and emotionally. My mom represented one of the strongest people I will ever know while also showing us true love.

Claire proceeded to dig deeper into my father's death, and I played along with it. "I was only fifteen when my dad died. It was the day after Thanksgiving, and I was watching TV in our living room while he watched TV in his bedroom. He came out to get something to eat and asked me to check the mail. Being a teenager, I rolled my eyes and went back to watching my soap opera. I would get to it when my soap was done. The phone rang, and given that it was 1986, the call came through a landline in our house with a cord attached to a wall. The call was for my dad, so I yelled his name and waited for him to pick up the receiver in his room. I yelled again. I became agitated because my dad always had trouble hearing and could never hear me over his TV. I put the phone down and ran into his room, and there he was… sprawled out on his bed, face up, no shirt on. His face was purple, mucus was coming out of his mouth, and his abdomen was distended and pure white."

Claire listened silently, taking it all in, not writing anything down.

"I stood in disbelief. My dad was 6'4, 280lbs. I couldn't move him if I tried. I thought, *I'm supposed to give him CPR, but how do I do that? But if I give him CPR, then I couldn't call 911.* So I ran to the phone to call 911, but the caller was still on the other line. I yelled and screamed for him to hang up so I could make a call, but he wouldn't. He wanted to know what happened and what I needed. I hung up on him, ran outside where my neighbor was washing his car, and screamed for help. The rest is pretty much a blur. The ambulance came, and it seemed like forever before they brought my dad to the hospital.

"Ironically, while this was happening, my mom was down at the Ambulance Corps building. She was a volunteer Ambulance Corps driver and was on call that day. She was using the bathroom when the call came in. The fellow volunteers recognized the address as our house, so they got into the rig and left without her. I'm not sure what the right way to handle that situation was, but leaving her at the station alone, knowing it was her house, probably wasn't the best approach."

Claire continued listening.

"Years later, I asked my mom about that day. She told me, 'I was in the bathroom when the call came in. Over the scanner, I heard our address, and the call came in as possible DOA (Dead on Arrival). I tried to run to the truck as fast as I could, but my colleagues were already gone. I didn't know what to do, so I jumped in my car and prayed that someone was visiting our house. I prayed it wasn't your father. I drove as fast as I could to our house.'

"I don't remember ever seeing my mom or my sister that day. My sister was upstairs the whole time, and I didn't know it. I don't know how we got to the hospital.

"When we arrived at the Emergency Room, I saw one of the EMTs walking toward the ambulance and throwing down his stethoscope in disgust. That's when I knew my dad was dead. *How can this be?* I thought. *He was only fifty years old. What if I weren't so lazy and checked the mail as he asked? I would have found him earlier. I could have saved him.* Why do you want to know more about my dad's death?" I asked, after finishing my story.

"Your past often gives insight into your future," she said. "Your father's death was traumatic, and how you handled it is a window into how you would handle the next tragedy."

I was mad. *How could she say that? I just lost my husband, my kids' father, my best friend, my life!*

"Since losing John wasn't your first trauma, your brain had already been rewired to deal with it, and you can pull knowledge from that experience," Claire explained, "It will not be easy, but our past experiences help us navigate new trauma." I found this hard to believe, but I hoped there was some truth to it.

The sudden and unexpected loss of my father had a profound impact on my mental health. It was a trauma that I never fully addressed or processed, and it continued to affect me in ways I didn't even realize until I met Claire.

If you know anything about growing up Irish Catholic, you know that nothing is ever discussed. Tragedies occur, traumatic events happen, but no one shares their feelings or lets you discuss yours. You are expected to endure any event that happens to you, feel it without tears or emotion, and move on and go back to school or work within three days. We had a two-day wake and a funeral on the third day when my father died. We buried my dad on my sixteenth birthday. It is just how the calendar fell. There was no discussion about avoiding my birthday; it just had to happen that way.

Girls rank their Sweet Sixteen birthdays as slightly more special than the others, but I woke up on mine knowing that I had to attend my dad's funeral. Still, I was excited; it was my special day. I remember my mom coming up to me at breakfast, and I guess I was expecting a "Happy Birthday," but instead, she patted me on the back and said, "Today is going to be tough," and that was it. Nothing else was discussed on that day or any other.

This was back in the '80s. Therapy was not commonplace, and it never crossed my mom's mind to bring me to a therapist or even buy me a book about grief. Why wouldn't I be able to handle the shocking, unexpected death of my father? Historically, our families endured painful experiences, and it was expected that we stuff down feelings and handle them. No one had a conversation with me about the fact that I found my dad dead, and maybe that could be traumatic for me. We didn't talk about sadness and death, and my feelings about losing my father at sixteen. My siblings didn't bring it up either; we just moved on. They were hurting just as much as I was, so how could we help each other? I never saw my mom cry, not even at the wake or funeral. My mom was the toughest person I've ever known.

I have always had immense respect for my mother. I never blamed her for the lack of guidance after my dad's death because I knew she did the best she could. She was ill-equipped to deal with sadness and tragedy because people before her didn't address it either. I will never know how she kept her emotions private. But this woman also never gave up. She took what she had learned and experienced and became the best mom and grandma she could be. Her mothering modeled unconditional love and sacrifice. I am grateful for her strength and resilience, and the lessons she passed on to me.

I knew early on that I did not want history to repeat itself. I was not my mom. I was not as strong as she was. She held back her tears; she never had a tantrum, nor did she scream or get angry at the world. On the other hand, my children saw me cry after John jumped. They saw me sob, bawl, punch pillows, scream, and break down while driving, doing the dishes, at a library program, while shopping for groceries, and at a birthday party, and this was all in the first two weeks after John jumped. So, I couldn't follow in my mom's footsteps even if I tried. When it came to showing emotion, I let it out. I was okay with that. Something inside me told me that it was healthy to show my children emotion and that it was okay for them to show it, too. Claire helped me analyze my upbringing and compare how my family handled trauma versus how I might want to handle it differently with my children.

Our sessions that followed were about analyzing my trauma and the PTSD that comes along with experiencing such an event. I spent many sessions crying over the unfairness of what happened to me, to John, and to our children. I would plead my case for a different outcome.

"I would give anything to do that morning again. To see John's smile again and look at his beautiful blue eyes. I took him for granted that morning, but I shouldn't have. If only I could have had just one more day with him."

"What would you say to him if he came back for one day?" Claire asked.

"Just how much I truly loved him with all my being, how much I appreciated everything about him, and how much I miss all the little things that made him and made us."

"Don't you think he already knows that?"

"Of course, but I want to say it again."

"I think you just did. Your problem is that he can't answer you back."

In that moment, my spirituality shifted to believing that John was still with me, and would always be, in a new form I could trust.

Claire's presence, patience, and guidance in my life have been instrumental in my healing process. She has helped me navigate the most difficult moments of my life and has shown me that it's okay not to be okay and that seeking help is a sign of strength, not weakness. I look forward to talking with her every two weeks. When things come up during the week, I mentally note them and know I must discuss them with Claire.

If there's one piece of advice I give to widows or anyone struggling, it's to: find your Claire. I lucked out because I clicked with her instantly, but that doesn't always happen with the first therapist you meet. It can be exhausting to find your Claire, but it is well worth the effort.

Find your Claire.

Brendan Cawley and Jack

CHAPTER 11

FDNY Support

When John jumped, it changed my connections to many of his friends and the firehouse family. Although the FDNY takes care of their own, my relationship with them would never be the same. Like a scarlet letter no one wants to wear, I had a new title: the widow. I missed John, and I also missed all the firehouse stories, the humorous antics, and even the stories about the runs he used to go on. One day, I was connected to the inner workings of a firehouse, and the next day, I did not know what was going on in the firehouse family I had come to know so well. I would mourn that connection, too.

Not long after John's funeral, the firemen from John's house asked if I would be up for a visit from Brendan Cawley. Brendan was the probie firefighter who survived Black Sunday. I couldn't even believe he was out of the hospital, never mind wanting to visit me.

He walked into our house gingerly with a sling over his shoulder, and his face looked like he was on the losing end of a bar fight. He reminded me of a younger version of John and was so soft-spoken and kind to my kids.

"Catch!" Jack yelled and threw a Nerf football at him.

"Jack! He can't play catch right now; he is hurt."

"What happened to you? Did you fall skiing? My dad skis."

I began to apologize, but Brendan went right with it.

"Really? I bet your dad is a really good skier. No, I wasn't skiing, but I did have a fall."

He looked at me with a nervous laugh. I laughed back. The other firemen who came with Brendan took the kids downstairs to play while we spoke.

"First, I am so sorry about John. I really wanted to attend the funeral, but they would not allow me out of the hospital."

"Don't worry about it. I can't believe you are even here. I appreciate you taking the time to see me."

"I don't know exactly what you are going through because I never lost a spouse, but I did lose my brother in the 9/11 attack, and all I wanted was information."

"Oh my God, Brendan, I'm so sorry. Was he a fireman? What was his name?"

"Yes, his name is Michael. He was a fireman who responded to the World Trade Center. He was one of the 343 firefighters we lost that day."

"Your poor parents... and then to have to deal with this." As much as I was grieving my husband, the thought of grieving one of my kids was too much for me to bear.

"So, I understand how important it is for you to have all the available information. I can give you what I remember. As you know, I was not with John in the apartment and found out after I jumped that he had to jump, too.

"The Saturday night shift before the fire was my first twenty-four-hour shift. My first interaction with John that shift was at 1 a.m. when we came back from a run. My job as a probie is to make sure there is always fresh coffee on, but I thought no one would be drinking it at 1 a.m. But when I went into the kitchen, John was making the coffee. I ran over to him and took over the responsibility. I apologized for not completing one of my probie jobs, and he just laughed and started a conversation with me. We ended up sitting down at the kitchen table, talking for a while, and found out we went to the same high school, Archbishop Molloy."

"Oh wow! You're a Molloy guy? He must have liked you then."

"Yes, he definitely loved that I was a Molloy alum, and we ended up knowing many of the same guys. John said that he told a mutual friend of ours that he would keep an eye out for me."

I liked Brendan immediately; he was so kind and very concerned that I got all my questions answered. I felt horrible for him; he was so young on the job and yet had to endure a lifetime of both physical and mental pain.

We became friends that day, through a tragic event that gave me a cherished confidant. Brendan understood my trauma and talked me through a lot of my sadness. I leaned on him, and I'm not sure I could have gotten through the first year without his help. Brendan also kept alive a connection to the house that I didn't realize I still needed.

Maybe because he was with John the day he jumped, it was easy to open up to him. He shared the trauma so few could comprehend. Long late-night calls became common as we navigated my grief and his healing with much-needed humor, support, and unexpected understanding.

John had promised to look out for Brendan; maybe that was what he was doing on the day of the fire. However, Brendan looked out for the kids and me after Black Sunday. I am so grateful for his help and friendship, which continues to this day.

In March, John's Captain, John Sullivan, came for a visit. He wanted to give me updated information on the investigation firsthand. The Fire Marshals had begun their investigation into what happened, and it became clear that a series of events had created a perfect storm that led to John's demise.

Sullivan came to my house weekly for the first year to provide updates on the fire's findings and to check on my well-being, taking the motto "We Will Never Forget" as seriously as anyone could. The safety report took months to complete, but once it was done, he came over to explain it in full detail.

"Good afternoon, Eileen. The safety report is out, and I thought you might like an explanation of what they found."

"Come in, thank you." I had the sitter take the kids outside, not wanting them to hear the answers I so desperately wanted to hear. *Someday, I'll let them read the report,* I thought, but that will be many years in the future.

"As we expected, there was a series of events that caused John's death. The blizzard, wind conditions, frozen hydrants, burst length in the hose line, and lack of safety ropes all played a role. One of the causes of John's fire was that the apartments on the third floor and the fourth floor were subdivided into illegal apartments."

"What does that mean?" I was confused; anger bubbled up inside me.

"We call them SROs, single room occupancies. The original apartments were meant to have two bedrooms, but the tenants carved them into four bedrooms and rented them out. The tenants share the bathrooms and kitchen, and one person collects rent for the whole apartment."

"Oh, really, I never heard about these before." I was trying to be civil but could feel my face become hot and ready to explode.

"John knew these existed. Bronx firefighters know about these; they are all over the Bronx. People build partitions out of flimsy sheetrock that are not fire-resistant—to create rooms they can rent out within a single apartment. They bolt the rooms with padlocks to prevent theft by the other tenants they share the apartment with. Some of the rooms have no electrical outlets, so they run cheap extension cords under the sheetrock from another room to power their devices, overloading the circuit. These apartment buildings are not equipped to handle the additional electrical power required by these rooms. The outlets are overtaxed, and electrical fires start."

"They have to be illegal, right?" *Seriously? How can they get away with this?*

"Yes, but it's hard to enforce the code because the tenants would have to let us in their apartment when we do a building inspection. The landlords know this is happening, but they choose to turn a blind eye to the partitions and padlocks when collecting rent. Both are aware of the legal ramifications and how it poses a risk to tenants and firefighters, but their primary concern was ensuring rent was paid on time."

"So, no one cared about the risk to John or firefighters. This is a blatant disregard for safety and the law. They should be punished!"

"John had experience with these types of buildings. The firefighters have tools to break through padlocks, search for victims, and reach the fire source, but these apartments are often chopped up into mazes, making it very difficult for them to do their job. We go into a building being trained on what the floorplan should look like, and then we find walls and unsafe living conditions, all the while with heavy black smoke interrupting our vision."

"So, will anyone pay the price for killing two firefighters?"

"I know the Bronx DA is looking into it, and possible charges will be filed against those who knew about these deathtraps."

"What about the ropes? I keep hearing that John could have survived if he had a rope system. What do you know about that?"

"Personal safety ropes, the department made everyone hand them in back in 2000 because their shelf life was ten years, and that time was expiring. They were supposed to research a new type of rope system and reissue us new ones, but it never happened."

"Would the rope have helped save John's life?"

"It would have given him a much better shot than what he had."

"Are they getting those ropes now?"

"I heard they are putting together a research team to develop a new rope system."

"So John's death won't happen to another firefighter, thank God."

"John had no choice that day; he did nothing wrong. It would have happened to any of us."

Many firefighters took these findings about the SROs and the rope systems being taken away seriously. They all understood that if they were working that day, it would have been them.

The FDNY is made up of 10,000 strong and brave men and women, but I have found a population that might even be stronger: the families that stand behind them. Our family found a sense of unity and support among some widows. We met many families who have welcomed us into this "new club." One widow in particular, who had lost her husband in the 9/11 terror attacks, came to my house to check in with me. She had lost her husband a little over four years earlier. I wanted her to tell me that I had to get through four years, and it would improve. She was so put together and seemed to have figured it out. What I loved about her visit was her honesty.

"I'm going to be truthful, this sucks, and it doesn't get better for a really long time. When people tell you, 'it's going to be okay,' don't believe them because it isn't. Life will be tough for you until you find your new normal, and even then, you won't like it, but you have no choice."

"But you look so put together. When will the physical pain stop?"

"There are days that feel like it happened yesterday and days that you have a few good moments."

I didn't like what I was hearing, but deep inside, I already knew this. She didn't sugarcoat it and had the guts to tell me the truth. Finally, there was someone honest—who wasn't trying to make me feel better. And she never tried to compete with me.

Skating at FDNY event at Rockefeller Center

CHAPTER 12

Competition Of Grief

One would never put death and tragedy in a competition category, but believe it or not, the evil eye of jealousy plays out in mysterious ways. This concept of Competition Of Grief is not about who has suffered more but rather about the unspoken, sometimes unconscious, comparisons and judgments that can arise in the aftermath of a tragedy. I am a competitive person by nature. I played sports growing up, always wanting to win at all costs. But when it comes to competing with others for attention after a trauma, that's a game I do not want to win. If we are competing in that game, you can have the win; leave me out of it.

While there were dozens of other FDNY widows who were kind to me, I've also met women who felt competitive. We attended events hosted by different organizations for children and widows. For example, we were invited to skate at Rockefeller Center, attend the Christmas tree lighting, concerts, Toys R Us Christmas parties, seminars, baseball games, hockey games, and the Thanksgiving Day parade. I thought these would be great opportunities for my kids to be around other children in similar situations, but I sometimes felt a sense of competition.

Some widows would recognize me as an unfamiliar face and ask me, "What is your connection to the FDNY?" or "Are you a 9/11 family?"

When I would explain, "No, I lost my husband in the Black Sunday fire..."

Before I could continue, they would give us a look like, *Oh, so you aren't 9/11?* I began to see that some widows used the event as a platform to tell you how much more traumatic their loss was than yours.

I had a mom ask my children, "Where are your fire department's sweatshirts?" It was almost as if she were questioning whether we had the right to be there.

A common dress code was to wear a loved one's shirt, a quarter-zip sweatshirt, or a jacket. My kids looked at me like I forgot to dress them. I never chose to wear FDNY fashion myself, so I didn't think to buy some for the kids. *Where do you even buy that clothing?* John just appeared with it all one day. Katreana was so picky with her clothes that there was no chance she would wear that.

When celebrities attended these events, some families occupied all of their time. The truth is, I often didn't even know who the celebrities were, and my kids were too young to know, so I usually used that time to go to the refreshment table because the lines were shorter. As I attended more of these events, I saw the same widows repeatedly, ensuring their stories were heard. I noticed a trend; some of these widows made this one tragic event their whole life. It quickly became apparent that I did not want this for my kids. "Daddy's death will always be part of your life, but it is not your whole life," I told them. John would never have wanted that. Though his death was tragic, he would not want it to affect every aspect of their lives.

Still, I am very thankful for these planned events. They gave my kids opportunities they would never have been able to experience in a life where there was no death of a parent. These organizations are vital in helping you cope with the sadness of your existence while providing social events that two-parent families do not dominate. My goal in attending these events was to help my kids meet other children who could relate to them.

I put on a gracious, happy face, but in reality, these events sometimes depressed me. I did not want to prove my worth through tragedy. Standing alone while watching my kids have fun, I would often be the only widow from our fire, and it felt like I had entered a sorority party I wasn't invited to. The 9/11 widows had a common event that bonded them; I felt like an outsider. It would be as if they dismissed my loss and our fire because theirs was a historic, national tragedy.

Even though I connected to a few other women, admittedly, in the first few months, I put myself in a hierarchy of widows. Soon after John jumped, I was offered an opportunity to join a grief group meant to provide support and a safe space for sharing experiences, but I couldn't do it. I didn't want to share my story. I didn't want to hear others tell me how their story was tougher, sadder, or more burdensome than mine.

Initially, you think you are at the top of the hierarchy, and no one can tell you differently. No one could have it worse than you, in your own eyes. Your sadness is so palpable that you can't even imagine having a group conversation about grief and trauma because you can only see your own. Perhaps selfishly, this is how I felt in the rawness of my grief.

I had widows of FDNY members and other fire departments nationwide reach out to me to share their stories. It felt like some tried to push me off the top of the grief hierarchy.

Because I was not in my right mind at the time, I became competitive and wanted to shoot back at them. "My husband was my soulmate, and we loved each other. He had to make the worst decision ever made, and I now have four little kids to raise alone." But of course, I didn't.

It took me a long time to understand that there is no hierarchy and that competing with each other serves no one. Instead, I listened to their stories cordially and thanked them for reaching out.

Now, when I meet a widow, I let them tell me their story first, and if they ask me questions, I tell them about mine. I've found that widows would rather speak than listen. In the early days after John jumped, I wanted to speak, too. Now, I am happy to listen. As the years pass, looking at others' stories allows us to grieve with them without competition. It is important to understand where they are in their journey, and it is not based on time.

Some widows lost their loved ones twenty years ago, but when you speak with them, it feels as if it occurred last week. You can talk to other widows who lost their loved ones a year ago, and you can hear the growth and know they are well on their way to moving on. I said they are moving on, not forgetting. This is important to understand.

I have learned to listen more than speak. The grieving world can use more listeners than talkers. Sharing our experiences and listening to others can help us feel understood and less alone in our grief.

But when it comes to competing with your own family, it is a different story. Even with all I have learned, I can't understand everyone's feelings. Before John jumped, my relationship with my in-laws was very good. We spoke on the phone and visited them often. There was no reason to think that would change, but tragedy changes people.

Afterwards, I heard rumblings in the background that some of John's family members were complaining about not receiving recognition for losing a brother, wanting the media coverage I was resisting. Maybe they felt that because they knew him a lot longer than I did, they should be given a voice. I acknowledged that, but the love and bond of a husband and wife is apparently more newsworthy.

I never expected to compete with John's family. I did not wish to be a news story or on the front cover of all the major newspapers. I didn't want the attention; I preferred not to be seen or heard. Before John jumped, I was content that no one knew my name, happy to have the attention of one man and four kids. Then John jumped, and lots of focus on me. On the front covers of the Daily News and the NY Post, writers wanted to tell stories about John's family, even though they couldn't care less about our lives just twenty-four hours earlier. I received numerous phone calls from different media outlets wanting interviews. Television stations were parked outside my house for months, looking for follow-up stories.

For some reason, I agreed to do an interview on the *Today Show* the day after John jumped. What was I thinking? I was not in my right mind, and others influenced my decisions. Matt Lauer interviewed my brother-in-law and me in my basement. Why would I agree to this? Looking back, it seems bizarre that I did. My brother-in-law, a retired firefighter, showed up at my house early that day, dressed in his firefighter uniform. I looked like hell spending the first night of my new life in my bed without John, crying myself to sleep.

The camera crew showed up, and we filmed in my basement while Lauer was in the studio. We spoke to him via satellite.

"We are going LIVE in five minutes," the cameraman reports.

"What? Kieran is due to be fed in five minutes." I held him on my lap and prayed he would stay still. The producer wanted him on camera.

"He will have to wait until after the interview."

"Oh, okay, I'll tell this five-month-old that your milkmaid is doing an interview; you will have to wait."

The cameraman gave me a nervous laugh and started counting down.

"5-4-3-2-1, we are live."

"Joining us from her home in Pearl River is Eileen Bellew and her brother-in-law, Danny Bellew. John Bellew was one of the firemen who had to jump to his death yesterday in a fire in the Bronx. He and five other firemen had to make the horrific decision to jump from a fourth-story apartment building to escape a flashover. Unfortunately, Bellew and Lt. Curtis Meyran died of their injuries, while four others are in critical condition. Later in the afternoon, a Brooklyn fire took the life of firefighter Richie Scalfani. The day is now deemed Black Sunday, the first time in FDNY history that they had three line-of-duty deaths, in two separate locations, on one day. Thank you for joining us, Eileen and Danny."

Wow, that is such a sad story. Wait, this is my story! What am I doing here?

"We are sorry for your loss. Maybe you could give us some insight into John and what kind of husband and father he was?"

"John is an amazing dad; he is the type of dad every kid wants. He is super involved with every aspect of his kids' lives.

He worships them, and they are his life." I realized I was talking about him as if he were living. "My kids are so young, I want them to have this interview to always remind them how heroic their dad is and a reminder just how much their dad loved and worshiped them."

"Do you have an opinion about the FDNY taking back the ropes that could have potentially saved John's life?"

I let Danny answer this; I wasn't versed in fire department protocol and certainly didn't want to answer controversial questions.

What was I thinking? I hate all these questions. The answers are so obvious, and they just wanted a face to connect to the tragedy. And I gave it to them.

"When I was a fireman in the Bronx for twenty years, we were issued personal safety ropes designed to help us rappel down a building if we needed to escape. We were told to hand them back in in 2000, but with the understanding that the FDNY would issue a replacement."

"Do you think this could have helped your brother get out of the building safely?"

"Yes, it would have given all of them a better chance of survival and reduced injury." Kieran became squirmy, and I felt my milk let down. I prayed the camera didn't see the milk stain on my shirt. *Does my body language read: we are done here, Matt, time for me to feed John's son, and that I'm not sure why I agreed to this anyway?*

"Thank you for joining us, and may I speak for all the citizens of New York City and say thank you for your husband's supreme sacrifice and for your family's sacrifice to keep our city safe."

"Cut, we are out. Thank you for your time. We will get our equipment out of here quickly."

Looking back, I must have done it because I did not want my love story to end. I wanted my kids to have a record of how amazing their dad was, and this was a way for them to have their history on tape. I tried numerous times to get the tape from NBC, but no one ever got back to me. I'm not sure I could even watch it now. How cringy the whole experience was because I wasn't myself. I was a person going through the motions of shock, who was trying to honor her husband while giving my children a record of the moment that they don't even have now.

I participated in some of these stories and interviews because I felt an obligation to John, my children, and the FDNY, but after many months of this, I wanted out. I wanted my very boring, lonely life back. Problems arose, however, when others wanted to keep the attention going. Maybe it helped them to feel connected to John, but when your desires and needs start to part ways, friction occurs, and relationships splinter. We all had our own agendas, and mine did not mesh with the others.

The truth was, I envied John's brothers and sister. In those early weeks, they got to visit our house and wallow in the sadness of our home but not live in it. They could see John in every photo, his clothes in the room right where he left them. John's presence was everywhere, his DNA running through the kitchen, and the life he left was right before their eyes. But at the end of the day, they got to leave his home and return to their own. They escaped the sadness and returned to their lives. I, on the other hand, was still living in his home with all his things and his four offspring, and I had to take on all the responsibilities he once had. Our relationships fractured after John jumped, and perhaps they no longer felt the same connection to our family they had before.

One exception to any competition I might have felt was with his parents. I recognize how tough his parents' loss must have been, and I would never try to compete with them. Since they lived in Florida, we didn't see them much. I can't imagine losing a child; it must be the worst pain and heartbreak there is in this world.

My mom lost four children in her lifetime: twins when they were a few days old, then two of my sisters passed away from health problems in midlife, several years after John jumped.

Seeing firsthand how devastating the loss of a child can be to a parent, I will never compete with my mother-in-law and father-in-law. They win the competition. I admit I didn't do a good enough job supporting my in-laws in their time of need, but I just didn't have the energy, nor did I know how to help them. I wish that were different, but I could only do what I could and supporting them was beyond my capabilities at that time.

It shouldn't be the widow who helps the parents. This might sound selfish, but widows are not equipped physically or mentally to help anyone else except for themselves and their children during their time of loss. It should not have been my responsibility. Yes, we are grieving the same person, but our grief is on two different spectrums, and I had nothing to give. I hope to explain that better when I get to heaven. It is one of my bigger regrets, but I only had enough in the tank for myself and John's children.

Another competition where no one wins is the survivors' competition. Sometimes, you are thrown into a life-changing event with the personalities of people you never would have crossed paths with or chosen as friends. I only knew one of the other five firefighters who jumped with John that day. Some were luckier than John, and I envy their families. No one asked for this connection, yet people assumed our relationships would be positive. Our families would have to coexist for years, even though we did not choose to.

When I watched the survivors move on, improve every day through their rehab, I was once again envious. *Why couldn't that be John? Why did they survive, and John did not?* After many months of rehab, four of the surviving firefighters started traveling around the United States, presenting about the Black Sunday fire. They were telling their own story and John's. It infuriated me that they were speaking on John's behalf. I wished he were here to tell his own story. They didn't seem to understand my grief because they are still alive.

With the exception of Brendan, I struggled to be around the survivors and internally wrestled with what felt unfair—like their story became bigger when John and Curt died. Brendan just seemed to get it. He understood my rationale and empathized with my situation. His patience with my anger, sadness, and confusion was beyond valuable in my grieving process.

I still navigate all of this competition to create healthy mental well-being and happiness. None of this competition has served me well. Competition in grief seems bizarre, but it's present and has taken up a lot of space in my mind. For the sake of my kids, I performed many award-winning scenes where I acted like these people didn't affect me, but inside, I was screaming that I was hurting.

The competition of grief is complicated. Most of the time, people don't even realize they are doing it. People have their reasons for wanting to win at grieving. Maybe it proves that their loved one was special, that their loved one loved them back, that they need to hurt more than you do, or that they have some un-resolved guilt they are working through. The arena is ugly, and it can put you on your ass. I have my reasons for entering the competition arena at times. I competed to honor John's legacy and to strengthen my family's self-worth. You can choose to fight or get your ass kicked. I decided to fight, but the results were never victorious. Sometimes, you need to compete because it is better than sitting in sadness.

Even now, most of the time, I take the high road, sit back, and listen. Although I have cultivated self-awareness, it took years of growth and understanding, which I continue to work on today. If someone gets under my skin, I'll still lash out. The initial feeling may relieve me, but ultimately, I feel empty. In the end, no one ever wins in the arena of grief. We all remain in pain.

My mom and I

Chapter 13

We're Not The Suing Type

When I was fifteen, I got bitten by a dog on my ass. I was a newspaper delivery person, and one of my customers' German Shepherds bit me. I had just petted the dog when the owner gave me the money they owed for the week. After I took the money, I turned away and walked down the path. I felt something jump on my back. It was their dog attacking me. He took hold of my right butt cheek and wouldn't let go. I screamed, and the owner kicked him off me, but by doing so, he tore my skin downward since the dog's jaw still had a grip on my buttocks.

The owner screamed, "Kujo (this was seriously the name of the dog), get down, release!" I ran back to my bike as fast as I could and started pedaling.

Kujo's dad came running after me, begging me to stop, "Come here, are you okay? Did he break the skin? Let me help you." I felt the blood running down my ass and was not going to let a stranger look at my bare butt.

I went to the ER, where the police took a report and photos of my ass. Doctors couldn't stitch the four tooth punctures because of the fear of infection, so I still, to this day, have scars, probably ending my chances of being a bikini supermodel.

My mom asked the police officer, "Why are you taking photos of her?" As you can imagine, my fifteen-year-old self wasn't interested in people taking pictures of my ass.

The police officer explained, "We need these as evidence for my report and in case you file a lawsuit."

My mom told the police officer, "There is no need for that, we aren't the suing type."

So, when I was advised to consider suing the building owner and the City of New York for wrongdoing, all I could hear in my head was my mom saying, *There is no need for that. We are not the suing type.*

In the weeks after John jumped, it was explained to me that I had to file legal papers within sixty days if I felt wrongdoing had occurred. Since I had never sued anyone before, I didn't know what was coming my way. At that point, I didn't even know whether there was any illegal wrongdoing, but those SRO apartments seemed like they should be illegal.

Luckily, my brother-in-law knew of a law firm that was familiar with firefighting training and law. The day I met the lawyers was emotional. This was uncharted territory for me. As I sat with the lawyers, they explained the case to me. As I learned more, I became increasingly enraged and felt compelled to follow through for the sake of the kids and John. I hoped the kids would receive enough money to help pay for their college. Brielle was six when we opened the case against the building owner and the City of New York. I figured that was plenty of time to finish the case before Brielle went to college. The lawyers explained that our case would most likely take up to ten years to enter a

Bronx courtroom. I thought this was an exaggeration, but sure enough, they were right.

I wasn't the only person involved in this lawsuit, and that had both positive and negative effects on me. There were six families involved in the court case, and five of us decided to file with the same law firm. The other widow filed with another firm. You would think power is in numbers, but sometimes I didn't feel that way. Everyone had their own needs, agendas, and desired outcomes.

A couple of months after we filed, the lawyers decided that all the families should meet to discuss the case. We gathered around a large oak table in a conference room. Everyone brought their own agendas they wanted to discuss. While their concerns were about healthcare, my concerns were about managing a single-parent household. I was the only widow in the room and felt outnumbered. The dynamics of our relationships changed, and it was a struggle to balance our individual needs with the collective goal of seeking justice.

The meeting started to feel like a bad idea. "What about our health insurance? Will I be able to get physical therapy for the rest of my life? We are going to have health issues forever. How are we going to be supported with our needs?" Their questions were endless about how the lawsuit would support their LIVING needs. *Why am I here? How does this have anything to do with me?* There are four of them with very real needs, but no one has asked me about mine. I was just the widow.

I became agitated as this conversation continued. Only Brendan could see I was becoming frustrated. He kept quiet; he understood that my needs were not being addressed. I couldn't sit around a table discussing how we were going to meet the needs of the living best when my husband was dead.

The kicker of the meeting was learning that New York State law allows the wives of the living to be part of the lawsuit, but widows have no legal right to sue. So, my husband died, I was left raising our kids, and I had no right under New York state law to sue for damages. But the wives of the men who survived could sue for loss of services of their LIVING husbands.

I got up in the middle of someone talking and slammed my hands down on the table. "I'm out. I can't sit here listening to your needs when John is dead. I can appreciate your needs, but this was not a good idea. I'm happy you are all alive, but I'm going home to no husband, and four little kids with no dad." The lawyers tried to settle me down, but I was already done.

I stormed out of the room with no plan of where I was going. Luckily, Brendan followed me.

"Eileen, don't leave. I know this is hard, just stay."

"I can't. I can't listen to them complain about health benefits and how they are getting screwed when I would die for John to be in their place. This was a bad idea; I should have never agreed to this." I returned to the van that took me down to the city and went home.

After that meeting, the lawyers decided to update us all individually, and I wasn't invited to any more group meetings. Truth be told, I needed the other men. They were the only ones who could tell part of John's story. However, the reality was that no one would ever be able to tell John's story. Only John knows the real story, the actual trauma, and the absolute nightmare he went through. John would never get his day in court. I needed the other plaintiffs to fill in the blanks about what happened on the fourth floor that day to find closure in this painful journey.

CHAPTER 14

Inner Demons

After the funeral, my mind was in a tailspin, and I was thinking, *Screw the world. Screw fate.* How could God do this to me? I felt indestructible. God would not mess with me, right? He wouldn't dare take me away from my babies. I drove my car, thinking there was no way I could get into an accident. I had no fear of getting sick, no fear of test results like a mammogram or blood work. I had no fear of saying something wrong to someone, nor did I care if people liked me. My perspective was so black and white.

During this time, I had a clear vision of the world: there was either right or wrong, and I didn't allow the rest of the world's noise to cloud my thought process. I lived by the mantra: "Life on Earth is precious and can be gone in a second, so live in the moment."

Unfortunately, this mindset only lasted a few weeks. I wish it had lasted a lifetime. There are real benefits to avoiding gossip and rumors, staying focused on my life, and not getting caught up in the day-to-day bullshit that surrounds us. But this new thought process was short-lived. Fear came roaring in like a bat out of hell. I call it my inner demons.

Soon after John jumped, Brielle was to attend a birthday party. I had no intention of attending parties or any other social events for the rest of my life, until I received a call asking for my RSVP to the party. I was taken aback. It had only been three weeks since my husband died. I guess I was in shock that I was expected to attend a six-year-old's ice-skating party this soon. Yet, Brielle wanted to go, and I could not disappoint her. Children have a unique ability to visit grief in waves. It is a great coping skill. All of her classmates would be there, and it was important for her to make friends. Worried that my grief could affect her social life if we didn't attend, I agreed to go in a moment of weakness while looking at Brielle's sweet little face.

What was I thinking? I dreaded the day, but I pretended to be excited every time Brielle mentioned it. We had to get a birthday present, which may sound easy, but not in my current state of mind. This task required me to shower, make sure Kieran was fed so I didn't have to pull out my breast in public (which I did often and have no issue doing), get four kids dressed and into four different types of car seats, and drive to Target. Then, find a gift for a kid I have never met, guessing her size and whether she would like it. Then, pick out a card and wrapping paper.

Why did I RSVP yes? Oh yeah, I know why; if I chose to be a hermit (which is exactly what I wanted to do), it could have long-lasting effects on my daughter's social life.

The party was forty minutes away, so highway driving was required. Gone was my carefree *screw the world* swagger. My creative, anxiety-stricken mind took over.

If I don't drive her myself, Brielle will be part of a twenty-car pile-up on the way to or from the party. Her injuries will be extensive, and she may have to be airlifted to the closest hospital. Or she might not know how to ice skate and will be standing alone without any help or guidance. She may try to skate on her own, fall backwards, hit her head on the ice, and then be airlifted to the nearest hospital. She might be too shy to interact with these new friends, and her "shy kid" social status will follow her until she graduates from high school. Or maybe, when she takes her skates off, the blade will cut her, probably a main artery, and once again, she could be airlifted to the closest hospital. Clearly, I had to bring Brielle myself to ensure no helicopters were involved in a fun day at a birthday party.

I took Brielle to the party, but apparently, I didn't read the invitation very well. You participate in an ice-skating party with actual ice and real ice skates. Brielle wasn't an ice skater yet; she just learned to walk five years ago. This party meant the moms had to strap up skates and help their child. *Why didn't I just say no?* Because I wanted Brielle to go. She should have fun. *Why didn't I just send her with someone else?* I thought about that, but then my newly rewired, fearful brain took over, and I took her myself.

My plan to find a corner to sit down and have a good cry while Brielle interacted with the other girls and made lifelong friendships was not going to come to fruition. So I did what other moms did; I asked for a size nine and strapped them on. *Why did I say yes to this?*

I had no mom friends yet. Brielle had only been in kindergarten for six months and was my oldest child. I was in no shape to be social and had no desire to make friends. So I held onto Brielle for dear life, and we did the 1-2-3 glide method around the rink. Not only was I trying to help Brielle, but I wasn't a proficient skater myself, so I prayed that I would stay upright. As I tried to skate, I overheard the other moms' conversations.

"Did you hear that Jen's husband cheated on her?"

"Really? I wonder who it was with? Can you believe Tommy's teacher is absent again?"

"I know. The kids probably like the sub better than her."

Who cares!? This petty gossip felt so trivial compared to my own world. But soon, I got sucked in and started paying attention to the nonsense. It showed me that my headspace was open to new information, and it was nice to focus on something other than my own life.

After the second time around the rink, tears ran down my face. Maybe it was the pain of the rental skates wreaking havoc on my feet, or perhaps it was just sadness about what my life had become. Brielle looked up at me. I was falling apart once again in front of her, and she just ignored the tears.

One of the moms came over and offered to take Brielle around with her and her daughter. I took her up on the offer and watched Brielle skate away holding hands with her new friend. I should have been excited that my daughter was beginning her social life, but I couldn't see past my darkness. It didn't help that the birthday girl blew by me doing double axels at six years old.

I went to sit outside the rink, staring at Brielle the whole time to make sure she didn't fall. Thankfully, another mom approached me to engage in small talk. I got through the party, and I appreciated other moms reaching out to me. It was the beginning of making my own new relationships, too.

If I learned anything that day, it's that it's okay to say no if you are not ready to see the world. Instead, think about sending your child with a trusted adult.

The party was the start of my supersonic anxiety. I went from being indestructible to convincing myself that I would die. The narrative I told myself was that when Kieran turned eighteen years old, I would get breast cancer. I figured God would give me until the kids were old enough to care for themselves. It made me feel better because then God would take me to John, and we would be together again. It was a very sick thought, and as much as I love John, I would not want to leave my kids… Ever.

I made up lots of stories and predictions about my health, my kids' safety, and our mortality. I needed to tell myself these narratives before it happened. It was the ultimate defense mechanism, allowing me to continue living in a world I didn't always want to be in. This process was the only thing that could help me quiet the fears in my head. This way, I could plan how to live the rest of my life. It was an unhealthy way of thinking, but it matched the sadness I felt.

After John jumped, I felt entitled to skate through the rest of my life. Bad things should not happen to my kids or me. We had experienced the worst thing to ever happen to someone, so "smooth sailing from here on out" felt like what we were owed. But bad things didn't stop happening after John jumped. I still got into a fender bender. I still had a lump in my breast removed and was given a life-changing scare after a routine colonoscopy. My thoughts were on speed, and the inner demons, the evil of anxiety, took over. My every thought was controlled by fear.

I can tell you thoughts that might sound humorous because of their craziness, but these thoughts are very real in my mind. The anxiety is like a constant companion, whispering worst-case scenarios and keeping me in a state of perpetual fear. I could not predict the future, and luckily, most of my predictions did not come true. The majority of the time, my kids were safe, and I lived an uneventful life, but the inner demons never stopped warning me.

Most of my fears boil down to one thing: I never want to be surprised again. Some people love surprises, but not me. I find solace in the ordinary, never getting a phone call or text that shakes me to the bone. I wasn't prepared to lose John; I guess no one ever is, but I never want to be in that position again. So, my inner demons try to think of every scenario to avoid the surprise, to regain a sense of control in a world that seems determined to keep me off balance.

I'm a creative thinker when it comes to my children's safety. I've spent many of my days thinking about ways they will get hurt and then act out how I will handle it. My internal stories were thought out and filled with gory details and horrific endings. This thought process is endless. It does not stop. The rapid-fire neuron explosion in my head only ends when I get them back to me safely, but the break is short-lived because, soon enough, they are off again, living their lives out of my sight and out of my control.

I quickly discovered that as the kids got older, the inner demons got louder. My anxiety wanted control of situations, and when the kids were babies, I controlled everything. I decided when they ate, slept, what they wore, where they would play, who they played with, and what activities they would engage in. But each year, my control as a parent grew weaker and weaker. I soon realized I wasn't the most influential person in my children's lives. Some sassy middle school classmates were. You would think that as each year passed further away from the date of John's jumping, my anxiety and sadness would fade. The truth is that the opposite happened. As I lost control of everyone's actions, my anxiety became worse.

I needed help.

Kids at beach

CHAPTER 15

Anti-Anxiety Medications

As I lay in bed and pulled the covers over my shoulders, the clock said 10:15 p.m.

Did I lock the front door? What was that noise? Is someone trying to break in through the girls' room? Have I checked the fire alarm batteries recently? Who is driving Brielle to cheer tomorrow? Are they good drivers? Will they make sure she buckles her seatbelt? What is that noise I hear? I forgot to give Kieran his vitamins this morning. I got everyone else's, but I said I would go back and fight with him later. Oh no, here it comes... my brain starts spinning, the tidal wave of debilitating thoughts starts rushing into my brain. Most of the thoughts don't even make sense. It is the start of a panic attack, a very typical night in my bedroom. It's like I'm sitting in a subway car while another car passes by at 1000 mph. *Did I drain the bath water from the tub? What if Jack stumbles in there tonight to go to the bathroom, falls in the tub, and drowns? Let me double-check that. I might as well check whether everyone is breathing and whether their windows are locked. What time is it? Oh no, it's already midnight—I have to get to sleep.*

My thoughts sped through my head; breathless, I couldn't stop the motion. My hearing became super keen, and the room's vibrations sounded so loud even though there was no noise. The room began to spin. My chest had a heavy weight sitting right in the middle of it. The cold sweats bled through my pajamas. *Why can't I slow down my thoughts, my room, the noise?* My mind felt like a computer screen, with binary numbers scrambling up and down in an endless loop.

I have to get out of bed. I started pacing around my bedroom, trying to get back to feeling normal. *I might as well check on the kids one more time while I'm up. I could check the front door and all the windows one more time. I'll double-check that the fire ladders are easily accessible to the kids in case there is a fire. What is that noise?* I made the rounds through my quiet house, then went back to bed. *Damn it, it's already 2:07 am. I have to be up in 4 hours. I hope I don't oversleep my alarm. Let me check my phone to make sure I set the alarm...*

When Claire highly recommended that I try anti-anxiety medicine, I fought it and fought it and fought it. In the beginning, it wasn't even an option because I was still breastfeeding. Then, I was so adamant that I was not the type of person who needed prescription drugs to live in this world. I was strong, intelligent, and self-aware.

But I was also broken.

No longer the person I once was, it didn't seem like my brain would rewire back to normal anytime soon. I knew stress could harm my overall health, and I worried that if I didn't do something about my anxiety, I would become sick and die (of course), and no one would be there to take care of my kids. I realized I couldn't keep going on like I was, so I decided to give it a try.

I'm not ashamed about needing medication; my kids needed me to be on it.

Before, like most humans, I had my ups and downs with bouts of anxiety and sadness, but after John jumped, it was like my brain neurons scrambled to a different dimension. I knew, of course, that I would feel broken after such a traumatic experience, and life would be more challenging. I kept thinking it was temporary. I believed my body's nervous system would return to normal in a few months. Still, with every additional day, life became more complex, and my anxiety and stress compounded until I didn't even know who I was anymore. If I put my toddler's sandals on the wrong feet, I would break down inconsolably. I yearned for the days before John jumped when I could easily handle life's little things.

The body and mind I had on January 22nd were never the same after January 23rd. When John jumped, he took my stable mind and calm demeanor with him. I wanted my old brain back, and I was so angry that this trauma took that from me. People didn't realize that, in addition to the trauma of John dying, I had trauma from knowing my husband jumped from a fourth story window of a burning building, out of desperation because the heat that barreled down on him reached 800 degrees. Along with his death was the death of my brain from ages 0 to 35 years old. A brain that could handle most things, including putting my toddler's shoes on. So when John jumped, part of my old self jumped, too.

I miss the old me. She was carefree and loving, spontaneous and fun. I wish my kids had gotten to know her. They could have grown up with a mom who laughed more, worried less, and didn't burden them with her anxiety. I could have experienced their lives through a joyful lens instead of an anxiety-clouded one—one that didn't warn them about everything that could potentially hurt them. They would have liked the old me. We could have laughed more and felt the carefreeness of life instead of thinking of ways to circumvent my anxiety.

The old me would have sat back and watched Kieran pitch in his baseball games, wearing the same baseball hat as all the other kids, and revel in his victories instead of making him wear a skull cap, in case a line drive came back at him, cracked his skull, and put him in a coma for months. Instead, Kieran humored me and put on the embarrassing cap.

I could have cheered on the sidelines, like the other moms did, as Brielle was tossed into the air during a cheerleading competition. Instead, I sat silent, looking at the exits to make sure ambulances had enough space to get to her in case they dropped her. I watched every tumbling pass, praying she did not land on her head. My kids would inevitably absorb this stress. I knew it was up to me to get it under control.

Finding ten minutes to talk to a secretary to make an appointment with a psychiatrist, then finding a sitter to watch my kids, was a feat in itself. It all seems simple, but this was not easy for me, and a simple phone call could take me a week to complete.

"Press 1 for English."

"Mom, can I have milk in my sippy cup?"

"Yes, I'll get it for you. Jack, stop punching Kieran."

"Press 2 for an appointment."

"I'll stop punching him when he answers me about being the Red Power Ranger."

"Press 9 If you are a new patient."

"He is one, he can't answer you yet, just give him the sword, helmet, and gloves."

"Hello, doctor's office, can I help you?"

"Oh, hi, can I make an appointment? I'm a new patient."

"Take that, I hate Red Power Rangers, take that."

"I need some information. Let's set up your file."

"Oh." *It's gonna take ten minutes to set up my file,* "Umm, okay, I can try… Jack, stop swording Kieran; he is not the enemy. I'm sorry, could you hold on for a minute? Oh, I'm sorry, I'll get you your milk, Kat. I apologize; I'll have to call you back."

I finally got to make the call and went in to see the doctor. He prescribed me an anti-anxiety medication. Back in 2005, the idea of going on medication because of mental illness was not readily accepted as "normal." I worried that I would become a character in *One Flew Over the Cuckoo's Nest* and not be able to take care of my kids. I certainly did not grow up in a household where therapy or medication was discussed. No one discussed being on medication, and the conversation about mental health was not a thing.

The idea of medication added to my anxiety and guilt. I was not a drinker back then, never smoked pot or did any recreational drugs ever, and now I would need to go on a daily dose of sanity. *Shouldn't I be able to do this on my own?* Luckily, the medication did what it was advertised to do. I was not changed but tamed. I can't remember the exact medication they put me on twenty years ago, but I believe it was Prozac. All I knew was that it helped me function. Suddenly, the spilled milk no longer brought me to tears; my kids running around the house was normal behavior. Weeks earlier, I was ready for the day to be over by 9 a.m., and now I could at least make it to 5 p.m. It made me slightly saner. It took the edge off. There was still sadness, anger, and anxiety, but I could breathe again.

Six months after I started the meds, my insurance company insisted I go on a generic medication. It didn't work as well as the brand. On the day of the follow-up psychiatrist appointment, my babysitter canceled at the last minute, so I took all four of my loves to his office. If you've ever been to a psychiatrist, you know that the appointments take five minutes. They ask you five questions, and they write you a script.

I walked in with my kids, and we sat on the leather couch (seriously, just like in the movies). My appointment was at 10 a.m., but at 10:15, the doctor had still not entered the room. I am responsible for my kid's behavior for the first ten minutes; I blame the doctor for any bad behavior after that. My kids were one, three, four, and seven at the time, with the energy of most kids their age. They first started with somersaults off the leather couch, then some fighting with hair-pulling and pushing. Brielle found a pencil to use as a microphone and was doing some sort of singing and dance performance. Katreana sat on the couch while her brothers rolled on top of her, never breaking from her normal non-reactive personality. The longer we waited, the worse their behavior became.

I did what many parents do: I promised McDonald's if the behavior improved.

"Let mommy talk to this nice doctor for ten minutes, and then we can go to McDonald's." Well then, an argument ensued about either McDonald's or Friendly's.

"For the love of God, just be quiet, and we can discuss it in the car!"

When Dr. Fix Me finally showed up, the sheer terror that crossed his face when he walked in was unsettling. I calmed the kids down, and they attempted to sit quietly while he spit out the five questions.

"How are you feeling? Are you still having anxiety? Any stressors in your life?"

Is he serious? Do you see what is going on in here? I just nodded.

"Do you think the medicine is working? Should we change the dose?"

"I don't think it's the dose. The generic brand isn't helpful—"

Kieran jumped off the back of the very expensive leather couch onto my head.

Jack yelled, "Friendly's!"

I picked him up, put him on my lap, and, without missing a beat, explained that the insurance company had switched the brand and that the meds weren't working as well. I could see that the doctor was distracted and not listening. He seemed concerned about his leather couch and getting us out of his office as fast as he could.

At that point, Jack found a stress ball and started pegging Kieran with it. "Take that!"

Brielle continued to dance and sing into the microphone, "La, La, La, I'm singing!"

Katreana, as always, sat quietly, studying the doctor, who abruptly got up from his chair and grabbed his prescription pad. He looked at me, held the pen to the paper, and said, "What do you need? What do you want?" I think I could have asked for any drug at that moment if it meant I would leave with my kids as quickly as possible.

Given that I never attended medical school, I didn't know what I needed or wanted, so I said, "I don't know. What do you think?"

I walked out of the office, without any faith in this doctor, holding a script in my hand. I never filled the prescription or went back to his office.

It was eighteen years before I got back on anti-anxiety medication, when the kids started leaving for college, and I was on them for less than a year. Though deep down inside I knew they would help me, I had an inner struggle with my old self. The truth is, I didn't want to need medication. So, I told myself I could stay off of it.

I think medication is a very valuable tool to help people cope. I am thankful there are prescription drugs to help tame the demons, dull the anxiety that can rule your world and help you feel joy again. I may go back on them someday.

It took all those years for me to come to terms with the fact that my brain was damaged after my trauma. Claire explained to me that trauma causes chemical imbalances, and I couldn't expect myself to function the same way as I did when the balance was different. Life is already hard when everything is in perfect balance. Add the imbalances of your neurotransmitters due to trauma and anxiety, and it is a wonder we make it through the day.

I will never be the same person I was before John jumped. Trauma stole the old, carefree me, and I will always double-check that the front door is locked.

Jack playing football

Kieran pitching with skull cap on

CHAPTER 16

Our New Relationship With John

After John jumped, I couldn't go to Starbucks like we did all the time; it was too hard to be in a place where we had deep and light-hearted conversations and many cups of caffeine. But about a month after John jumped, I was so exhausted that I needed a coffee boost. I buckled all four kids into the minivan and made the trek to our spot. I turned right toward the store like I had many times with John in my car. I looked up, and in the sky, right over the Starbucks, was a massive rainbow in the February sky. There was no rain or even clouds, yet a beautiful rainbow stared back at me. I got chills because the last time I saw a rainbow was across Kieran's face moments before I told him his dad died.

I wondered if these rainbows were a sign from John, so I rushed to look up their symbolism. Spiritually, a rainbow means God's Promise of hope. So there it was, no longer God's Promise to us, but John's Promise. From that day forward, rainbows appeared during some of our brightest times and saddest times, constantly reminding us John is right there with us.

These rainbows give us hope and faith in our new life. We see rainbows at very coincidental times. One will appear on the kids' birthdays, John's birthday, during special occasions, or sometimes just on ordinary days, to remind us that Daddy is still with us, still here, parenting and guiding us through this life.

Rainbows have gotten me through some very tough times. I was a wreck the first time I dropped Brielle off for college. Brielle knew I would be, and I think I cried for a month straight. About twenty minutes into the four-hour drive home, I got a text from Brielle. Attached was a photo from her seventh-floor dorm window, and a rainbow was in the sky. "Don't worry, Daddy has taken over watching me now." And that is how I got through the car ride. I spent the next four hours talking to John.

"I tried my best for the first eighteen years, but now it's your job to watch over her," I said out loud. "I can't believe I just drove away. Did I teach her enough about life to be safe in college? I no longer have eyes on her. Please watch over her. Make sure she has fun, but not too much fun. Protect her from jerks, drugs, and bad decisions. It's your turn; I am passing her off to your watch. Thank you, my love."

His rainbow was John's message back to us: "I made a promise to you all to always be your husband and your father, and I will continue to do so from heaven."

John's birthday is April 15th. He would have turned thirty-eight on his first birthday after he jumped. On the morning of his birthday, I woke up around 3 a.m. in my room, and in front of his closet, at the foot of my bed, was a black silhouette. I had an eerie feeling that it was John watching over me. You would think I would have been frightened, but I wasn't. I felt calm in the room as I stared at this black image.

An overpowering feeling of tiredness came over my eyes as if someone was forcing me to go back to sleep. "John, is that you? Is that you?" I tried so hard to stay awake and be in the moment with John, but I could feel someone pushing my eyelids closed. I wanted to talk to him and ask him all the questions I should have asked before he left, but I had never felt so exhausted as at that moment, and my body forced me back to sleep.

I believe I woke up unexpectedly and caught John in the moment of being my guardian angel. The next day, I had a pep in my step and a lift in my spirits. I was hopeful because I thought more of these nights would come. Sadly, the black silhouette never returned. John visits in dreams, but no one is standing at the foot of my bed, or at least I haven't been awake for his visits.

This sighting was just the beginning of a series of coincidental events that showed me the universe is much bigger than we know. Six months after John jumped, a woman appeared at my door. It was not unusual for a stranger to appear at our front door; when your story is public, people feel they have some ownership of your life. They were usually kind, but since our lives became news stories, some felt connected to us and could be intrusive. I opened my door to this familiar-looking woman, ready to say, "Thank you, yes, very sad, we are doing okay, one day at a time." Instead, she had a look of panic on her face, and I didn't feel comfortable welcoming her in. Her hair was untamed, and her forehead was wrinkled as if in pain.

"John sent me here; he wants you to know things." She was slightly scary, and I thought for a second that it might be safer to close and lock the door behind me. However, something told me to listen to her and give her a moment to collect her thoughts.

"John came to me, and he wanted me to tell you a few things. He told me where you lived."

I took her outside on the front lawn. She told me, "You have to listen to me; if I don't tell you what he wants you to know, then I won't get rid of this debilitating pain in my head and neck."

I was intrigued and suspicious at the same time. Even though this so-called medium said John told her where we lived, I didn't think it would be too difficult to find out.

"John wants you to know he didn't want to leave, but he had to go. He loves you and the kids more than anything."

I decided to let her keep talking and see where it took me. My kids joined us outside and began to play with chalk on the driveway. I walked her over to the other side of the front lawn away from the kids, so they were unable to hear what she was saying. At first, what she told me was just basic information that anyone could have said or known. But then the real revelations began.

"John wants everyone out of your house, clear everyone out of your house. There are too many people coming and going and giving their opinions. Ask them to leave and pay someone to help you."

My ears perked up because I had the same feeling. I was so thankful for all the help and food trains, but I felt like I was losing my identity. The final straw was when someone tried to discipline Jack. *Oh no, you are becoming too comfortable in my house and think you can take over my job. That is not happening. Thank you for your help, but here is the door.* What I said was: "Okay, I've got this from now on. I appreciate the help, but I got it from here. Please call if you are going to stop over, and I will call you if I need help."

I couldn't ask people to fold my laundry or wash my dishes because they were being kind to stop over. But that is what I truly needed. If I paid a sitter, I could get the help I really needed.

"John also wants you to stop talking to the media." I felt exhilarated and connected to John as she told me this. I'd stopped answering all calls and media requests about a month earlier. John and I were still on the same page, even while he was in heaven. As kooky as this lady was, her advice was productive and not harmful. I wish I could remember every single word she said, but my mind kept going back and forth from, *this is crazy, why am I still talking to her? ...*to, *tell me more and more and more and let me ask him the questions I want to help me raise our kids the way we both wanted to!*

I was dying to ask her for John's answers that I desperately wanted: "What age are we letting the girls date? Do you want the kids to go to Catholic high school? Should we give the kids vaccines for HPV? Should we let the boys play football? What foreign language should we have them study? What's the length of grounding for the first offense of drinking? At what age are we getting them a phone? How far are we letting them go away to college? Do we tell them if we don't like a boyfriend or girlfriend?"

I stood there dumbfounded, letting the medium talk while trying to absorb it all. "John is okay. It took him six months to find someone like me as the go-between from heaven to Earth." Apparently, that's a rapid turnaround time for a spirit intervention.

Throughout the conversation, I could see that my kids began to feel uncomfortable with her presence. After a while, I said, "Thank you for your information, but we have to be somewhere, so I am going to ask you to leave." I felt so much excitement about the visit but still hesitated to believe whether it was all true or just a wacky woman needing to include herself in my trauma. She drove off, leaving me with this new connection to John.

I took the kids inside, and the answering machine had three messages from various media outlets. They wanted my comment on an upcoming press conference announcing the reinstatement of the Personal Safety System (ropes). This was significant because the department completed research and development of a new PSS rope system. I smiled, remembering her advice and didn't call any of them back. John confirmed what I already knew: I was done with the media.

Soon after we walked into the house, the kids wanted to walk up to 7-11 to get Slurpees. We were not in the store for more than two minutes when the medium walked in and said, "John told me where I could find you. He made me come back because he wanted me to tell you about other things." Earlier, I watched her drive away from our house, and we didn't take our car to the store, so it was clear she didn't follow us. I began to believe John really was talking to her. She said, "I tried to leave, but unless I tell you everything, the pain in my head and neck will remain." Even though it was slightly spooky, I loved that John was following us.

"You will be financially fine, so stop worrying about money. He is also insisting that I ensure the girls never go near the next-door neighbor's house. You always need to know where they are and who they are talking to." I found this odd because although we didn't have a great relationship with our neighbor, I didn't consider him harmful.

The medium continued walking back to my house with me. "I know this sounds odd, but he wants you to take down the flagpole and all the flowers surrounding it."

I gasped, "No, that doesn't sound weird at all." After John jumped, our neighbors approached me and offered to put up a flagpole. I knew John didn't care for this neighbor, but what was I supposed to say, "No"? I knew John wouldn't have wanted their generosity, or anyone else's, done out of pity, while making the giver feel better. I still had to live across the street from the neighbors, so I accepted the offer. His wife planted flowers around the base of the pole. When the medium said John wanted me to take DOWN the flagpole and the flowers around it, I knew she was truly listening to John.

Two weeks after the medium visit, my neighbor's son was arrested for soliciting underage girls in a mall parking lot. He was part of a sting operation in which he thought he was talking to young girls over the internet, but it was law enforcement. When I found that out, I almost lost it. *There you have it! John continues to protect his girls from above.*

I hoped John would understand that the flagpole had to stay up. I took down the flag hanging there, but he would have to compromise on this one. I explained to him, "I understand your request, but I have to live across the street and see these people. I will take down the flag, but please understand the pole needs to remain."

John must have understood, because a month after the medium's visit, I went to pick up the kids from school like I did every day. They wanted to play on the playground for a while, so I chatted with the other moms as a thunderstorm rolled in so quickly that no one had much time to react. It was strange because there was no mention of rain or storms earlier that day.

We rushed to the minivan and waited a while because the rain was coming down so hard it was unsafe to drive. The wind was blowing branches enough to bend them in half. We finally made our way home, and as we approached our house, I saw the effects of the storm. The one hundred-year-old maple tree that sat at the curb of our front lawn was uprooted and fell right on top of the flagpole. Somehow, the massive tree missed our house but snapped the flagpole in half, smashing the flowers planted around it.

Once I surveyed my house for damage, I understood what had happened. John heard me and understood that I could not fulfill his wishes on my own, so he took care of it himself. An unexpected storm demolished the flagpole and the flowers while I was away picking up the kids. It still blows my mind that he found a way to show me that he still had my back.

When I think I'm alone, I remember the maple tree and the flagpole. I sometimes think I spend all my time and energy trying to control what is happening around me, even though I have nothing to do with any of it.

I told Claire about my visitor, and I thought she wouldn't believe any of it, but she was intrigued instead. I was confused because we had discussed seeing a psychic or medium earlier, and she wasn't a fan of going to one. After I told her about my visitor, she clarified that she wasn't opposed to mediums in general. She said, "I believe John sent you the medium visit as a gift, so you could feel she was truthful. Paying for a medium leaves you questioning its validity."

As time passed, I read books about people who received similar visits, and it took their loved ones much longer to locate both the receiver and the giver. It feels good that John worked diligently to find my receiver/giver. It wasn't really about what she told me; it was more about him finding someone to let me know he is still my partner, just in a different way.

Every once in a while, I see the medium around town, and we never say anything to each other. It would have been easy for me to befriend her and hope that John talked to her whenever I was nearby. But how would that help me live a healthy life? I would live my life hoping John would tap into her again, waiting to hear from him, or, worse, running all my decisions by her first. If he needed to tell me something, he could use her again. She knows where I live and where I buy Slurpees.

Rainbow outside our house

CHAPTER 17

The New Normal

During the first year, waking up in the morning was the hardest part of my day. The first minute was suffocating. I would roll over, and for half a second, I would forget the modern tragedy of my existence and look for John. Initially, I would think he was just at the firehouse completing a twenty-four-hour shift, but then reality would stab me in the heart. *Could this really be true that I was left to raise our kids alone?* Once I realized it was not a dream, I turned to the baby monitor. *Please don't light up, give me five more minutes.* No more rolling over and asking John for an extra five minutes; it's now on me, every second of every minute now belongs to me.

Climbing out of bed, I began my day, completing task after task to be checked off. Four different schedules had to be followed. Each job is monotonous, with tasks completed after task in a numbing, comatose state. Every cry, every scrape, every meal prep, every diaper change, every car seat buckle, every bath, every bottle, every problem, every everything is all mine.

One of the tasks I hated the most was changing the toilet paper roll onto the springy stick. I know that sounds ridiculous, but once I realized that I was the ONLY person in the house who could figure out the spring mechanism to put a new roll of toilet paper on, I realized it represented my new life. It was a reminder that I'm on my own, and if we want to wipe our asses, it would be up to me.

I had to create a new normal, a new ebb and flow that did not include John. To fill our days, I signed my kids up for every sport, every library program, every town program, and anything to get us out of the house and keep us (me) busy. I thought I was being a great mom. I was giving them many opportunities to learn and make friends. What I was really doing was avoiding our home, keeping myself numb to emotion, and staying away from a place that screamed, "John lived here."

But no matter how busy I kept our family, the pain of losing John would sneak up on me. Around 6:30 p.m. every night, I would hear John's car pull up in the driveway, hear his car door shut, and even hear the front door creak open. "Daddy is home!" I almost yelled numerous times. I often thought, *maybe it really is him, maybe he is coming in to watch us*. This was our new normal, keeping so busy that exhaustion replaced mindfulness.

This routine worked for a while, but I would often crash on rainy days when all events were cancelled, forcing me to sit in deafening silence. It was on those days that I missed him the most. People understand the sadness and grief, but few understand the true loneliness. All my plans, my whole future, were mapped out until they weren't.

The mom my kids used to have was no more. I was no longer confident, present, and self-assured. Yes, I was there, I did the chores required to keep the household moving, but when you lose your husband, you also lose time. Time to sit with your children, to laugh with them, to play with them, and to talk to them.

I spent most of my days racing through chore after chore, looking forward to 9 p.m., when everyone was bathed, and bedtime stories were read, so I could take a deep breath. Not only did I think about sitting in the loneliness after the kids went to bed, but I also projected about my future loneliness once the kids no longer needed me.

There were many tough days that first year, but I can vividly remember a day in February that destroyed me to new levels. Since I was still breastfeeding Kieran, I had not gotten my period back. It's nature's way of giving you time to provide all your nutrients to feed your child. You have to be careful during this time, as you could become pregnant during your first menstrual cycle. I was very much aware of this as it happened to us between Jack and Katreana.

So, in February, the thought crossed my mind: *Maybe I could be pregnant.* It was about the same time frame after giving birth that I had become pregnant with Katreana. As sad as those days were, this idea gave me a glimmer of hope that I might be pregnant. *How amazing that would be! I could still have another piece of John, even though he was no longer with me.*

I would discuss the idea with him at night, "I hope you have one last surprise for me, as tough as it will be, please let me be pregnant. I want one more opportunity to be a mom to one of your kids." I was aware the conversation was crazy, but I was desperate; I needed something to believe in. I needed some joy and a sense of reconciliation with faith. Every passing day, my hope grew that I would receive one last gift. I even planned where I would fit a fifth child in our small Cape Cod house.

But then it happened about one month after John jumped. I was in the shower, and there it was… blood. *No! I want one more! This can't be the end.* I was devastated as I sat in the tub, sobbing while the water poured over me. My dream was over, my hope of one last gift vanished. It destroyed me, grieving a child that did not even exist. It was my last hope, my last piece of John, taken from me. Heartbroken, my grieving started all over again. I had to accept that John was not coming back, not even in a mini version of himself, and mourn my chance to be a mommy to one more person. John jumping decided this for us.

The jump ripped the conversation about having more children out of my future, along with many other discussions that should have been shared between two parents. In the past, I ran all decisions by their dad. During the first year, I spent the day making mental notes of things I would discuss with John when he got home.

Oh, I have to tell John the car is rattling. I saw his college friend at the store today. Jack's teacher said he did great in school today. Should I sign Brielle up for softball? But our discussions never happened. You spend nights wallowing in loneliness and self-doubt that you can make all the parenting decisions on your own, with no one to run the pros and cons with, relying on one broken brain to run things through, to make life-changing decisions, and try not to ruin four little humans along the way.

The first year was just about surviving; there was no "being in the moment" and reveling in their beauty and brilliance. I had just enough energy to survive. So, when I lost John, I lost many precious mommy moments that would have been priceless memories.

When I had to fill out medical forms for Kieran, it came to the part that asks for the ages he babbled, crawled, walked, and what his first words were. It's all a blur. I was so numb during his milestones. I know Kieran was taken care of. Damn it, I continued to breastfeed him until he was a year old. But I can't remember his developmental stages. I would make up dates that I knew were in the normal range. I didn't want the doctors to think I wasn't a good mommy, but the truth was that most of the time, I couldn't focus or feel anything.

It must have been clear to me that his precious first year was slipping away quickly while I was dealing with my misery, because I took a ton of pictures of him. It was like I knew I was missing his life, so I wanted a record of it to revisit later. We joke that he was "raised by wolves." But we joke to mask the sadness. I was robbed of Kieran's first year, and I can never get that back.

I still had trouble falling asleep every night, so a glass of wine would relax me and help me get drowsy. This was how my ritual began: get all my loves settled, put them to bed, pour a cold glass of white wine, put my feet up, and take a sip. The demons that ruled my world would drift away for a moment.

Oddly, this made me feel closer to John. It was as if I took on one of his enjoyments and made it my own. It was my time with him. We talked (I talked, he listened) about the day and the kids. We figured out parenting strategies during those glasses of wine. By the time I took the last sip, I was ready to fall asleep.

The biggest truth I learned in my first few years was that there was only one other person in the world who cared as much as I did about our family. Only John would care as much as I do whether Jack will score a goal in his soccer game, whether Brielle will write a sentence in perfect penmanship with a detailed illustration using many different colors, whether Katreana reads before kindergarten, or whether Kieran is the quarterback on the flag football team.

What would John say? I can hear him in my mind: "Jack has a career as a professional soccer player. Brielle is brilliant; she will probably be the next best artist in the modern world, given the way she uses color. Should we have Katreana skip a grade? She is already reading, and I don't want school to be too boring. Kieran has the smarts to be the quarterback and is so athletic."

I imagine having to bring him back down to reality: "Yes, our kids are awesome, but they are probably just normal, regular kids." We would laugh about it and enjoy his projections even if they were a proud parent's fantasy.

There was obviously sadness and grief after John jumped, but no one prepares you for the loneliness. You can be surrounded by many people and still be incredibly lonely. You find yourself every once in a while having a good day, and then you can string two together, but the loneliness never goes away. People can be happy, sad, and lonely at the same time.

There were people who were willing to fill my loneliness if I let them in. Everyone was kind but didn't know what to do with me. I didn't know what to do with myself. I could choose to keep everything inside, stay numb, or I could begin to open up.

I eventually started sharing the littlest things I would have normally kept to myself, telling people about daily moments that happened. I just needed someone to care and listen. Now, when I left the pediatrician's office, my sister, Patricia, got the phone call. She cared about what the doctor said about my kids. It made the loneliness sting a little less. I started telling the local barista that Brielle was graduating from kindergarten. People were kind and seemed to care. I also discussed with my local mechanic which car "we" should buy, as if he would ride in it with us daily. I probably overshared with the kids' teachers and took up too much of their time at parent-teacher conferences, but they were the only ones I had to discuss my children's academics with. I was blessed to have many great teachers and friends who cared about my kids.

I would call my friend Laura after the kids were asleep and tell her every detail about my day, even though she had kids of her own. She was my saving grace. Laura gave great advice that I still remember and repeat to this day: "Don't blame your kids for the genes you gave them." And "What's in the cat is in the kittens." These sayings saved Jack. They rattled in my head whenever my kids misbehaved. Laura is an amazing friend; I could not have survived the first year without her. Find your Laura.

This all started gradually, but once I let the floodgates open, I couldn't stop it. Did folks need to know Kieran was obsessed with Thomas the Tank Engine, Woody and Buzz, and Spider-Man? Did they need to know that Jack could add and subtract at age four, and that he insisted on wearing his alligator rain boots 365 days a year? Did people need to know that Katreana had an eclectic style and wore a fake-fur cheetah coat since she was three years old? Or that Brielle was a master manipulator and could get everything she wanted from her siblings? Like convincing Jack to ask Santa for the Wii so she wouldn't have to use up one of her presents, even though she would be using it, too.

All these precious moments were happening in my life, and though I yearned to share them with John, I was lucky to have others who listened. And maybe, at times, I overshared, but I yearned for adult conversation. These conversations helped me exhale. I was a balloon filled with pent-up air, released into the universe. I quickly realized that what I put out into the universe was returning to me. When people started sharing their own life experiences with me, I welcomed their stories and struggles.

I remember the first time I laughed, like really laughed, after John jumped. My sister and I can make each other laugh at the dumbest things, and then we can't stop. I will have tears of laughter rolling down my face, and I can't catch my breath. This often happened to us as kids in church, and we would get yelled at when we got into the car after Mass. One day, after John jumped, I remember starting to laugh and feeling so strange that this emotion had escaped me for so long. My abdomen began to ache from the contraction of my stomach muscles, and I was physically bent over with laughter. It's one of those times that the laughter becomes contagious with everyone surrounding us. I don't even know what provoked the episode, but it was probably so silly that it wouldn't appear funny to anyone else.

After I recovered from the fit of laughter, an enormous feeling of guilt came over me. *How could I be laughing? My husband died.* I looked around. *Who had seen me do this? They will think I'm happy and don't love John.* It took the wind out of me. I had conflicting emotions: joy and guilt simultaneously. All of this is part of my resilience journey, showing that it's okay to feel conflicting emotions and that resilience isn't about being strong all the time but about learning to live with and accept all your feelings.

My maternity leave with Kieran, which was to be one year, was extended to two years after John's jump. I then made the difficult choice not to return to teaching, especially while my kids were young. My struggle was choosing between all the effort and investment I put into my post-grad education vs. my need to be there fully for my family. I chose to support four children at home over 120 in a classroom.

When you make yourself available and share your story, others respond in kind. Opening myself up to the universe and being exposed to people's opinions might be one of the scariest things I've done since John jumped. Once you conquer this fear, your world will be less lonely. It didn't always go smoothly, and I risked getting the look of *Why are you sharing this with me?* But on those days, I told myself they might not have gone through a similar experience, which is why they didn't understand. I might have acted the same way if John had not jumped.

Everyone has a story. The world is full of people going through struggles, maybe it's their first year without their husband, first year being divorced, first year without their mom, first year being an empty nester or just diagnosed with an illness. Don't assume you know the severity of sadness people might be experiencing. Be empathetic to strangers because your patience could make a difference in their lives. Understanding where people come from and how we can make a difference is always worth the risk. All we can do is try.

The first year was definitely the most challenging year of my life, but I discovered that sadness, grief, and loneliness can bring personal growth and life lessons that make me a better person. The first year was just the beginning of many lessons to come.

Kids summer after John jumped

Sitter Kristen with Kieran

CHAPTER 18

It Takes A Village...

"Hi, I'm not sure if you remember me? You taught me in sixth-grade." The young girl standing at my door looked familiar. It was three months after John jumped.

Most of the time, I would ignore people knocking on my front door and pray that they would eventually go away. I rarely showered and certainly did not want to make small talk with anyone.

"Of course, you're Kate."

"I am so sorry about your husband. I just wanted to drop this card off and offer babysitting, free of charge, if you ever need it."

"Oh, thank you so much, Kate." We chatted for a minute, and then I excused myself. "I really appreciate you stopping by."

The truth is, I was thinking about hiring a sitter. I had so much help after John jumped, my mom, my sisters, and random people walking in and out of our house. I was in such a fog in the beginning that I didn't even notice. In reality, I needed everyone's help. I was physically there but mentally gone, lost in mourning. My priority was to survive each day and ensure the kids were fed, clothed, and bathed. It was a primitive time in our lives. Nothing fancy, just survival.

Most of the time, I didn't feel like getting up in the morning and doing any of those things. The kids' little voices would stir, and I would roll over to see John not there. My new life would come rushing back to me, filling me with dread. I wanted to pull the covers over my head and never get out of bed. I had dreams of going back to sleep and shutting out the world. But I dragged myself out of bed and never missed a day as a mom. There were days I wanted to quit, there were days I wanted life to pass me by, but I didn't let it. When it all seemed too much to handle, I depended on my village.

I appreciated all the townspeople, but over time, I felt as if I were losing control of my house and my life. The longer they helped, the more comfortable they felt. When people came to help, I wouldn't tell them what to do. I wanted to, but I couldn't. I spent my days thanking them for being there, even if they didn't do much. I couldn't ask them to cook dinner, do my laundry, or take out the trash, even though that was exactly what I needed. I had no energy to do these simple tasks, but the guilt of asking others to do what I did three months earlier prevented me from asking for help. But things changed when I realized it was time to take back my home. As difficult as it all was, it was still my life, and I was losing control over it. My house may never be clean, laundry may never be done, and my kids may never be fed all the food groups at every meal, but I needed control back. I needed to sink or swim.

Where is the card Kate dropped off? I need to call her. This is how my village grew.

John and I never used sitters; we only had family members sit for us. I trusted them, and they were free. Once we entered the parenting world, we made everything about our kids, including our social outings, so we didn't often need help. We went from hanging out at bars to hanging out at zoos, parks, children's museums, and G-rated movies.

Our bedtime changed from 2 a.m. to 9 p.m. The kids were mine and John's, and a committee wouldn't raise them. I wanted our kids to have that special relationship with an aunt, an uncle, and a grandparent that most other kids had. I wanted them raised by me, with the help of their dad in heaven. Their relationship with our extended family would continue to be just that, a special kind of relationship, not a disciplinary one.

Now that the dynamic had changed, I needed to alter my philosophy and trust others. Little did I know it was the best thing I could have done for my kids.

I heard the car pull up. I knew it wasn't John's, but the sound brought me relief. The car door slammed, and my mind settled; my heart stopped racing, and the immense responsibility for four kids' safety was now dispersed. The door swung open with an urgent swing. My SOS arrived.

"Good morning!" It was Kate. She got to work immediately, without even stopping to chat. She started picking up the plastic VHS cases that Jack had opened and had made into a tower. Then she moved on to putting all the dress-up clothes back into the toy chest and meticulously returning every Lego piece to the bin. She did this within five minutes of entering my house, a task that would have taken me a whole day to complete.

The kids learned quickly to just let Kate be Kate. She would get around to talking to them eventually, but she had a list of chores in her head to complete. I certainly didn't get in her way, either. She could see the big picture; I was living in a mess and couldn't see it. It was like passing by the laundry basket on the steps twenty times before realizing it was there. Kate was a tornado, swirling in and putting everything in its place. There is something about living in a house with some order that helps you think clearly. I only wish Kate could have done the same with my thoughts and anxiety.

Katreana notices Kate and runs to her, "Kate!" and jumps into her arms for a hug.

"Morning, go run and get your brush. I'll help you get ready."

Kate turns to me, "So what's on tap for the day? It's Wednesday, will you be bringing Kat to the library program? I will be here with Kieran. I'll go get the library books to return."

"Um, yes, that's right, it's Wednesday, isn't it?" I finish cleaning up the breakfast dishes, and as I turn around, Kate has already stripped two of the kids and begun dressing them for school.

"Any particular outfits today, or are we letting them choose again?"

I give Kate a look; she knows what I am thinking.

"It is not worth fighting Katreana. She can wear whatever she wants, and if Jack wants to wear the alligator boots again, even though it's not raining, I am okay with that, too."

Kate was more than just a babysitter. I could tell her to vacuum, make waffles, or attempt to comb Katreana's hair without feeling guilty about asking for help. She wove into the fabric of our lives without stepping over the boundaries of discipline.

Most of the time, I didn't even leave when she came. Sometimes, I would go to the gym or take one kid to a doctor's appointment without bringing the whole crew. But often, she just came with us, so I had two sets of eyes on the four kids. She allowed me to give my kids a life back. She let me talk to other parents and build new relationships instead of always running after my kids. We could go to the park, we could go shopping, we could go out to dinner like other families, without my crippling anxiety breaking me down into tears.

Kate was a beacon of light, a ray of hope, a new adult who brought positive energy and a touch of OCD tendencies into our house. We have so many "Kate stories" that the kids still reference today. She took the yolk out of their egg salad, made up games that helped Jack memorize his sight words, she read the Junie B Jones series ad nauseum, she wore a garbage can top for protection when pitching wiffle balls to the boys, she would allow Kieran to be Kieran by littering the kitchen with shopping bags to simulate rubble on the tracks when he was pretending to be Thomas the Tank Engine, she would call him only by the name that he was emulating that day, she would bring levity to stressful traveling by singing into the Big Ass Fan in the Jamaican airport just at the right time before my patience snapped. Most of all, she was just Kate—the person who saved me and showed me the beauty of life again.

Fortunately, I was blessed with many other angels who came into our lives. Kristen joined our crew a few months after Kate. She was an outstanding counterbalance to Kate. Kristen's personality was the most "mommy-like"; she worried about each child's safety and protected them as if they were her own. She was vested in every aspect of their lives, both socially and physically. She was like a second mom, worrying about them.

One might start the day, and the other might finish it. They would text each other information that the other might need.

Kate: Are you working today?

Kristen: Later

Kate: There is a load of laundry in the dryer

Kristen: OK, on it. Jack has a baseball game tonight, so I will probably be home with the girls to give them a break from attending another baseball game. Eileen can bring Kieran.

Kate: Sounds good

One year, my sitters even surprised me by bringing the kids to get a family photo for Christmas. They took them shopping, packed fancy clothes, had them change in a bathroom, and took a family photo. Apparently, some of the kids were not very cooperative, and in the end, the sitters had to beg the photographer, "Just take the damn photo! She doesn't expect perfection!" This meant so much to me—not only the photo but also teaching my kids the importance of showing love to their mom. It also gave Kate and Kristen a dose of reality and their future photo shoots with their own kids.

Soon, Kristen and Kate got real jobs. So, we later added Christina, Kelly, Blathin, Sam, and Tommy to our crew. All of them added their special talents to our days. They were my crutch, keeping my sanity and making me laugh. If we could not have John, we had people who loved, cared for, and guided my kids through a new normal—a single-parent home that relied on others to keep joy in our household.

When the boys became tweens, I sought out a male sitter, which was uncommon at the time. My boys needed someone who wanted to pitch, catch, throw, run, wrestle, and break up fights. Tommy was just that, and a fantastic role model for them to see. He gave the boys an outlet to be boys with some proper refereeing. He knew how to balance their personalities to keep everyone playing. Each sitter had strengths, and I relied on them to share their talents so my kids could benefit.

Kate and Kristen will often send us texts and photos of memories they think of, like when Kristen fell off the snow tube, bruised, and mortified, and Brielle wrote about it for the whole fourth grade to hear. Or how we made s'mores in our fireplace, and Kieran ate all the chocolate when no one was looking. I love these memories because I forgot some of them, and they still make me smile. Maybe their childhoods weren't so bad?

My kids joke that the babysitters raised them. I never mind when they say it because it's true. It takes a village, and I equipped myself with the best townspeople anyone could ask for. I don't know how I went from never having a babysitter to employing a gaggle of them. They might have been the best decision I made as a parent.

Many of my sitters are moms now, and sometimes I watch their kids. We often discuss the good old days and laugh about the memories. They give me credit for giving them the freedom to help raise my kids without imposing too many rules. I never realized that I did that. I let their strengths shine, and my kids benefited from all the styles.

Sometimes you need a village to raise kids, and I am so thankful I found my townspeople. Thank you to my village for all of your help. Thank God I was open to allowing others to influence my children's lives. Here, I thought I was the only one who could best influence them when, in fact, my sitters gave them the best of themselves and enriched their lives immensely. Find your townspeople.

Kat, Kate, and Kieran

Family photo that the sitters surprised me with at first Christmas

CHAPTER 19

Christmas

A funny thing happens when your kids' dad gets taken from their lives early. You want to ensure they feel no sorrow, so you do what every financially capable mom would do—shower them with gifts. Lots of them. I felt that large boxes wrapped in fancy paper and decorated with oversized bows would mask what we all knew: their dad would not be with us on Christmas morning. I had to put together those stupid toys that always had extensive manuals and one fewer screw than I needed. I paid sitters to watch the kids while I went to Toys R Us and bought every toy in every aisle. I counted to make sure they all had equal gifts: 5, 10, 15 each. How many would be enough to hide that their dad wasn't there? After all, Santa had to prove to them that it wasn't their fault that their dad was gone. Santa knew they were very good this year, but sometimes being good still gets you a shitty deal. So I spent two months going from store to store, ensuring everything on their list would be under the tree. I would not, and could not, spend Christmas morning looking at little disappointed faces.

A glimmer of hope had started arriving by mail in November. We received crocheted angels and butterflies from all over the United States. I don't know how they got my address, but all colors, shapes, and sizes would show up in our mailbox with a note of sympathy.

"Please take this angel as a sign of hope. We are sorry your fireman, your dad, and your husband will not be with you this Christmas but let this be a reminder that he is watching from above."

I didn't know what to do with them all. Since I had no motivation to take out our ornaments and didn't want to decorate the house after John jumped, we decided to use the gifts as our ornaments and place them on the tree branches. I put Christmas music on and lit a Yankee candle that smelled like Christmas cookies, and I thought maybe the kids wouldn't realize I was faking my way through this holiday. Since I let the kids do all the decorating, only the bottom half of the tree got covered.

Mostly, I remembered how our Christmas lights were still up when the limousine drove past our house on its way to the cemetery on January 27, 2005. Someone said, "John was so proud of this house. What do you think John would be saying right now?"

All I could think of was how John would have said, "Those Christmas lights should already be down and put away by now." They were a reminder that all chores led to me. It took me another month to take those stupid lights down. I certainly didn't want to put them back up again less than a year later. I tried so hard to be in the spirit for the sake of my kids, but the anniversary of John's passing was fast approaching.

In December, we went to the mall and waited in the long line to get the photo that every family celebrating Christmas has.

That day, like all the years before, started with high hopes, but soon Jack pulled Brielle's adorable braids, which took me twenty minutes to brush and style. Kieran spilled the sippy cup of chocolate milk all over his Christmas sweater. Katreana would only agree to wear "comfy clothes," so she wore mismatched leggings and a shirt, while Brielle wanted to wear a chiffon twirly dress with red Dorothy sparkling ballet flats. Jack is still pouting over me screaming at him for ruining his sister's hair. No one at the mall pointed to us and said, "Look at that beautiful family." To top it off, Santa said, "Make sure you are good boys and girls for your Mommy and Daddy!"

What?! My kids thought, *surely Santa knew that Daddy died.* I began to sweat and quickly moved them away from the podium, changing the subject before anyone asked why Santa had mentioned their dad. *Where was the Santa from Miracle on 34th Street who could sing Dutch to the little girl? Santa had to know their dad died; he is watching, isn't he?*

Despite the challenges, I was determined to keep the spirit of Christmas alive in our home. I spoke highly of Santa and all the wonderful things he does. It's hard to cry when you're talking about Santa Claus, so I used him to lift our spirits and get through the holidays. We talked about Santa (and their father) watching over us and how we should always be on our best behavior. December often brought me the best-behaved kids, thanks to the promise of Santa.

Christmas is a stressful time of year because every TV show or commercial questions Santa's identity. *Why does every storyline have to be about whether we should believe in him or not?* I don't know how often I would quickly turn something off when the storyline shifts to doubting there is a Santa Claus. I always welcomed December 26th, knowing I had finished another year of keeping the dream alive. Even to this day, I've never told my kids his identity "might be" a fantasy; we just never discussed the possibility that Santa got some help from parents. Santa is still very real in our house, and he is no longer a person but a spirit.

When Christmas Eve came, the kids were so excited, but all I could think of was how much I missed having a partner to wrap presents and assemble all the toys. John had a tradition of reading *The Night Before Christmas* either before bed or before going to work if he had to work on Christmas Eve. Even if I wept through the reading, I needed to keep that tradition alive. First, we got the carrots, cookies, and milk ready for Santa and the reindeer. Then, I put on their Christmas PJs and read the story to them. I was never the thespian type, but I should have won an Academy Award for that reading. I fought back tears and gave a fabulous performance. I acted my way through most of that year, and Christmas time was no exception.

I put the kids to bed and gave them one last hug and kiss. I knew I still had a few things to assemble, wrap, and then put it all out under the tree. I leaned down to Brielle for one last kiss, and she said, "Mommy, you have been so good this year! Santa is going to bring you so many presents!"

At that moment, my stomach dropped, my heart began to race, and my palms were sweating. I smiled at her, "Well, Santa is very busy making toys for all the good little boys and girls, I'm not sure about parents."

"Oh, no," she said, "Santa cares about everyone, and I told him that you are the best mommy, so that he will bring you lots of presents."

I realized I had no gifts from Santa prepared for myself in the morning. Of course, my siblings and mom would have gifts for me later. But no Santa gifts. Panic set in. *Would I have enough time to pull this off before morning?* I went into my closet, picked out clothes, shoes, and jewelry I thought the kids wouldn't recognize, then took my exhausted body back downstairs and started wrapping gifts for myself. I threw things in Christmas bags, rewrapped gifts I had already received, and re-gifted them to myself. I needed to make a pile like their pile. *Why did I buy them so many gifts?* It was one of the darkest nights I have ever had. Sitting there, letting the tears pour out, and feeling sorry for myself, was easy. It was one of many lonely nights of my new life. This sadness was my new reality. Santa couldn't help. And even worse, the January anniversary was right around the corner.

The following Christmas was better, and we created a new normal. We added traditions, and the kids shared their opinions on what they wanted to include and exclude throughout the month. It was a little easier, but there was always an absence felt on Christmas morning when only I could smile about all the trouble I went to for a gift. I had some challenging items for a few years, as Kieran would invent toys and expect them under the tree. I would ask, "What store did you see that toy in?" He would answer, "I have never seen it in a store. I invented it, but I am sure Santa and his elves could build it for me."

Kieran was a huge fan of Santa. Every year, he would make gifts for everyone, walk around the house with an enormous red sack, and drop them off to imaginary people in our home. When he went through the kindergarten-screening process, the teacher asked, "What do you want to be when you grow up?"

"Santa Claus."

"Oh, that's sweet," the teacher said, "Is it because he brings toys to all the good little boys and girls?"

"No, it's because he never dies," Kieran replied.

The teacher was astonished at his answer. At that point, I realized that all the people who told me that it was a good thing my kids were so young when their dad died, because it wouldn't affect them, were all wrong. Even at four years old, Kieran knew about death and dying. He was already thinking about death because he had already learned that it was a possibility from birth.

The guilt of the trauma never really goes away. I know Santa spoils them with way too many gifts, and it shouldn't take all day to unwrap them, but this day is more for me than for them. Christmas Day is the only day of the year that you are allowed to stay in your pajamas, drink coffee, eat breakfast at noon, and listen to Christmas music. It is the one day of the year that my anxiety is in check. We don't go anywhere and sit together around the living room laughing. Just the way their dad would have liked it.

Grief doesn't take a day off at Christmas; it's a constant, and new facets creep up on you over time. I look back and regret that I hadn't wished Christmas and my life away so quickly. At the time, I was just trying to survive, but when you wish your life away, you suddenly long for it back. Though I wish I could have John with us every Christmas, he indirectly taught me the true meaning of Christmas. We all need a little Santa in our lives.

Christmas photo - second year

CHAPTER 20

Plaque Dedication

The landline rang in the chaos of the house. I yelled to Brielle, "Can you pick it up and just ask who it is?"

"Hello, this is Brielle. Who are you?"

"Hello, I am Michael Bloomberg. Is your mom there?"

"Mom, a man is on the phone, and he wants to talk to you."

"One second, I have to clean up this mess."

"Hold on, my mom is cleaning up Kieran's spilled chocolate milk."

I grab the phone, out of breath, "Hello."

"Hi, Mrs. Bellew, this is Mayor Michael Bloomberg. I have made it a tradition to reach out to line of duty widows before the New Year to check in with them and to once again thank them for their supreme sacrifice for the City of New York."

"Oh, hello, thank you for the call." *Again, I'm thanking this man.* Talking to him took me right back to the waiting room at the hospital the day John jumped. "Yes, the kids are getting big, yes, I'm holding up the best I can..." I kept the call short and went back to cleaning up the mess.

As I took down the 2005 calendar, a wave of sadness came over me. In one way, I wanted the worst year of my life to be a distant memory, but I also wanted to reflect on how much growth we accomplished. A few people came over for a New Year's Eve party. As midnight approached, we went outside, where I had a small bonfire set up. Brielle, Jack, and Katreana were still up, and we decided to have a Year in Review ceremony.

I ripped January off the spiral binding and held it up in the air, "Let's throw January in the fire first! The worst month of our lives! Good riddance!"

Jack yelled, "Let me do it, I hate that month!" He crumbled it up and threw it in the fire. We all cheered.

We then ripped February off, Brielle yelled, "I want to do this one! I hate February when Daddy wasn't our Valentine!" And she tossed it into the fire.

It was Katreana's turn; she looked at me for help because she was unsure what John had missed in March. I whispered to her. "I hate March because Daddy missed the St. Patrick's Day Parade!" She repeated what I said and tossed it into the fire.

"I'll do April, I hate that Daddy missed his thirty-eighth birthday," I said.

"But we still had cake, and we will always have dessert, right, Mom?" Brielle piped in.

"That's right, Daddy passed up dessert the night before he went to heaven, so along with teaching us many things, a big one is to never skip dessert. And that's a good reminder, Brielle."

We ripped the rest of the year off month by month, crumbled it up and talked about something we hated about each month. "When Daddy missed this... When Daddy missed that..." I was trying to symbolically get rid of the worst year of their lives, acknowledge their pain and let them verbalize their loss. After mentioning many of our losses, we began to talk about some positive things that happened to us.

I started with, "Daddy is so proud of how well you are doing in school, how you have made so many friends, how you helped around the house this year."

Brielle added, "How I have lost three teeth this year."

"Yes, he is so proud of you for that."

Jack added, "How I can hit a baseball really far."

"Yes, he is so proud of you for that."

Kat said, "And how I didn't cry when I broke my elbow."

"Yes, definitely then, but it was okay to cry..."

I needed 2006 to feel different. We grabbed an extra dessert and raised our sippy cups to the starry sky and said, "Happy New Year, Daddy! May 2006 be a better year!" All I kept thinking was: *well, it can't get much worse.*

As I woke up on the first day of 2006, I hung up the new calendar and the anniversary stared right back at me. One more obligation to get through; it couldn't come fast enough. The ceremony will mark the end of the year-long obligation to honor and uphold tradition.

The FDNY always marks the first anniversary of line-of-duty deaths with a plaque dedication at the firehouse. John's plaque describing his supreme sacrifice would be unveiled and then affixed to the firehouse wall along with Lt. Meyran's. These plaques remain as permanent fixtures to represent what firefighters do for the citizens of the City of New York. It's a tangible symbol of the common saying, "We Will Never Forget." My kids and their kids and their kids can visit Engine 46 and Ladder 27, long after I pass, to see John's legacy and witness the brave DNA they were created from.

Hundreds of people would come together once again to honor John and Lt. Meyran. Important fire department heads were scheduled to speak about the day, along with lots of pageantry and sad music. I think I dreaded it because it reminded me of John's funeral. Once again, dignitaries speaking on John's behalf who did not really know John. Celebrating a one-dimensional aspect of his life. My kids must listen about their father, the firefighter, and to the description of that terrible day. In a couple of hours, all the work I did to keep them from hearing details of the fire would be undone by the dignitaries' speeches. All of my work could be destroyed in one ceremony.

How can I flip the switch on this day? How can I make this mean something more for my kids than what is planned? I wanted them to see a celebration of him, not a morbid bell-ringing, bagpiper-playing invocation that only brings sadness to their small, impressionable minds. My job was to skew the presentation in any way I could.

John's wishes that he did not want dignitaries to speak on his behalf rang through my mind. *He was so much more than his job. I want the world to see that.* I began reflecting on my family's year-long journey, resentful that John's life was synonymous with a firefighter who died in the line of duty. It occupied only ten of his thirty-seven years on Earth. Being a fireman is not how I remembered him, but how the world saw him.

I decided that if I were going to bring my kids to another formal ceremony, I would make it about John as a person, not only a fireman, or I would not go at all. With the help of a good friend, we created a photo montage video set to music that best represented all of John's life.

I told the Ceremonial Unit my concerns, and about the video we created, "I cannot attend one more ceremony with my children that only represents John as a firefighter. They are going to grow up thinking that is all he was. I'd like the video shown at the dedication."

"That's never been done, nor would they allow it. It's not how we do things."

"Okay. That's fine, but I will not attend, nor will my children."

All hell broke loose. "The wife and children have to attend. They always do!"

"I understand, but I am not attending unless you show the video. I cannot subject my kids to another depressing, sad event surrounding their father. This video shows who their father really was, yes, a brave firefighter, but he is so much more, and that needs to be celebrated, too."

I received numerous phone calls from the fire department's higher-ups, urging me to attend. An assistant to the Chief of the Department even visited me in person.

"I came here to explain how things would work for the plaque dedication." He went through the whole ceremony and pleaded with me to come.

"Look, I will not attend unless we show this DVD," I said, calmly, "Let John's plaque dedication be a first. No one understands the protocols and ceremonial institution of the FDNY better than I, but what the department doesn't understand is the toll and trauma these events have on my children. They lost their father; they didn't lose a firefighter. You're concerned about how the fire department will look if I don't attend. I'm concerned about how my kids' father will be forever ingrained in my kids' minds. If you want us to attend, you must let me show them the whole story, not the one written in the papers."

The Chief said he would give the DVD to the Chief of Department, Nicholas Scoppetta, and let him decide. Scoppetta called me less than twelve hours later.

"Good morning, Mrs. Bellew. I watched the video and totally understand why you would like to share it with the department. I will make sure it is shown at the plaque dedication."

I thanked him and began to wonder whether the kids needed new clothes for the ceremony.

As the day came closer, I felt both dread and relief. The dread was surrounding the spotlight I would be in for the day. The relief was that it would all be over in twenty-four hours. I hated the media and photographers. They snapped endless photos and hoped to catch us at a vulnerable moment when you shed a tear and look hopeless. Their job is to capture a raw, private moment and then make it public by plastering it in their newspaper. It was as if shedding a tear proved how much I loved John. I could hear the shutter mechanism open and close as the cameras captured the seconds of my life. My kids were prime targets. They were cute, young, well-dressed, and innocent-looking. Photographers loved keying in on them during these sad events. Like all kids, they were also unpredictable, misbehaved, and occasionally had tantrums. I hoped they didn't make the six o'clock news for it.

On our way down to the plaque dedication, I remember praying that someone of great significance would die, another war would break out in the Middle East, or any breaking news would be more important than this event. I knew I was only important if it was a slow news day, and our lives were used to fill a sixty-minute news program. I knew they would use me to fill a forty-five-second news story or to sell papers if there wasn't any big news that day. In the early days, the press came around often, but eventually the phone calls for comments became fewer and fewer. Then, another memorial event or something about our court case would come up, and they would be interested in me again. Thank God I saw this pattern.

The day of the plaque dedication, there was chatter that news outlets wanted comments on the FDNY's reinstatement of the Personal Safety System that could have saved John's life. I had no desire to speak to the media and would let others talk to them who did not mind the spotlight. After they got their sound bites from the other firemen, they rushed away to make their deadlines.

On our drive home from the firehouse, I heard on the radio that there had been an armed robbery in Queens. I'm not sure if John had that much pull up in heaven yet to keep our event off the news. We received a tiny segment on the news that night. And, of course, they showed me wiping away a tear. A tear that I clearly remember trying to wipe before they could capture me. The other video was of Kieran playing with a baseball that he refused to leave at home. He spent the entire ceremony playing imaginary catch with the firefighters, who stood at attention.

I placed a lot of stress on myself before, during, and after these events, and they took a toll on me physically and mentally. At the end of days like these, I was exhausted. All I wanted to do was turn off my brain and sleep, but if you know anything about trauma, a good night's sleep never happens again.

For the record, everyone loved the video and thought it was a great way to celebrate their son, brother, firefighter, and friend. Maybe we made a change for future dedications: Celebrate life, not loss.

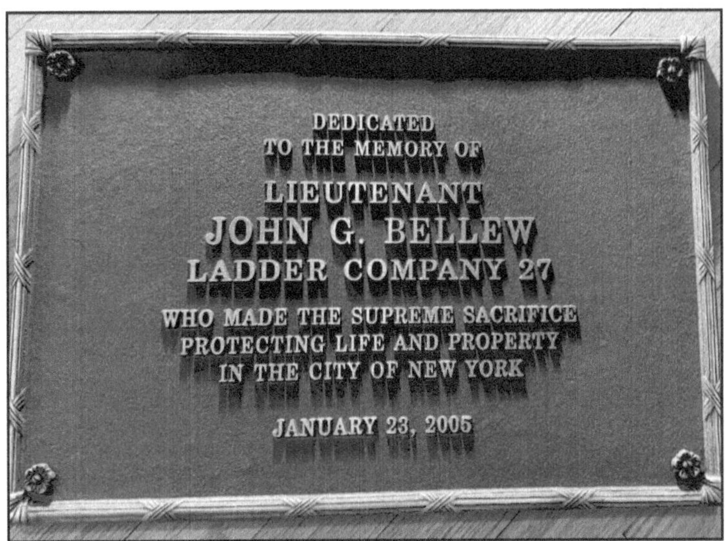

Plaque hanging in John's firehouse

Kat and Jack visiting John's firehouse

CHAPTER 21

The Timeline Of Grief

Time is so subjective. Everyone has their own opinion on how much time people need to grieve. When it comes to grieving, I don't put a clock on it. I am still grieving John and our life together. It doesn't take up every minute of my day as it used to, but it's still there. When I'm doing anything involving the kids, I think about what he would do, how he would react, what advice John might have given, and most of all, how proud he would be of how they turned out.

Society does have a clock, however. It started ticking from the moment John jumped. The people around me had their own clocks, based on their experiences and losses. It's not that people aren't unsympathetic; it's just that they want others to be okay, not needy. They are willing to give you some empathy, but in my experience, beyond three to six months, they are done. I had tremendous support initially and didn't need to lift a finger. But after two weeks, even though the Dinner Chain Train keeps dropping food off, you are expected to move on. The irony is that this is when you most feel like staying in bed. When the adrenaline wears off, the well-wishers return to their lives.

I hated that everyone went back to their lives. I couldn't understand how they could.

A couple of weeks after John jumped, we drove into New York City to meet with lawyers. I remember people honking at us and flipping us off. I thought, *don't you know, I just lost my husband?* I got to the lawyer's office, and the secretary was rude in her deep smoker's voice, "Why are you here? Do you have an appointment? Go sit over there, we will get to you when he is ready for you." *I just lost my husband; it took everything for me to get down here.* She was clueless about my grief.

Brielle returned to kindergarten a couple of weeks after John jumped. Her teacher, Mrs. M., called me to tell me that, unfortunately, during Show and Tell, the Monday after John jumped, a student came in and told the class that "Brielle's dad jumped out of a fourth-story window because he was on fire and died." What idiotic parents thought it was a great idea to expose their five-year-old to this information? I hadn't even told Brielle this was how her dad died. I planned to tell my children the details, but only when it was age-appropriate. Thank God, Brielle wasn't in the classroom, but now her classmates all knew what I tried to protect her from. As a result, I kept Brielle home from school an extra week to allow the story to fade. I will never forgive those parents.

Three months after John jumped, I helped out at Katreana's preschool and sat next to another mom. We were cutting out shapes, and she began to tell me how annoyed she was that her husband still goes to help out the widow of his best friend, who died on 9/11. This mom thought it was ridiculous that her husband needed to help this woman four years after her husband died.

"Oh, that is so nice of him. I just lost my husband three months ago," I said, thinking I would stop her before she completely humiliated herself. I thought she would be apologetic and embarrassed.

"Yeah, I know," she replied. Apparently, her grieving time frame was less than three months. She continued to complain about the grieving widow.

Six months after John jumped, I was still in deep misery over losing him. Even though I was still seeing Claire, my family was concerned and set me up to see a hospice grief counselor. Their love for me was reflected in their fear that I would never move on. I hesitantly agreed, thinking I was going crazy since I couldn't function. The counselor was lovely. She confirmed that I was not crazy and should not be expected to move on from my loss faster than I was capable of.

"Have you had sex yet?" she asked.

I was stunned by the question. "What? Was I supposed to have sex already?"

Her husband had died in a bus accident, and she told me she'd had sex six weeks after he died. Which means I should have had sex at least three-and-a-half times by then. *Great, I couldn't even do traumatic grieving correctly.* Just what I needed: to feel unattractive while mourning my husband. I was only thirty-five, yet the thought of having sex with someone besides John was bizarre.

"I can barely shower, let alone think about having sex with another person," I said.

She is kidding, right? Not sure when the last time I shaved my armpits, and I'm still wearing a nursing bra.

"When people feel such extreme sadness, they yearn to feel the opposite, a feeling of extreme ecstasy. Seeking out sexual pleasure after a traumatic event is not uncommon." She continued to explain that everyone has their own scale of emotion. We reach for comfort in surprising ways.

I understood the concept, but her suggestion of having sex was so far from my existence at the time. She said my devastation meant that at one point, I had felt extreme happiness and euphoria. Although the sadness is brutal to go through, it means I was on the other end of this scale at some point in my life. It gave me hope that maybe I could get back there again.

I assumed the second year would be an easier path. Unfortunately, the second year was more challenging in some ways. Maybe it's because, with every passing day, I was further away from the last time I saw John. Perhaps it was more difficult for me to remember the tone and inflection of his voice, the exact shade of blue in his eyes, which side of his hairline the strong cowlick was on, or his infectious smile. Maybe it was because new problems and challenges had arisen, and I still didn't have John's opinion on it. Perhaps it was because the rest of the world expected me to move on.

I started living life as a single mom, not as a widow. When the second year began, I thought I had conquered acute grief, but unfortunately, the second year just brought more sadness and loneliness. There is no way to sugarcoat it; with every passing event, holiday, birthday, I would remember the year before, which was torture. The second year represented my new life, a new beginning, not a year I just had to get through.

I began to see the pattern for Brielle; she needed safety and a sense of control. But there were some things I could not control for her. She developed a massive fear of thunderstorms. Before John jumped, they did not bother her; after John jumped, she had full-fledged panic attacks when storms rolled in. The other kids slowly came to feel their grief over time, and it was reflected in their behavior in different ways. They each had to learn how to deal with loss in a world that had already moved on. They learned the hard way that the world has its own time frame for grief. The everyday struggles of growing up were compounded by their loss, but people lose sight of this truth.

One day, I pulled the sliding door open to see Kieran chasing Jack with a wiffle ball bat in the backyard.

"Kieran, stop hitting your brother," I said, very nonchalantly, since this is a regular occurrence, but this time I noticed they were both running around in just their socks—socks with holes in them. *Oh shit, that's right, I was supposed to buy socks today.* I have no energy as tomorrow is Father's Day, a day I am trying to just get through, even though it wasn't the first one without their dad, it's still rough.

"Boys, come here, we have to go to Target."

"Nooooo, I don't want to, I want to play, you go." Jack runs away.

"Jack, I have no help tonight, we all have to go."

"Kieran and I want to finish our game!"

"Sorry, get in the car." Jack pouts his way into the car and continues to complain. The girls jump in, and Brielle helps me with Kieran's car seat. I drove to Target feeling sorry for myself while listening to the Kid Bop CD for the 1,000th time.

When we pull into the parking lot, Jack refuses to get out, still complaining about our errand.

"Let's go, buddy."

"No, we wouldn't have to be here if you could stay on top of the laundry."

Brielle covered her ears. "Jack, why would you say that?"

Tears began to swell, and my face became flushed. *Wow, that stung.* It felt like I had smoke coming out of my ears while I reminded myself that Jack is just a kid, a kid who is hurting as much as his mom is. Still, I was pissed.

"Fine, you want me to stay on top of the laundry!" My voice became louder with every word I spoke. "OK, fine, let's get the effing socks, go home, and figure out how YOU will all help me stay on top of the laundry."

I stormed into Target, with the kids running to keep up with me. Not looking back, confident that they were following me, I knew they saw how angry I was. I grabbed the fucking socks and didn't say a word on the drive home.

When we got back to the house, I made them sit at the kitchen table with paper and pencils. "Write five ways you can help me stay on top of the laundry." Brielle had to help Kieran with his list; they did not leave the kitchen until the lists were complete.

Losing my cool during the first couple years as a single mom was inevitable. We were navigating this new life together, all of us struggling with our loss. I was mindful that my sadness often turned into anger, although that awareness sometimes came after my anger was projected onto the kids' behavior. I'm sure they got yelled at more times than warranted, but they survived.

There is no standard time frame for grief. People who haven't experienced trauma don't understand that. Our loss is forever, and the ramifications of the loss end up being a lifetime of fixing broken hearts and expectations. My kids were affected by watching other kids' dads chat on the football bleachers about their kids' performances. They were affected when moms and dads were sitting together in the audience for concerts, plays, communions, confirmations, and graduations, while only one parent represented them. My boys didn't have a dad to answer man questions, and their mom had no experience with these issues. When my girls couldn't attend the Father-Daughter Princess Dance in elementary school, I chose not to attend the Mother-Son Luau Dance because it wouldn't be fair to the girls. It broke my heart.

There are endless examples of when my kids felt the loss of their dad. People see time as the fix for sorrow, and I see time as the enemy. The more time that has passed since John jumped, the more things he has missed and the less advice he has given. His loss in our lives is immeasurable. College graduations, walking down the aisle, and becoming parents, all these future events will hurt, too.

Grief is a lifetime sentence, and we are paying the sentence with no chance of parole. We do not want pity, but it wouldn't hurt to acknowledge all the times their loss affected our lives and all the future events, too. John's jumping was not a single event. It was a consequential event that altered our lives daily. My sweet, silent heroes.

None of us escapes grief in our lifetime. Be patient with those who are grieving. By honoring their timeline for healing, hopefully yours will be honored when it is your turn to grieve.

Kids on beach at sunset

CHAPTER 22

Living With An Anxietyholic

Before John jumped, my kids lived a pretty normal existence. They lived in a bubble where they knew nothing about the wars taking place, robberies, crime, or any other craziness in our world. My kids were too young; they played outside, they went to preschool, they got filthy, and we went on vacation. The biggest struggle for them was to avoid the road outside our house, where people regularly sped to get to the other side of town. I wish I had sat back and enjoyed that time in my life. But most of us don't take a breath to be thankful for the life we have at the moment. I certainly didn't.

I recognize that life is short, and I am thankful for what I have. I cherish every moment with my kids, who are growing up way too quickly, but it was a journey to get here. My kids have stories that will make you laugh at my absurdity, but with each example, I felt strongly that I was doing the right thing at the time. None of the stories are exaggerated; it's what goes through the minds of those who suffer from my type of PTSD. You can't turn it off. When trauma takes over your life, you can't just ignore it. Or at least I can't.

When Brielle was eight, she was invited to her first sleepover birthday party. I heard the girls would be sleeping in the basement, and my first thought was that there is usually only one way out of a basement in case of a fire. Firefighters refer to this as a means of egress and recommend two in any location. I thought about it all night, but I couldn't resist calling this mother, whom I didn't know well, to ask her such a crazy question. If I hadn't, I would have been up all night.

So I texted the mom at 10:30 p.m.:
> Are there two ways out of the basement in case of
> a fire? :-)

She must have thought I was nuts and probably crossed Brielle off her daughter's list of future friends.

The lovely woman reassured me:
> Yes, there are two ways to exit. The girls are fine,
> they are safe, and they are having a good time. :-)

When I picked Brielle up in the morning, the first thing she told me was, "We slept in the basement, and I made sure I knew the two ways of egress." Thankfully, Brielle was not crossed off the list and remained friends with the little girl.

I have many stories of my anxiety affecting my kids, but I never looked at it that way. I saw it as me protecting them and ensuring their safety. For example, my kids had fire rope ladders under their bedroom windows.

I conducted fire drills.

"When I yell FIRE from the hallway, pretend there is a fire. Wake up your sibling and go to the window. Begin to unravel the rope out of your window. Make sure the hooks are attached to the molding on the window sill." I listened attentively at the door.

"Kieran, this is serious. I hear you playing with your Legos. We can play with them after the drill."

Panic set in. *Can I trust that they can do this independently? Stay calm, isn't that the first rule in the Stop, Drop and Roll videos?*

"If this were a real emergency, you would lower yourself out the window onto the ladder feet first and hold on tightly to the rope. The nice fireman will be at the bottom to help you to safety. Did you finish?"

I walked into the girls' room, and the ladder was deployed perfectly. I checked the boys' room, Legos everywhere. *Additional drills will be needed.* I saw it as taking the fire plan that most families do up a notch. It is not lost on me that I equipped my children with ropes, a life-saving device that their father should have had. When I renovated my house, I added a balcony to my bedroom. It looked aesthetically pleasing, but since all the bedrooms were on the top floor, we would also have a balcony to escape to in case of a fire.

After John jumped, I became obsessed with watching my children sleep to ensure they were still breathing. I put it in my head that, in heaven, John would want one of them to join him so they would develop SIDS and pass away in their sleep. Brielle was asthmatic, so during her episodes, she would sleep with me, and I would be up all night watching her little chest go up and down. I made Kieran sleep in my bed well after the age at which SIDS was considered a risk. It didn't stop there. I would lie in my bed trying to fall asleep and get it in my head that one of the others had stopped breathing. I would go to their bedrooms and stare at their chests. If I found one of them sleeping on their stomach, I would flip them over. This ritual lent itself to many sleepless nights.

After John jumped, I had the thought that one of my kids was going to become paralyzed. Maybe because of the likelihood that John would have been paralyzed if he had survived the fall. I allowed Jack to play Pop Warner football even though I find the sport violent and detrimental to a kid's brain health. I convinced myself he would be okay because he would be on the defensive or offensive line. However, one day, the coach changed his position, moving him to linebacker. Jack got clocked by another player and was laid out on the turf. I had a full-fledged panic attack on the sidelines.

"Whose number is that? I can't see the number?" the other parents asked, but I knew exactly who it was. I never actually watched any of the games; I watched his number move around the field. So, when he got hit, I knew immediately it was Jack. When he started playing, I had told him, "If you ever get hurt, move your extremities around so I know you are okay." He was not moving. I started looking for an ambulance and checking out the vegetation to make sure a helicopter could land on the field in case he needed Medevac to airlift him to a specialty hospital for orthopedic injuries. Thankfully, after a few minutes, he got up and walked off. This was Jack's last football season.

Kieran played flag football. I rationalized that he would not get hurt since no one gets tackled. Tell that to the other five-year-olds who must not have gotten the memo. I watched from the sidelines as Kieran got pulled down and trampled without any safety equipment. I became the enraged mother that Tik-Tok videos are posted about. I ran on the field and screamed at the other coach. "This is flag football; no one is supposed to get tackled. Didn't you teach your team the rules? You'd better hope my kid is okay."

Kieran got up, unharmed, and continued playing. While walking to the car, I got a few double takes and snickers, "That's the mom."

It wasn't one of my finer days, but God help anyone who thought they could hurt one of my kids. The inner rage and fear made me stronger and fiercer than anyone on that field. Don't mess with a mother trying to protect her babies.

Brielle was a fantastic tumbler and cheerleader. She competed all over the United States. I held my breath every time she stepped on the mat and entered the air. Still, I paid for the tumbling lessons and cheerleading teams. I had determined kids, and I didn't want to get in the way of them following their dreams. My rationale was to pay for them to learn how to tumble properly, which will keep them safe. So, I paid for trainers, watched from the sidelines, and slowly died inside. If I allowed my kids to participate, then my anxiety was not affecting them; it was just killing me.

Jack and Kieran were pitchers. A pitcher stands very close to a batter. I watched many news stories about pitchers getting nailed with a line drive to their head or chest and experiencing head trauma or going into sudden cardiac arrest. I needed to protect them as much as I could. I made them wear heart guard shirts that sit tight over their heart and are highly uncomfortable and hot. And of course, I made Kieran wear that skull cap. Was it cool to wear? Absolutely not. Did it make Kieran stand out compared to the other kids? Absolutely.

I hated telling Kieran that I found new protective gear he needed to put over his baseball cap to protect his brain in case of a line drive. His response, "Ummm, it covers up my team name, and I have never seen anyone else ever wear anything like this." I shook my head and smiled. He just looked at me and said, "OK, Mom, I get it."

While Katreana wasn't doing dangerous sports, I found a way to include her in my web of obsession. The school system, by law, has to notify the public when a sex offender relocates into our surrounding towns. I noticed one moved in across the street from Katreana's Art Studio, where she took classes. So I, of course, warned her about not trusting any strangers, and I sat in the parking lot with two eyes on the art studio door just in case any pedophile felt a need to borrow a pencil.

One day, I spotted a man walking around the building and walked into the studio. I jumped out and walked right in behind him. Katreana saw me and knew what I was thinking.

"Mom, he is Abbey's dad, and he is picking her up early. I'll meet you in the car after class." I knew I had embarrassed her, but I couldn't help myself. I got back into the car and replastered my eyes on the door.

I give my kids a lot of credit. They knew what they were dealing with and just did what I asked, even at the risk of looking different from their peers.

I warned my kids about oceans and pools, too. "Don't dive into the ocean because of sandbars or a pool unless you know it's very deep," my inner Science Mom explained, "Topography of the ocean floor changes with every wave, so when a wave is coming at you, turn and duck under it. Rip tides are another very dangerous situation. Even the strongest swimmers can get caught in them. Don't fight them, swim parallel to the shore." I would listen to the weather to see how the tides were so that I could warn them about any impending danger. And don't get me started on possible hurricanes brewing in the Tropics. "We have a Category 2 Storm brewing in the tropics off the shores of Africa, which could be at the Jersey Shore by next Tuesday."

The greatest anxiety was when my kids went off to college and went on Spring Break. I couldn't track the tides or nautical winds. I imagined the kids getting into accidents, active shooters in their schools, and plane crashes when they were traveling alone. Sometimes, I would prioritize my worries, warning about getting drugged or roofied by some boy or even girl in a bar. Since they usually stay in shady, low-budget motels, there would definitely be a text telling them not to sit or lean on the balcony railing, since it's probably rusted and hasn't been secured or inspected since it was built. I warned the boys about not getting into bar fights because one quick blow could have them falling on concrete and creating a brain bleed, causing immediate death. The girls should not help break up a bar fight because they could fall on concrete and create a brain bleed, causing immediate death. I bought those strips to put into their drinks to test for drugs (though I am sure they never used them). Of course, I equipped all of them with pepper spray and high-pitched keychain alarms for their walks home, and if, for some reason, they didn't remember one or ten of the things I warned them about, I was sure to text them reminders.

Ironically, my kids got caught in a riptide during a vacation in the Dominican Republic. It was a very powerful one. They were in the ocean with their uncle, while I was on the shore watching them ride the waves (so I thought), until I saw two lifeguards dive in and swim to them. Even though we were at a beach with lifeguards, and there were no red flags to warn us, it still happened. My kids always mention that it seemed like I didn't care because I wasn't reacting. I was in shock. Surprisingly, I remained calm during the incident. But once everyone

was back at shore safely, I squeezed them so tightly and handed the lifeguard all the American money in my wallet. "Gracias,
gracias, gracias, you saved my family!" He took the money and
looked at me like, Crazy American. As I walked away from the
lifeguard stand, my panic attack began. I could barely breathe,
my heart began to race, and my thoughts were spinning out of
control. *Okay, let's add ocean swimming to the list of activities we
will never do again.*

When you have experienced trauma, you are very much
aware that it could happen again. I try to block out that memory
altogether, and even writing about it now makes me sick, but I
should have learned something from that experience. Bad things
still happen regardless of your planning and warnings to your
kids. We had discussed riptides and how to get out of them, but
until you are in them, you don't know how you will react. I will
be forever grateful to that lifeguard who did his job and saved all
the people who mean the most to me.

The saying "small kids, small problems" holds true with
anxiety. Big kids mean considerably more anxiety. I was hoping
to outgrow it once they were no longer within my reach. But
what I didn't realize was that I lost control of every movement
they made. The college sent safety alert texts intended to reassure parents about campus safety, but they only heightened my
attention. Every time I got an alert about a sexual assault, I would
immediately text my daughters to make sure it was not them. My
son went to a city school, so sometimes, I would get texts about
shootings close to the campus. I would call him (because I knew
I wouldn't get a text back), and he would say, "Oh yeah, I just
passed the yellow crime tape, lots of police activity."

Why couldn't my kids have moved to a farm where I would
only have to worry about them falling off a horse, getting struck

by lightning, or having a tractor accident? Instead, all four of them now live in different parts of New York City where I need to worry about crazy people pushing them on the subway tracks, random violence, protests, homeless people spitting in their faces, locking the vestibule doors behind them when entering their buildings, walking into the bike lane (if you ever visit NYC you would know that the most dangerous place to walk is the bike lane), making sure you have checked the license plate of the Uber you have called.

All of these, along with anything else I can think of, are sent out as daily text reminders. I know it's extreme, and I try not to remind them of all the dangers that could come their way, but it's difficult to stop.

Claire once had me do a very valuable exercise. She told me to ask my kids to list all my concerns before I reminded them of any danger. My kids listed numerous things that they assumed I would warn them about. The list was much longer than I would have given them. The point was that they already knew all the dangers to look out for and MORE, so I did not need to tell them daily. This exercise made me extremely sad. I have placed vicarious anxiety onto their once carefree minds.

I lost control of life's predictability after John jumped. 1 + 2 no longer equals 3 in my life, so I have to control every other logarithm of possibility for safety from now on. And the truth is that my kids have not been immune to unsafe events. Jack got hit with a 70 mph pitch to the face in a baseball game. A wanted gunman was arrested outside Katreana's apartment five minutes after she came home. Kat had to jump into a liquor store because a creepy man was following her, and she got help from the store owner, and got spat in the face by a homeless man during the height of COVID. Kieran was on a Greyhound bus driven by a ninety-year-old man who seemed to be falling asleep at the wheel while driving back to New York from a baseball trip to Myrtle Beach. Thank God (and John) that they all survived these incidents. The point is, I cannot control dangerous situations, and bad things will happen to them; I just want to minimize the possibilities.

They didn't grow up not feeling danger. So when people say, "Your kids were young, they won't even remember," I find it insulting and wrong. My kids knew in a split second that life can change. They are aware that their mom is an anxietyholic, and they have to navigate being a child of one. They grew up in a household of people who were sad and anxious. As much as I tried to shield them, the environment and people's aura entered their cells by osmosis. They have the added stress of dealing with their mom but also protecting her. I was blessed to have children who cared about my every moment, yet no child should have the burden of responsibility for their mom's happiness. I wish I had not placed vicarious anxiety onto them, but maybe it was inevitable, or maybe I could have done a better job at getting myself help before hurting them.

My kids are empathic, kind, caring, and self-aware people. They show me so much compassion, love, and patience. They understand my disability and tolerate me. They saw firsthand what PTSD does to a person's mental health, yet they accepted me for who I have become and handled my craziness with beautiful compassion. I am sure their life circumstances shaped their personalities, and I am very thankful for any positive traits they all received on a terrible snowy day in January.

My anxiety is always with me, and I have tried numerous ways to handle it. I tried meditation, which I am not very good at, but someday, I'd like to master it. I've tried yoga, somatic stretching, talk therapy, exercising, EMDR (only did one session), massage, no sugar diet, gave up alcohol, supplements, tea drinking, basically, you name it, I've tried it. It's possible that my anxiety could be worse if I didn't do all of these things, which is why I keep trying. I research often, and I'm a sucker for every Instagram ad that might be useful for me. (Now that I have written this, I will get 100 more ads to try their products.) Talk therapy has been vital in saving my life. I couldn't imagine where I would be if I didn't have Claire. I know I will continue to fight against my thoughts. Life is worth the fight.

I was lucky to have found Claire and clicked immediately, but that doesn't always happen. I took my kids to six different types of therapy, but none worked for them. A group of Columbia University students came to my house to play with the kids and do talk therapy. That didn't work. I took Brielle to a pediatric psychologist for six sessions. Brielle didn't say one word for six weeks. The psychologist was friendly but ended therapy as she didn't think Brielle was ready yet. So that didn't work. We tried an arts-and-crafts group therapy program and a hospital-based play therapy session, along with two other therapists. None of it worked.

One extremely valuable program for two of my kids was the Big Brother and Big Sister program. The FDNY had its own chapter where firefighters or people connected to firefighters could become a Big. Jack was lucky to have Patrick as a Big Brother, who took him to ball games, built birdhouses, and took him to McDonald's. Katreana's Big Sister, Shannon, would take her to lunch, paint pottery, or go to plays. Their time with them was invaluable because my kids had one-on-one time with an adult who cared about their lives and made them feel special. My kids still have a relationship with both of their Bigs. Katreana was even in Shannon's wedding. I am so thankful for these compassionate treasures.

Along with my gratitude, I found the process of enlisting professionals to help my kids exhausting. It's not easy and very time-consuming. At the time, we needed help. There weren't many good pediatric options available to them. The process increased my anxiety as I knew how essential it was for them to get professional help, like I had. Claire warned me that finding the right fit could be a long process, and she was right. After years of trying numerous types of therapy, we finally found some good fits. In the end, it is worth the effort. It's a field that could benefit from more options for families in need of assistance.

My anxiety shaped their lives. They certainly wouldn't have as many stories about how nutty their mom is and how she projected her anxiety onto them to keep them safe. Of course, it was all out of love. It's similar to addiction; no one wants to be addicted, but it's hard to stop. We are all the sum of our experiences, both happy and traumatic. I pray that I have given them more happiness than anxiety, but only time will tell.

You raise your kids to the best of your ability, and you try to protect them from harm. When trauma occurs to you early on in motherhood, it has a profound effect on how you handle situations. My kids didn't know any different, but as they grew older and understood anxiety better, they understood the world I brought them up in.

Kat and Brielle cheering

Jack pitching (before I discovered a skull cap protection)

PART III

After After John Jumped

After, after John jumped was my true new beginning.
When the rise begins…

CHAPTER 23

Criminal Trial

Four years after the fire, the court case was finally called.

John's firehouse arranged transportation and a companion for me to and from the Bronx for the six-week trial. Every morning, a new firefighter would appear at our door, "Good Morning! I'm Tom (Eddie, Joe, fill in the blank), and I'll be driving you to the courthouse today. Here are some donuts and coffee." Some guys I knew and could ask about their family; some I had never met, and I would get to know them as we drove to the courthouse.

"I like chocolate donuts," Kieran said. "Are you driving my mom? Do you have a van outside? Did you know my dad?" He interrogated each firefighter, and if I had a repeat driver, they always remembered to bring him a chocolate donut.

The transportation from John's firehouse was a huge help. It took the worry out of parking and traffic.

But still, the trial was an emotional roller coaster for my kids. They were used to me being around all the time, waking them up, making them breakfast, packing school lunches, and picking them up from school. Now, I would have to leave the house at 7:30 a.m. to reach the courthouse at 9 a.m. My mom came over to watch the kids before school. A babysitter came to help after school. Though the schedule was demanding, it was imperative that I be present at the trial to represent John. Unlike the other firemen, I didn't have the opportunity to be on the stand and defend John's actions, so I did the best I could by sitting in the courtroom and serving as a face for my husband.

Walking into the Bronx courthouse for the first time was scary. I had to go through metal detectors and be screened. This became my morning ritual for six weeks. Our courtroom was on the bottom floor at the end of a dark hallway. I had never been in a courtroom, so it all seemed very surreal. I walked in, took my seat, and looked at the defendants for the first time. I had heard their names, but this was the first time I saw their faces. They were the people John protected. They never turned to look at me during all six weeks I sat there. John ran into their building to help save their lives and property, but their reckless actions killed the person who took an oath to protect them.

The District Attorney's investigation led to the indictment of four individuals. The owner of the building, the landlord, the tenant who subdivided the apartment on the third floor, and the tenant who subdivided the apartment on the fourth floor. They were all charged with two counts of manslaughter. These individuals were aware of the danger they were putting firefighters and others in, but their greed overrode the safety of others.

"This case underscores the crucial need for accountability in our society," the Bronx DA, Jeffrey Gluxman, emphasized, "Particularly where lives are at stake. This is an ongoing issue in the City of New York that needs to be addressed before it happens to a civilian or another firefighter."

Unlike most cases, there were two sets of defendants on trial at the same time. To save money and time, the City of New York tried the four defendants simultaneously, with two separate juries. So, instead of twelve jury members (plus two alternates) sitting in the courtroom, there were twenty-eight. As the case played out, sometimes one set of jurors was asked to leave the courtroom when specific evidence was presented, and other times the other set had to leave when different evidence was presented. It was difficult for me to figure out why one jury couldn't hear specific evidence while another jury could. All I knew was that no matter what evidence was being presented, it was clear that they were all at fault for the death of my husband.

I took a seat in the second row, a seat that would be mine for the next six weeks. I would hear every detail from that seat, every audio tape that echoed the pure hell John and the firefighters went through, and every piece of evidence. I tried to make eye contact with all twenty-eight jury members to show them there is a family connected to John. Five of us were left behind because of the reckless actions of the four defendants. I sat there wanting to scream, but I had to be civil. *Look at me! I am right here! I am the widow of John Bellew! We have four kids! The defendant's reckless acts killed the man who protected all of you!*

Over the six-week trial, the DA called many firefighters and experts to the stand. There were electricians, fire marshals, construction engineers, tenants and, of course, the firefighters who were at the fire. They had diagrams of the apartment floor plans, graphic photos of the rooms after the fire, pictures of the windows through which they jumped, and the courtyard where they landed. They had the radio transmissions that lasted about fifteen minutes, building up to the first Mayday, called by Lt. Meyran.

After morning proceedings, we would go to John's firehouse for lunch. I loved being in his firehouse; it made me feel close to him. I got to sit at the kitchen table where he ate so many meals. Taking in the place where he loved to work, I immediately understood why he never minded going to work. The laughter and antics that took place daily were both entertaining and comfortable. It was John's second home. After lunch, we went back to the courthouse for the afternoon session.

I can't remember every detail of Gene Stolowski's testimony, but it was the most graphic and disturbing. Gene was a veteran and a friend of John's. "We got the ticket around 8 a.m., we were First Due, which means we would be on the fire floor. John Bellew, the chauffeur, took a turn down a street that would get us to the fire the quickest, but when he saw a box truck blocking our path, he had to back the rig out. Between the snowbanks from the blizzard the night before and the box truck, he could not get the rig through the street. John went around the block. At that point, I knew we had something. I told Brendan, the probie, 'Mask up —we have something.'"

My heart began to pound, as this was the first time I had heard Gene give details of the day. I looked at the stranger next to me. *Can he hear my heartbeat? I have waited so long to listen to the details, but now I just want to run out of here.* It is almost as if once Gene said it out loud, it really did happen. Until that moment, the truth was buried in my brain, and the kids were protected from it. Since I did not revisit the details of John's death, the kids were protected from them. But now Gene's testimony would be in the newspapers the next day, removing my shield. *Can we stop this? I'm not ready to have this out there yet. I don't have enough barriers set up to protect my kids. Please, Gene, STOP!*

"We pulled up to the box, and Ladder 33 got in before us, which made us now Second Due."

This chain of events is significant because if there had been no truck blocking the roadway, then John could have gotten to the fire first, which would have made their responsibilities on the fire floor. No one on the fire floor dies that day. And John comes home.

"John secured the rig, and we now had to report to the floor above the fire. We got our equipment and climbed up to the fourth floor, passing tenants as we went up the stairwell. I remember hearing reports on the radio about a trapped baby on the fourth floor, so our immediate job was to search and rescue to find the tenants. At first, the fire seemed very routine. Once we entered the apartment, we immediately saw it was an SRO."

The DA stopped him, "SRO. Can you please explain to the jury what that means?"

Gene continued, "Single Room Occupancies, they are all over the Bronx. It means the apartment is divided into separate rooms. Each room had a padlock to prevent residents from stealing from each other. The tenants share a bathroom and kitchen."

The DA looked at the jury for confirmation that they understood the concept. It appeared the jury was aware of this situation. "Why is this dangerous to firefighters?"

"This situation adds a risk to firefighters. Even though we train for these circumstances, you never know what you are walking into. I showed Brendan how to break the padlocks to gain access to the illegal subdivision rooms and continued searching and venting the windows. Lt. Meyran showed Brendan how to use the thermal imaging camera to detect fire in the walls and had him look for the fire escape in case we needed it to evacuate."

Do I really want to hear this? I knew we were getting to the point where everything went wrong, so my heart was pounding even harder, and my palms started sweating. *I know what happens, but do I really want to listen to this? I waited four years, and all of a sudden, it was not enough time.*

"There was a slight extension," Gene said.

Gluxman stopped him, "Please explain what that means to the jury."

"There was smoke coming up from the third floor, but not heavy smoke. It was a typical fire—nothing to worry about. At that point, my Vibra Alert went off, indicating that my air tank was running low. I told Lt. Meyran I was okay, but we went to find a window. Lt Meyran called on the radio to have the roof send down a mask for me. Brendan found the fire escape, but it was a few windows over, and a wall blocked our access to it."

"Why didn't you just go to the fire escape?"

"The fire escape was not in reach, like I said; they butchered up the floor plan, and the fire escape access was not where it should have been. A wall blocked our means to use it. And then all of a sudden, everything just went from a typical fire to deadly in a matter of seconds. Lt. Meyran called for Maydays on his radio; the heat was barreling down on us, and the temperature went from hot to unbearable. We were all running out of air. Lt. Meyran called for more Maydays, but then the flashover rolled toward us, forcing us to jump."

As Gene retold his story, I knew that John was not with him, and that was the tough part for me. Once John secured the rig, he chose where he was best needed. John could have stayed with the rig, gone to the fourth floor, or gone to the roof. I was told no one was surprised when John chose to go to the floor above; he heard reports that a baby was missing, he knew their house had a probie in the crew, and John was never one to shy away from the adrenaline rush of being at the most dangerous part of the action. But John's exact path is known only to him; he does not speak in the transmissions; he only talks to two Rescue 3 firefighters while on the fourth floor. His true story is developed only through others. I needed these other firefighters to give us a glimpse of what John's story is.

Waiting patiently for the others to testify was all I could do to piece together his story.

You could hear a pin drop in the courtroom as Gene recounted the panic and trauma he had to endure with Lt. Meyran and Brendan. Lt. Meyran led the way, as a true leader does; he rolled over the child guard that was in the window and dropped first. Brendan was next, and then Gene. Their only other choice was burning to death. The unfathomable decision they had to make was to endure tremendous pain from landing or let the heat and fire burn them to death.

I sat in my chair sobbing, alone. Gene sat in that witness chair, clearly still recovering from his physical pain, knowing he would never get over the mental trauma he had gone through. He was amazing. I'm not sure how he was able to keep it all together while I was falling apart, wishing John were up there telling his side.

Gene's testimony was extremely powerful and moving. My heart broke for Gene; there would not be one day for the rest of his life that he would not think of that day. We both share this burden.

Two firefighters from Rescue and Brendan also survived the jump. All of them testified about what happened that day, along with firefighters who investigated the fire, and others who were at the building. The story unfolded as a series of unfortunate events that culminated in a disaster. The third floor was the fire floor. Firefighters kept losing water due to burst length in the hose line, and frozen hydrants caused by the blizzard. An investigation found that the hoses were improperly stored the night before and that ice had accumulated in the lines. Since the third floor had no water to fight the fire, they pulled the fourth-floor charged hose, leaving them without water. If water pressure hadn't been an issue, the fire would not have had a chance to burn through the ceiling into the hidden room on the fourth floor.

As mentioned above, the hidden room, due to the illegal partitions, hindered the firefighters from finding the burning room because of the added walls. It was revealed that the refrigerator was blocking the hallway leading to the room engulfed in fire, which ultimately caused the flashover.

Eventually, the firefighters from Rescue 3 testified about the SRO and their repeated searches of the kitchen. They searched for victims while smoke continued to billow from the floor below. Firefighter Pat McKenna from Rescue 3 bumped into John in the kitchen.

"We must be missing something. It is hotter than it should be," John said to McKenna.

Skilled firefighters use all their senses to determine how to handle a fire situation. They feel the heat on their ears to determine if the fire is changing from a controllable state to one that is getting out of control. What they were missing was the hidden hallway behind the refrigerator, which led to the room that was beginning to burn from the floor below. The original room on the third floor burned for several minutes, and since they could not get any water on it, it burned through the ceiling into the illegally partitioned room on the fourth floor.

If the tenant had not built a wall creating another apartment, or used a refrigerator as a door, blocking access down the hallway for the firefighters, they would have found the source of the fire and retreated until they got water on it. Instead, the room burned for several minutes until a source of oxygen ignited it into a flashover. The ball of flames rolled down the makeshift hallway, over the refrigerator, out of the kitchen where John was standing. John's only choice was to run from the ball of fire towards a window.

Brendan confirmed these findings with his testimony. "I saw the fire escape from a distance out the window. I tried to break through the wall with a can so we could reach it. But soon my Vibra Alert went off, and everything blew up on us. It was like a wall of fire that pushed us out the window. We had no choice, Lt. Meyran told us in a calm, convincing voice, 'This is the way we are going out,' so I did what I was told. I went next, and Gene came after me."

The DA then played the fire's transmissions to the court as evidence. I listened carefully for John, knowing he was not on them, but I still prayed to hear his voice just once more. The tapes lasted 15-20 minutes, with a lot of back-and-forth about the water pressure issues. However, it sounded like organized chaos until it wasn't. Then the Maydays started. It felt like an hour from the first Mayday til you hear Lt. White in the back of the building screaming for help.

"Mayday, mayday, mayday, Ladder 2-7 mayday!"

"We need a hole in the roof, or we are going to lose the top floor, Paddy!"

"Mayday, mayday, mayday, Ladder 2-7 mayday! We are bailing out of here!"

These were Lt. Meyran's last words. And then an eerie silence. But then we heard the saddest transmission. Lt. White screamed into his radio as he reached the back courtyard, where they all jumped into.

"A fireman just jumped out of the fourth floor of the building, two firemen jumped, holy shit, three, four, five, six firemen just jumped out of the building…massive EMS needed, we need massive help and buses…" Lt. White screamed while fighting back tears. I hear the anguish in his voice—the desperation—and tears start flowing out of my eyes. I looked at the jury, then at the defendants, but there was no response. *How can they hear this and not react?*

After much investigation, it was determined that John was the second to jump. He jumped out of the window closest to the fire escape and the source of the fire. *Did John think he was jumping onto a fire escape? In an apartment that wasn't chopped up, would the fire escape be at that window? Did John think he was the only one who had to make that decision, or did he know his other brothers were bailing too?*

We don't know many details about John, but we do know he was most likely on fire, as evidenced by his turnout gear turning from black to reddish brown. He was at the kitchen doorway when the flashover occurred. The firefighter that John spoke to face-to-face seconds before the flashover bailed out the apartment door into the hallway, to safety, while the window was John's only choice.

John jumped with his air tank still strapped to his back. The weight of the air tank most likely pulled John backwards while he fell, causing him to land on his back. His injuries indicate this as he broke over twenty ribs, his right femur, and numerous vertebrae. I couldn't stop thinking that his death is worse than all the people on death row. *Clearly, the jury members would see this.*

After Brendan testified, he was allowed to sit in the courtroom for the remainder of the trial, which was a relief to me. I had someone to sit with who cared as much as I did about the outcome. Brendan also included some comic relief in a very heavy atmosphere. When it was all too much, I could rely on Brendan to break the tension with morbid humor.

The two firefighters from Rescue 3, Firefighter Jeff Cool and Firefighter Joey DiBernardo, were the fifth and sixth to jump from the two other windows on the back of the building. Their windows were farther from the fire source, so they had a few seconds longer than the others before making the horrific decision to jump. Cool carried a personal safety rope he purchased himself (not department-issued), so he threw it to DiBarnardo to tie off to a substantial object to help him rappel out. The rope helped reduce the height of his fall, but he still dropped 30 feet. DiBarnardo was the last to jump. He used the rope, but it broke, so he took a significant fall as well.

They got to tell their story while I sat quietly in the courtroom. They were being heard, and John was not. Relying on them to tell the whole story left me empty and unsatisfied. John's story was never truly told. They got to express their hurt, sadness, and journey publicly; how the fire changed their lives. In contrast, I could not tell John's story at all. *HELLO! I'm over here! No one is talking about John! You know he was there, too. John jumped too! He broke most of the bones in his body and missed out on his kids' lives!* I never got to share an impact statement or got to tell John's side of the tragedy. The firefighters had no idea I was competing with them, but I was, internally. The depth of competition is often not publicly seen, but its jealous eye is eerily present.

Once the prosecution rested, the defendant's lawyers began to plead their case. I was curious how they would handle this. I sat back in my chair with my back up against the seat, clutched the side rails and stared down the defendant's lawyers. *Don't you dare blame John or the other firefighters for this. Don't twist this story around to make your clients somehow innocent.* I was ready for war.

The lawyers did not go after the firefighters; instead, they attacked each other and the City of New York. We were stuck in a ping-pong match, listening to the landlord and building owner blame the tenants for installing the illegal partitions. The tenant's lawyers blamed the landlord and building owner for being aware of the situation and never instructing them to remove the partitions. The landlord was well aware of the walls, but as long as the rent was paid, it didn't matter to him that they were risking their own lives and firefighters'. Both defendant lawyers took shots at the City of New York for not protecting their firefighters by not supplying them with proper safety equipment that could have saved John and Lt. Meyran's lives. The DA allowed this banter to continue because it helped prove each defendant's guilt in our case.

The defendant's lawyer called up an expert about the personal safety ropes.

"Why did the City of New York have the firefighters turn in their personal safety ropes in 2000?"

"There was a ten-year life span on that equipment, and they needed to be replaced. The firefighters were ordered to hand them back in. The department was researching a lighter system, but they never got around to purchasing new ones."

"The fire took place in 2005, correct?"

"Yes."

"Can you explain to the jury why the FDNY did not replace the life-saving ropes for five years?"

"I know they were looking into it, but I do not know why."

"Would you agree that if these men had life-saving ropes on Black Sunday, then they could have evacuated safely and we would not be here today?"

"I don't know."

Outfitting 10,000 firefighters with a new personal safety rope was a significant expense for NYC's budget. The longer they put it off, the more money was saved for New York City. If John had the personal safety rope, he could have tied off to a radiator and safely exited the building. He would have had a chance at survival.

Both Cool and DiBarnardo also testified about how they used the personal safety rope to help reduce their falls. Their testimony confirmed the importance of firefighters carrying personal safety ropes.

As both sides finished arguing their cases, I sat there exhausted. Mentally reliving Black Sunday day after day took a toll on me. Every person who testified relived their experience, and I was left to piece together John's story. All along, I was sitting there wanting to scream. *What about John! No one is mentioning John! John was there; he had to jump, he was on fire!* I tried to clear my mind on the way home each night so that I wouldn't bring toxic energy into the house.

I was confident that John's life would prove meaningful in the judicial court. His life could help stop illegal subdividing in the Bronx and elsewhere. John's name would undoubtedly be remembered as someone who made the supreme sacrifice and helped revolutionize building codes. I hoped that people would stop putting civilians and firefighters at risk for the greed of money as a result of this trial. These thoughts comforted me during my darkest moments.

When the closing statements were finished, I felt confident that the DA had done a great job presenting their case of manslaughter against all four defendants. I was also aware that each set of defendants did a great job accusing the other defendants of wrongdoing. We left the courthouse wondering when the jury would return with a verdict.

Brendan and I hypothesized, "If the jury comes back quickly, do you think that means they will have a guilty verdict? What if they deliberate for a really long time? Does that mean they are struggling with the evidence?"

All these questions rattled in my head. We debated every which way the juries could be thinking. It was so helpful to have Brendan, who shared my level of vested interest. When the jury asked for particular testimony or specific evidence to be reread, we questioned, "Why are they asking for that? Is that good or bad for our case?" The DA kept us informed of any evidence they wanted reviewed or of testimony transcripts they wanted reread. We spent our days sitting around the firehouse waiting for news. *Did the DA do enough? I could have taken the stand and proved our case. They could see how passionate I was about losing John and how he lost his life due to the negligence of the defendants.*

A few days later, we received a call informing us that the verdict in the case against the tenants was to be read. My stomach turned, and I felt a momentary sympathy for the defendants. I understood why these defendants did what they did. They were making ends meet, and this helped them pay the rent. But they also had to know how dangerous it was to risk people's lives.

On the contrary, I had no sympathy for the landlord or building owner. They didn't care about their tenants and were well aware of what was going on in their buildings. They didn't care about human life as long as they received their monthly rent.

When I entered the courtroom to hear the verdict, the atmosphere was different from that on previous days. The walls were lined with court officers. There must have been thirty court officers when there were only two in the past. All stood at attention in their starched white shirts and pressed blue pants. The room was packed with more people than ever before. Media and firefighters were present for the verdict. I sat next to Brendan, and the other firefighters were close by. I tried to read the jurors' faces as they entered the courtroom. *Were they looking at me? Were they smiling at the defendants?* The landlord, building owner, and their lawyers weren't present. The judge emerged from her chambers and began reading the verdict.

I felt physically ill watching this all happen in front of me. I couldn't believe I was in a courtroom watching total strangers decide the value of John's life. If they were found guilty, people would know that John's life meant something, even though I didn't need a verdict to tell us that. The City of New York would show the world that firefighters' lives matter.

If they were found not guilty, it would be a crushing blow to me. My heart would once again break. John went to work every day, protecting the safety of this jury and their homes. He responded to every call: an elevator being stuck, a child being sick, a car accident, or a false alarm. John was there to respond to their needs at 2 a.m. or 2 p.m. and on holidays. John took his oath for them, to protect them, to care for them, even though he didn't know them. He died for them. Indeed, they understood his sacrifice for them. His kids' sacrifice for them. My sacrifice. There are four children without a father because he chose to run into that building to look for a baby and put out a dangerous fire in their homes.

My heart was beating so loudly that I was sure everyone could hear it. Firemen came over to give me a reassuring pat and tell me, "We got this." Brendan gave me a look like, "Do we?" A wave of uncertainty came over us. *Where was my confidence I had moments ago?* He sat so patiently with me that I sometimes forgot he was still in daily pain because of his injuries. He never let on that he suffered physically and mentally because he was always quick with a joke and always made sure I was okay. I am certain that John and Brendan would have been good friends if they were given the chance.

After what seemed like forever, the judge was ready to read the verdict. The two defendants rose, and she read the charges. I can't remember how many charges were filed against them, but it didn't matter because all I heard was: *"NOT GUILTY." "NOT GUILTY." "NOT GUILTY."* They were acquitted on all charges.

I was shocked, but mostly crushed. My heart broke in two. How could this be? I sat for six weeks, didn't miss one day of testimony, and heard all the evidence. I was sure they would be found guilty. Where is the justice? I bent over my knees and cried. I didn't plan to react like this. I planned to sit quietly while they said "Guilty" and not show emotion. Two people's fates were on the line, and I planned to sit quietly while they learned of it. But now emotion overcame me. My husband's life meant nothing to this jury. This jury represented the People of New York City, the city John protected; he meant nothing to them.

How could they not make the defendants responsible for the loss of a beautiful life, husband, friend, brother, son, and father? I couldn't help but sob, but not as loudly as the squealing I was hearing. I looked over at the defendants, who were screaming in excitement.

The woman was shouting, "GOD IS GREAT, HALLELUJAH! GOD KNOWS BEST! HALLELUJAH! GOD IS GRACIOUS!" The man was jumping up and down, his arms in the air in a sign of victory, an enormous smile on his face. They both needed translators throughout the trial, but for some reason, their English had become perfectly fluent. Somehow, this upset me.

One of the court officers went over and told them that there were men dead because of this trial and that they should think about being more compassionate. It did not matter to them; they continued to celebrate my husband's death.

I had trouble breathing. I wanted to jump over the wooden divide and punch both of them. *Do you understand that you killed my husband? You are celebrating killing my husband and getting away with it!* A day earlier, I had empathy for them, and now they were boasting about getting away with it. I looked at the jury, and no one made eye contact with me. *You cowards! Look at me!* I wondered if they, too, were living in apartments like the one that took John's life. How could you possibly be objective and come up with this decision? Explain how my husband left his family so he could protect your family from harm, and you couldn't honor the supreme sacrifice he made for all of you.

The jury was thanked for their service and excused from their duties to return home, while I returned to my broken one. The tenants were free to go, too. They left the courtroom, speaking to the press and telling them, "God is good, God is great." At the time, it felt like God only works for people who willingly put others in danger and don't have to pay the price. It seems the justice system works in the same way.

I couldn't leave the courthouse through the same doors as the victors. Not because I was a sore loser; I just couldn't speak to the press at that moment. I knew I couldn't say anything about my disappointment in the verdict. I thought of my kids at that moment—and needed to take the high road. We didn't need a ten-second sound bite to follow us around for eternity. We were better than that. Whatever I would have said wouldn't have brought John back. The press didn't care about my crushed heart. They wanted my ugly, crying face planted across the nightly news. I wasn't giving anyone that part of me. I chose to use the back door to escape. Escape to my house without John.

A day later, the other jury was ready to render its verdicts in the landlord's and building owner's cases. Once again, I returned to the room that, forty-eight hours earlier, had caused me such heartache. The court officers lined the room again, and the press waited outside the doors. I sat in the same seat as I had for the last six weeks. Today was slightly different; a new defendant, the building owner, was finally seated in the courtroom. I suspected she had come to the trial once before, but wearing a disguise. She wore a big hat, wig, and sunglasses, but we saw her speaking to her lawyer in the courtroom. I'm not sure who she thought she was fooling or who she thought cared.

The jury came in, and, as on the other day, there was a thank-you ceremony for the jury members and other court protocols. The judge read the verdict: the landlord was "GUILTY," and the building owner, "GUILTY." I took a deep breath and felt some relief, realizing that John's life meant something. Once again, I chose to go out the back door and not talk to the press.

The other firefighters at the fire were there to speak with them and discuss their satisfaction with the verdict.

I didn't feel as much satisfaction as I thought I would with this guilty verdict. John was still gone, and none of it changed my loss. I was able to go home and tell my kids that the people responsible for taking their dad away would pay some sort of price. We would have to wait six months to hear the sentencing.

Six months after the verdict, I returned to the Bronx courthouse for the sentencing. Once again, I saw the landlord, his lawyer, the Bronx DA, and the judge. The judge read a lengthy explanation of the law. I didn't understand a lot of it, but I was just waiting to hear what the sentencing was for playing a role in two men dying. And then the final dagger shot straight through my heart.

"So with that law in mind," the judge announced, "I am reversing the verdict for the landlord and building owner. They will not be held liable for the death of the firefighters and are free to go without penalty."

What the fuck?! How could she change what the jury decided? Why did we go through a six-week trial if she planned on deciding the verdict anyway? It was insulting and hurtful. She explained in law jargon, so I never got an explanation in layman's terms. I would've loved for her to explain her decision to my kids. She could tell them how she let their dad die without anyone being responsible for all the wrongdoings that went on that day. *Would she find this to be true if it were her husband or son who ran into that burning building?*

How do I explain this outcome to my kids?

How do you raise kids to be law-abiding citizens and have them believe in a judicial system that failed their father?

I can only speculate why the judge reversed the decision. There seemed to be bias in one jury, which let people in similar living arrangements go free. The judge found bias on the part of the other jury against the landlord and building owner, and that, in turn, the defendants did not receive a fair trial. So, how is any of this fair for John? In the end, no one pays the price for playing their part in killing two firefighters—ultimately three—as Joey DiBernardo died of his injuries years later.

When I sat my kids down after the trial, I looked at each of their faces and began with... "Life is not fair... and if anyone knows this, you guys do."

For years, I sent a Christmas card to the building owner. I knew her LLC's address from court papers. My Christmas cards always had a large photo of my kids across the front. On her card, I would simply write, "Thinking of you this Christmas. I hope you are thinking of us. Bellews." I never missed a year. I know she got them because, at one point, my lawyer mentioned that her lawyer had a folder with all of them. This gesture was my way to get my message to her: your actions of greed tore apart a family and took away a loving father. Since I never got to take the stand and testify, I allowed a photo every year to represent a thousand words.

**Hallway Created by the Construction of an Illegal Partition Wall in Apartment 4L
View from kitchen facing toward rear fire escape window**

Illegal wall built on the fire floor

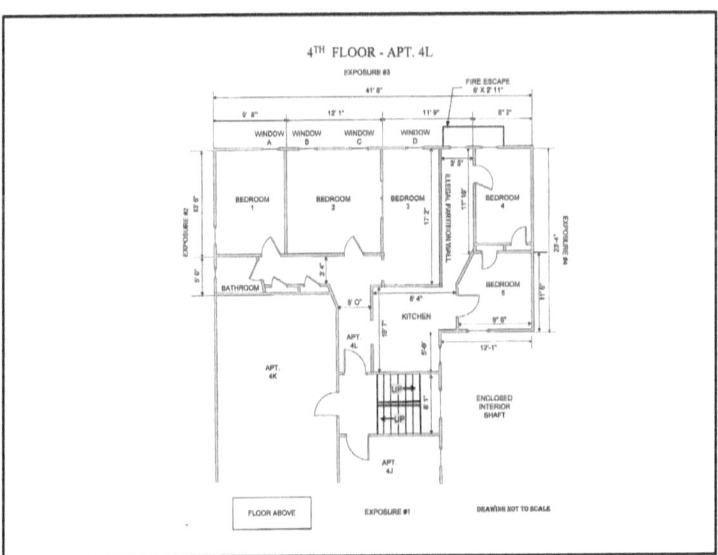

Diagram of the fire floor

CHAPTER 24

Dating

"Ugh, the thought of dating again makes my skin crawl," I said when I started discussing the idea with my friend Marie a few years after John jumped.

"It will be fun! We can analyze your dates, dissect all the things you like about them." I knew Marie was being sarcastic. This new journey would certainly be more fun for her than for me. What she meant was: "I can't wait to hear about your dates so we can evaluate their potential; we will have so many laughs."

I was happy to be her entertainment.

As much as I wanted to feel like a woman again, the thought of being interested in anyone other than John was mind-blowing. My list of potential boyfriend material criteria had changed significantly since I was twenty-three, and on my first date with John. My expectations had changed considerably since 1993. Back then, I wanted a tall, handsome, well-built person who wanted a family, had a job, siblings, and a car. In my early twenties, I didn't want a boyfriend who had a drinking problem, was a smoker, or was divorced. He preferably didn't have any kids, but most of all, was someone who could make me laugh. Looking back, this was pretty specific, but I was young and naive, and the population of available men was in my favor.

Fast forward fifteen years, and my expectations needed to be revised. I still wanted a tall, handsome, well-built guy. He needed to want a family (or be okay with my ready-made family), still needed a job, siblings were not a must, still needed a car, definitely could not have a drinking problem or do drugs, vape, or smoke, could not have a criminal record or any restraining orders, and not be a pedophile (but I think that is just obvious). He could be divorced and have kids. Once again, a non-negotiable trait was that he had to make me laugh.

The last time I looked for a potential boyfriend, (even that word makes me cringe. Do you even use that word at thirty-eight years old?) My hair had no gray in it, I had no crow's feet around my eyes, my breasts had not fed four kids, I was getting eight hours of beauty sleep, and I was 30lbs. lighter. My stomach was taut and tan since I could wear a bikini. Now my midriff was as white as my ass. Oh, yes, and a minor detail: back then I did not have four kids to work into a conversation.

"Yes, I love exercising, reading, cooking, and a small detail about myself is that I have four kids that I adore, love, would do anything for, and if you ever meet them and you look at them cross, I will kill you."

After meeting John, I was happy to never need to play the dating game again. Never having to make small talk until you got to the real questions, which had significantly changed. "Have you ever been arrested? Have you ever killed a woman on your first date? Do you normally drink four glasses of wine before the meal comes? Do you plan to pick up the check, or will there be an awkward silence until I reach for it?" And my newest question I would add to the arsenal: "Did you ever have asthma?"

So, this should go well.

One thing I did know was that I was too young to live out the rest of my life alone. My mom was fifty when my dad died, but it didn't cross my mind back then that she was young and should date. I guess I thought she was "old," but looking back, my mom deserved to have another companion. She had so much love to give, and it would have given her great comfort. My mom unknowingly taught me that I did not want the same thing for myself. I was well aware that though my kids needed me now, they would eventually leave me. The fear of being alone, even though children surrounded me, was always at the forefront of my mind.

The scariest part of dating was putting myself out there. My confidence was different from when I met John at twenty-three. I was naive in my youth, and now I had to be guarded; not only did I have to protect myself from undesirable people, but I also had to protect my kids. Little did my dates know they were dating five people.

Reentering the world of dating was like landing on another planet, where you feel like an alien, and your potential dates don't resemble the people you dated fifteen years earlier.

The first date I went on was with a very nice, young police officer named Pat. I had a conversation with John while I drove to meet him. "OK, you need to help me out here, since I can't have you, help me find someone I can spend time with. Wean out all serial killers, criminals, married men, and all-around losers. I don't have the time or energy to sift through jerks, so if you could, direct me to someone who will fill my time on Earth until I meet you again."

I was surprised Pat was interested, seeing that he was at least five years younger than I was. The date started strongly; he was very easy to talk to. By dessert, he brought up religion. *Well, this is odd. I haven't done this in a while, but I thought the topic of religion was more of a third-date talking point? But I went with it.*

"So, what religion are you?" he started with, "Do you have a strong faith?"

Well, probably not the time to bring up my parting ways with God. Yes, I'm Catholic, and God and I are at odds right now. He decided to take my husband away from me and my kids one day in a hospital room in the Bronx. I often scream at him and question the whole concept of religion. I decided against that route. "Yes, I'm Catholic and have a strong spirituality." That should save me for a while. I do have a strong spirituality, but I'm not sure if saying that I pray to my dead husband fits into a first date conversation.

"I am very spiritual as well," Pat said, "and I'm a deacon at my church."

Well, nice knowing you, Pat. I'm pretty sure we are not a match. I have the utmost respect for you, but I can guarantee that we are not a match. You are a much better person than I ever will be, and I cannot be saved at this point in my life.

Pat told me about all the charities he is part of and the good deeds he does in his community. *Did I mention, Pat, we are not a match?* I would like to be that type of person, but I know I am not, at least not at this point in my life. *And that I talk to my dead husband?* One date down, and I lived to tell the tale.

As I drove home, I reconvened with John and said, "OK, not a bad first date, but I do not want a saint."

I wish I could say that all my dates were as easy-going as Pat, but they weren't. Some guys were just fun, some were just fun to look at, but most were not worthy enough to introduce to my kids. I thought that going into dating, I had so much baggage that no one would want to date me. It turns out there are many men out there who have a lot more baggage than I do.

At times, dating was exciting. I was surprised by how many men did not care that I had four kids. My kids always came first, and their schedule dictated my dating schedule. So if you were willing to fit a date in between cheer practices, basketball games, art lessons, school events, baseball games, cheer competitions, and babysitters' availability, then I was all in. It was rare for any of them to meet my children. If they did, they were introduced as my friend. If they weren't willing to throw some sort of ball around to Jack and Kieran within the first five minutes of meeting them, it was a huge red flag.

Most of the time, though, dating was just like it was in my early twenties. There were plenty of cringy moments, but plenty of sweet ones, too. In the beginning, I found myself being attracted to more of the bad boy types longer than I should have. It bothered me when they did not call or text back. It was like I reverted to my sixteen-year-old self and had to relearn the dating world all over again. I picked some real "winners," but the distractions helped to break up the daily grind of mommy responsibilities.

The main difference at thirty-eight was that if I was interested in someone, I had to reach out to let them know. In my twenties, the guys would approach me, and I would decide whether to pursue. Now, I had to do the approaching because if I waited for them, I would be sitting home alone for the rest of my life. I think, naturally, men do not approach widows. I think we are a category that doesn't get many looks, almost like we have the plague. I must have been a difficult read. "Was she really looking to date? She is sort of giving off the 'don't mess with me' vibe." I have been told I give off an unapproachable look. I was so closed off to the dating world for years that I had to relearn how to make my persona appear accessible to those approaching me.

Getting to know new people was enjoyable, but within a date or two, I had an inner voice that said, "waste of time," or "I could do one more date." I allowed a few to stay on longer than they should have, for pure entertainment. I also had some that blew me off. When that happened, my insecurities reared their ugly head, and I questioned who I was. *I guess I'm not pretty, funny, or engaging?* You would think that all I went through and all the years of growth would squash the insecurities, but they came rushing back. I would let them enter my thoughts even when I knew the guy was a loser.

Dating doesn't change, no matter what your age; it can be fun, and it can waste your time and headspace. I assumed I would continue with this routine until the end of time because I enjoyed the companionship on my terms but had no intention of ever marrying again. John and I had a beautiful marriage, and the thought of sharing that with someone else was the furthest thing from my mind.

For two years, I dated a variety of men on and off. But someone (John) had different plans for me and my future.

In 2009, a family nearby lost their mom, who was fighting a terrible disease called Scleroderma. I did not know them personally but had heard of their loss. Many months later, I was walking into church and saw a brick with her name on it in the courtyard. I couldn't get their family out of my mind. Feeling so much sorrow for them, I knew firsthand how much her loss must have affected them as a family.

In the summer, I emailed Kevin, the dad, to introduce myself. "If you ever want to talk, I'm available," I wrote. Many weeks passed before I heard back. Then we corresponded about different grief topics. Most of our emails were rather morbid. "This is how I handled the first summer without John…" I wrote, "I found therapy helpful for me…there are plenty of days when I still don't feel like getting out of bed… try and plan to do things so the grief doesn't creep up on you…" I tried to help him the way other widows helped me, but the reality was that no matter what you write in an email, it still all sucks. I could paint a picture of life getting better soon, but I would be lying.

There would be weeks between correspondences, and with each one, I felt like he was doing much better than I ever was at the time. I kind of hated him; he was much more put together and seemed to have grief figured out. *Was I really helping him?* Every warning sign I mentioned, he would say, "I'll keep an eye on that; we aren't having those issues."

One night, we spoke on the phone, and I thought, *I really hate this guy. Maybe he should be counseling me?* I was giving him all these warnings and predictions, and I got, "I am not finding that, everyone seems okay. Yes, I see what you are saying, but I'm doing okay. I'm busy coaching my son Luke's basketball team and working. My daughters, Lauren and Leanne, are busy with school. Leanne is looking at colleges." I wanted to hang up. *Now, I really hate him. How is he so put together? I am supposed to be the one who has it together five years after John jumped, not him.*

Weeks passed after our phone call, and I got an unexpected email: "I really enjoyed our phone conversation. Would you like to go to dinner sometime?" My first gut was, *no, not really. We will continue our morbid conversations about grief in person. Why would I agree to that? He seems like a nice person, but he will have all the answers, and I do not. I will have to get a babysitter, shower, and put on makeup. And by the end of the night, I will feel bad about myself.*

When he invited me to dinner one night, I already had plans to meet friends. *I could ask the sitter to come a little earlier, and the shower and make-up would already be in the prep.* So, I said yes.

As the day approached, I was running around so much with the kids that I regretted saying yes. I warned the sitter that the night was a two-parter. "I will come home from the first dinner, but I will be heading back out to meet friends once this guy drives away."

My sitter gave me a big smirk and head bob as if he thought I had two dates planned for the same evening.

"It is not what you think."

The sitter smiled and shook his head some more, "Aha, I get it, not to worry."

When Kevin arrived, Kieran answered the door, shirtless and covered in chocolate pudding. "Who are you? Are you my mom's friend? Are you taking my mom out to dinner?"

Kevin laughed, looking surprised, "I'm Kevin, I am your mom's friend, and yes, we are going to dinner." He got to witness the chaos I referenced on the phone firsthand. I grabbed my coat, and we were off.

"Any suggestions for dinner?"

I reluctantly responded, "Would you mind if we chose a restaurant a few towns over? You know, small town, big rumors." I'm not sure if I insulted him, but he agreed. We sat at the bar waiting for our table, "I'll have an amaretto sour," he said to the bartender.

"What?" I blurted out, "What are you drinking? Who drinks an amaretto sour? Who are you, my grandmother?" The words just flew out of my mouth. I had never shown my sarcastic side before. I quickly took a sip of my Pinot Grigio.

He laughed, "What should I order? I like the sugary drinks."

"Not sure, but there has to be something behind that bar that doesn't make you look like you are eighty years old." I took another gulp of my wine; it looked like I might need some liquid courage to get through this night.

Luckily, the night took a much brighter turn. Although I made fun of his drink, he took it in stride and laughed at himself. *Good start, there is a sense of humor in that grief-stricken body.* Something strange happened; he started asking questions about me and my life, and none of the questions had to do with death, dying, or tragedy.

"Do you come from a big family? I think I know your brother, John. Where did you go to college?" The conversation was not about grief and sadness, but just a regular conversation. He was charming and engaging, and he quickly became someone different from the person I had been corresponding with for the last few months. There was a definite pivot from widow talk to human talk. *Wait, this feels more like a date? Was this his intention all along when he asked me to dinner?* The evening flew by, but in the back of my mind, I had to get to my original plans for the night.

"Would you like to go to another bar for another drink?" Kevin asked. *Has his amaretto sour gone to his head? He's on a date. Does that mean I'm on a date with him?* The truth was, I wouldn't have minded going to another bar, but my friends were waiting, and that would mean I was agreeing this was a date. I was not sure if I was ready for that.

"Sorry, I have to get home."

He gave me a quick "not sure what this was" kiss on the cheek, when he dropped me off. *What was that? That was not a grief dinner? Did we discuss anything related to grief, sadness, trauma, or our pain? No.* I was confused. I'm pretty sure that constitutes a date.

"I don't know what just happened?" was the first thing out of my mouth when I met up with my friend Kris. "I agreed to go out to dinner with the guy I told you about, whom I've been emailing about the loss of his wife. I thought it was going to be a grief pow wow—like you and I have had many times—but it wasn't. I think it was a date?"

Also a widow, Kris wanted to know everything.

"The man I went out with tonight was not the same Kevin I had been emailing with. This guy was cute, funny, charming, and interesting. His only downfall I could see so far was his choice of beverages."

"Love finds you when you least expect it."

I toasted my friend the way John always did, "Good to be with you!"

Over the next few weeks, the calls and dates became increasingly frequent. It was my first time dating a widower, and we communicated with great ease. I understood I could never compete with his first love, Liz. Kevin understood he could not compete with John. We did not want to.

Kevin had three kids. I wanted them to remain his priority, as I made clear from the beginning that my kids would be for me. He understood that they would always come first in my life. Blending families is hardly ever easy, and for us, there were many challenges. As much as I wanted all our kids to share a relationship with one another, the age difference and their attachment to their mom made this really difficult. Even though it had been nearly a year since she passed, I understood that they may not have been ready for their dad to move on.

Ultimately, we felt as if John and Liz had something to do with getting us together.

It took John five years to find Kevin for me. I hope John didn't bombard Liz immediately when she got to heaven but gave her some time to adjust. "Hi Liz, my name is John. Welcome to the Pearly Gates. I have been watching over you and your husband for the last five years, and I have a plan that I think works for all of us." John would convince Liz that their soulmates were better on Earth with a companion until we each meet again.

Sometimes love finds you when you aren't looking for it. And sometimes you have to look beyond the amaretto sour.

Kevin and I when we were dating

CHAPTER 25

Hawaiian Wedding

Bounce, bounce, bounce! The kids jumped on the backyard trampoline on a warm day in May 2011. Yes, it is a death toy that I allowed my children to play on, all the while I predicted emergency visits for broken elbows—another example of letting them be kids, while all along dying inside.

Bounce, bounce, bounce, they continued to play as Kevin approached them. It was over a year and a half since our first dinner together, and Kevin had been intertwined into their lives.

"Can I have a serious conversation with you guys?"

"Sure."

"OK."

"Do I have to stop jumping?"

Three of them respond. Brielle just keeps jumping.

"Yes, why don't you guys come sit over closer to me?" Three of them sit down, but Brielle keeps jumping. Maybe she sensed the moment and wasn't ready for it. Kevin lets her be and continues. "You know I love your mom very much, and I love you guys. I wanted to ask you guys if it was okay to ask your mom if

I could marry her?" Kevin pulled out the ring to show the kids. Brielle never stopped jumping.

"Wait, you guys aren't just friends?" Kieran said. Kat and Jack looked at each other.

"Yes, we started out as friends, but now I would like to marry her and be part of your family."

"Well, there are a few conditions," Jack said, with a smile. Brielle kept bouncing.

"I don't want my mom to change her last name to yours." Katreana piped in, and Kieran agreed, "Yeah, no last name change."

"And no more new siblings that aren't already born." Kat blurted out.

"Oh, okay, interesting. I understand. Your mom keeps your last name and no babies." They all nodded in agreement.

I'm not sure if Brielle was ever part of the original conversation, but it wasn't the last one we would have about how marriage might affect their lives. We reassured them that life would not change as they knew it. I would not allow that. Yes, I loved Kevin and wanted to be with him for the rest of my life, but only if my kids' lives were enhanced, not changed.

Once Kevin got the approval from the core four, he moved on to my mom. I'm sure my mother never expected to have this conversation twice on my behalf. My mom was a real pushover with all of her in-laws and was so happy to see me find two amazing men.

A couple of weeks later, Kevin got down on his knee and proposed. It was simple and beautiful. He knew I couldn't handle a considerable fanfare, and if he did that, I would have said no. I sensed it was coming, and the anxiety that he would plan something elaborate gave me panic attacks. Kevin was comfortable with fanfare; he doesn't mind attention. I would say he even likes it. He grew up with lots of positive attention showered on him. He was a college basketball superstar. He led the country in scoring and free-throw percentage in '87 while playing basketball at West Point.

Now we were engaged! It felt weird to be wearing a new ring showing the world I belonged to a new man. Honestly, I struggled with this at first. At times, I still do. I love Kevin, and yet, I still have a relationship with my first husband. Kevin still has a relationship with his first wife. My heart has many scars on it, but it has also grown. Over time, Kevin helped heal those wounds and gave me a new opportunity to love again.

Months and months passed, and I was learning to be okay with the idea of getting married again while enjoying the prospect of a new forever with someone other than John. Kevin met John's parents and all of his extended family. I had no worries that they would love him. Some might say they liked him better than me. That would not shock me. John's mom had one request of my new fiancé: "Please take care of those little ones." Kevin, of course, reassured her that that was his plan.

The idea of planning a wedding was so overwhelming. *How would we ever get married? We have so many family members and friends that would all get an invite. No church could hold 500 people except St Patrick's Cathedral, and I'm pretty sure that is booked for the next ten years. How much would this wedding cost?* So, I did what worked for me: I ignored it. I put it out of my mind and was content with being engaged. *Do we really need to get married? It doesn't change anything. Let's just wake up one day and say, "we are married," and that would be official.*

But one day in December, my sister, Patricia, saw a contest on *Live with Kelly* on ABC. Kelly Ripa announced, "One lucky couple will get married on our show, in beautiful Oahu, Hawaii! Thirty of your closest family and friends will join you on the biggest wedding giveaway ever! Just write to us about your love story and why you deserve to be our Hawaiian Dream Wedding Couple!"

Patricia called me. "You guys should enter; you have the perfect love story."

"Yeah, right. Only hundreds of couples will enter, and they are going to pick the middle-aged, widowed couple with seven kids. I'll tell Kevin, you know he loves that kind of stuff." I told Kevin about it, and then promptly put it out of my mind.

But Kevin got right on it; he wrote about my loss, his loss, and how we found each other.

> Dear Kelly,
>
> To fall in love once and marry your best friend is an amazing feeling. It's a dream come true. Falling in love a second time, after all of your dreams are tragically shattered, and marrying the love of your life, is even more amazing. That is the story of Eileen Bellew and Kevin Houston.
>
> In January 2005, Eileen's world was turned upside down in an instant. Her husband of ten years, John Bellew, one of New York City's Bravest, lost his life in a catastrophic fire, which became known as Black Sunday. Married in 1995, Eileen and John had a life full of love and four beautiful children, ages 6, 3, 2, and 5 months, at the time of John's

death. He continued sharing about Black Sunday and John's tragic passing.

Inspired by her four young children, her little angels, Eileen kept her family moving forward despite the difficulties, sadness, and emptiness that surrounded her daily. Over the last six years, she has watched her two daughters and her two sons grow and mature into wonderful, well-adjusted children, all the while reminding them of John's courage and bravery, as well as the many great traits he displayed as a father.

In January 2009, Kevin's world was also toppled. Immediately after graduating from the United States Military Academy in 1987, Kevin married his high school sweetheart, Elizabeth. Kevin and Liz were married for twenty-one years when Liz succumbed to a long-term illness, a rare autoimmune disease called scleroderma that eroded her quality of life over five years. Kevin and Liz also lived a charmed life, full of love and happiness, with three fantastic children who were 20, 16, and 13, when their world crumbled. Over the course of five years, before her death, Kevin became Liz's primary caregiver as she steadily lost her independence and ability to do everyday tasks we all take for granted. On January 3, 2009, the physical toll that scleroderma took on Liz proved too much. Kevin's worst fears had arrived. He wrote about gathering his children at the hospital to share their mother's prognosis, and about her peaceful passing.

Kevin, too, drew inspiration from his children, and together they have moved forward amid the same difficulty, sadness, and emptiness that the Bellew family endured. Although Eileen and Kevin grew up in the same small town and were only five years apart, they had not previously met. In late 2009, Eileen and Kevin met and enjoyed a casual dinner, unaware that something very special was happening. They soon thereafter fell in love. They have had an overwhelmingly great experience of finding in each other the person they wanted to spend the rest of their lives with, despite the enormous losses each endured.

Eileen and Kevin, and their families, frequently look to the skies for mindful and loving signs from John, who sends rainbows, and Liz, who sends soaring hawks. Those are the loving signs that tell them John and Liz are always nearby, looking out for them, and reminding them of happy times, past, present, and future.

Eileen and Kevin are most deserving of a Dream Wedding in Hawaii. Despite the horrible tragedies that befell them and their families and sent them into emotional free falls, they have rallied, collected themselves, stayed positive, and risen to dream again. Smile on them and send them soaring in the Rainbow State, Hawaii, for the Wedding of a Lifetime.

I thought he did a beautiful job, but how many people would be entering this contest? Maybe hundreds? He sent it in, and I put it out of my mind again.

A week later, we were sitting at Starbucks when Kevin got a call from a producer on *Live with Kelly*. They asked for me, assuming I wrote the letter, so Kevin handed the phone to me.

"Hi Eileen, this is Christine from *Live with Kelly*. I wanted to talk to you about the letter you wrote about the Dream Wedding Contest."

"Actually, my fiancé wrote the letter, but I could answer any questions you might have."

The show loved that Kevin wrote the letter and continued to verify and ask questions about our story.

"We love your story and would like to allow you to compete against four other couples for a chance to win a dream wedding in Hawaii. How would you like that?"

I think my heart stopped. *Wait, what? Seriously, we have a shot of being on TV and getting married in front of millions?* "Oh wow, seriously, that's incredible. Thank you for the opportunity!"

I hung up and told Kevin. "Oh my God! Amazing! We are going to win! I know it! This is so cool, we will get married in front of millions on TV! This is great!"

All of a sudden, reality hit me. *Is it really? In front of millions? I'm not very likable, and the world could rip me apart. I have spent the last five years avoiding the media and now putting myself in the limelight.* Panic set in. *But we haven't won anything yet; four other couples will definitely beat us. No need to worry about anything yet.*

From that moment on, things moved fast, really fast. A producer came to my house with a camera crew and started interviewing me, Kevin, my mom, my best friend, my sister,

Kevin's family, and his best friend. They wanted photos and cute stories about us. But what is cute about a middle-aged couple? We sent a few photos of us with our kids.

While I was not attached to winning, in the back of my mind, I thought, *this would be perfect, I wouldn't have to plan a wedding, and it would be nothing like my first wedding, something different, something unique just for Kevin and me.* But who was I kidding? The chances of us winning seemed so out of reach, even though it still was a one-in-five shot.

The experience was surreal. All my past experiences with the media were surrounded by sadness and sorrow, as they always tried to get a shot of me crying, but this was a celebration. They didn't want me crying; instead, they wanted the opposite: uplifting, sweet, and funny Eileen. I wasn't sure if I could do that either.

A week passed, and the five stories were featured, one each day on *Live with Kelly.* They didn't show us our pitch beforehand, so we saw it with the rest of the world. It was tough, and very vulnerable, to put myself out there, plus how many pounds does the TV camera put on you? Our story went out to the world, and now we waited to see if people liked it. I knew I shouldn't read the comments on their website, but it's like a train wreck—you can't look away.

"I don't like their story; the other stories are better."

"They are too old to win a wedding in Hawaii."

"She doesn't even look like she likes him." What was I supposed to do, make out with Kevin on camera? Would that prove I love him?

Back in 2012, the social media craze was just beginning. To vote for us, you had to vote through your email. We watched all the other stories and thought they, too, had beautiful stories worthy of a Hawaiian wedding. Voting started on a Friday night after the last story was shown and ran through the weekend. *What am I doing? I fought to get the media out of my world, and now I'm inviting them in.* It did feel different this time, a happy occasion, on my terms.

As the weekend inched by, the vote was always at the forefront of my mind. It was out of my hands, like so much in my life I couldn't control. But the idea of someone taking over all the responsibilities of my wedding felt liberating. For my first wedding, I was thrilled to pick out flowers, the church, the music, the venue, the dresses, the menu, and the honeymoon. The thought of someone else doing all those things for me the second time around was exhilarating.

On Sunday morning, I received a call from a producer who wanted to set up a Skype call with all the contestants for the show the next morning, so they could put us on air immediately if our names were called. Ironically, the next day was January 23rd, seven years since Black Sunday. *Is this a coincidence, or is John sending me a sign?* He wanted to change my mind about that date from a tragedy to a happy occasion.

Monday morning came, and I got the kids ready for school. I acted like it was any other day; I didn't want them disappointed if we didn't get picked.

We signed on to Skype, and the producer came on the screen.

"Okay, can you see Kim and Kelly waving to you?"

Ummm, you mean Kim Kardashian? "Oh yes, I see Kim and Kelly waving to us." As if this is commonplace, Kim Kardashian gives me a quick wave as if she knows us. But then they turned our monitor to face a doorway. We could no longer see the set. *So, is that it? Were we not the couple getting picked?* I thought four other couples were waiting to hear their destiny, too. Did they have a better view of the set than we did? I think it was about an hour from when they set up our call to the announcement of the winners. Waiting was torture.

"Here we go! We are going to reveal the winners of our Aulani Hawaiian Wedding!" Kelly finally announces.

My heart is pounding. Kevin and I are sitting in front of a small laptop screen, still facing a doorway, and we can barely see Kelly and Kim. Kelly hands off the honor of announcing the names to Kim.

"The winners of the Aulani Hawaiian wedding, with thirty of their closest friends and a week-long honeymoon at the beautiful Disney Resort of Aulani, are… drum roll please…

JUST SAY IT ALREADY!

"…Eileen and Kevin from Pearl River, NY!"

Our monitor quickly turns to get a better view of Kelly and Kim.

"Oh my God! Oh my God! I can't believe it!" As I jumped up and down and screamed, Kevin was laughing and keeping his cool, as he always does. I sounded like a lunatic, but I honestly didn't think this would happen to us.

"How do you feel?" Kelly asked.

"I am shocked! I can't believe it!" *Oh my God! We are really doing this. I am getting married again.* Panic began. *I have to go on TV again.*

But this time, on a totally different trajectory, it would be one of the happiest days of my life. Time was ticking; there were twenty-three days until we had to leave—so much to think about, so much to decide. My first thought, though, was: *How do I let my kids leave me in Hawaii after the wedding, while we stay for our honeymoon? They can't get on a plane without me.*

It's one thing to enter a contest with hundreds, even thousands of applicants, agree to give up all control of planning your own wedding and agree for it to be broadcast over a major network for millions of people to see. But it is another thing to win that contest and have to go through with it. I was going from hiding from cameras to putting it all out there. *I'm crazy to agree to this, right?*

After the celebration with my new friends, Kelly and Kim, the phone calls started coming in, "We will need the names, birthdates, and ages of your guests. Are you able to come into the studio next week to be part of the show? We have to set up a time for a dress fitting." Question after question was coming at me as if I had the answers. Five minutes earlier, I had no idea when I would get married, and now I would be married in a month. *How many pounds does the camera put on you? I guess the diet starts right now.*

Kevin was so excited, and I didn't want to rain on his parade, but my anxiety took over. *Who will watch my kids when we are on our honeymoon? How will they have everything they need when we are away? How much school will they miss? Who will watch the dog? How will I let them get on a plane without me?* They had never gone on a plane without me. I had never been away from them longer than a day.

This time should have been blissful, walking on air and flying down the aisle like a Disney princess, but my brain doesn't work that way. My brain wants to flood me with intrusive thoughts of harm and anxiety. This wasn't fair to Kevin; he deserves a wife who is not broken.

"Champagne for everyone!" Kevin popped the cork. I took a sip and relaxed. *Maybe this is how I'll get through, let the champagne keep flowing.*

We were invited to the show three times before we left for Hawaii. The first time was intended to introduce us to the viewers. Daniel Radcliffe was guest hosting, so Katreana skipped school to meet the one and only Harry Potter. Kat had read the series twice, so this was a once-in-a-lifetime dream. She was ecstatic, and he was so nice to her. We sat behind the curtain to be called out, and all I kept thinking was, *do not trip, do not stumble over your words and do not curse. This experience was surreal. Whose life am I living right now?*

The following few times on the air were to meet Derek Hough from *Dancing with the Stars,* who was to teach us our wedding dance. I did a simple box-step slow dance at my first wedding and probably struggled with it. Derek might have been given the impossible task of making us look coordinated and talented to perform a simple dance. We ended up having a few lessons with him, and I might have remembered one twirl and one spin. I do remember that when watching back all the footage they chose to air on the show, the dance got very little airtime.

In another competition we played a game show called Newlywed vs Nearlywed against Jerry O'Connell and Rebecca Romijn. Crazy right? *How is the Stand By Me actor I grew up watching, playing a game against me on TV?* We won, and our prize was Colbie Caillat singing our wedding song, "Fallin' for You." So crazy.

The most surreal pre-wedding activity was picking out my wedding dress. Since Disney owned the TV station, a sales rep offered me a choice of ten wedding dresses named after Disney Princesses. I showed up at a bridal shop with my mom, Kevin's mom, my girls, and Kevin's girls. I was forty-two years old, trying on Ariel's, Belle's, Cinderella's, Snow White's, and all the other princesses' dresses.

My concern was that they did not make princess dresses in my size. My waist size grew a little larger than the last time I bought the "sample size" wedding dress off the rack, which needed no alterations. This time around, we might need a fairy godmother or at least a skilled seamstress to create my dress.

As I began to try them on, Carson Kressley spun in with high energy and pixie dust. "Well, what do we have here? A beautiful bride who will be walking down the aisle in Hawaii?" *Oh my! Carson Kressley is going to style me? Does he know what he signed on for?*

I looked at my mom, who had no idea who he was, and I knew what she was thinking: *Is this guy lost? Why does he have so much energy?*

Kelly and Carson spent the afternoon with us picking out a dress that best suited me and helped me jazz it up so it wasn't so white. This was not my first rodeo, and I needed to represent that. We put a light-blue sash with sequins around my waist. I can't remember which princess I was, I think Ariel, because it was a mermaid-type dress. Despite the names, the dresses were beautiful.

Carson then tackled my mom and Kevin's mom. My mom was seventy-six at the time, and I'm pretty sure she never saw the show *Queer Eye for the Straight Guy*, but they hit it off. He was so kind to her and treated her like a queen. I think my mom and my mother-in-law, Jean, stole the show; they looked spectacular. The girls picked out their dresses, and we were on our way. Check it off the list. And we were another day closer to letting my kids go on a plane without me.

I really wanted to marry Kevin, and I knew he was having a ball with all the planning and appearances, but in the back of my mind was the dread of leaving my kids on a plane without me. My whole family would be on the same plane as them, so the issue was not parental supervision; it was that my brain was wired to see the plane go down over the Pacific and my whole life going down with it.

Kevin could see my anxiety as the days passed, "Why don't we just keep them with us on our honeymoon? We can take them out of school, get another room, and change their flights."

I thought about it, I considered it, but how could I do that to Kevin? His honeymoon with my four kids? And who was I kidding? If they stayed, I would get a connecting room to ensure they weren't alone.

Claire and I had many sessions over the days leading up to the wedding. "So what is your biggest fear about them going on the plane home without you?"

"Isn't it obvious? What if the plane crashes and they die? I could not live with myself."

"OK, I get it, so what would you do?"

"I would kill myself; I would commit suicide if my children died."

"Well, okay, then you have a plan. If that happens, you will commit suicide."

And just like that, I felt so much better. I had a plan, and I was in control. If my children died, I would join them in heaven. God would have to give me a pass with how I chose to leave; he would clearly understand that I could not live on Earth without them.

I was happy that Kevin could have a real honeymoon because he deserved it. I told him my plan. "Well, I would not want you to leave me, but I understand." Somehow, I found a man who understands this brain, and I was going to marry him.

The day finally arrived when all thirty of us loaded on a plane to Hawaii. It had been such a whirlwind that I'm not sure I really processed that I was getting married. I was happy to have the opportunity to do all the traditional planning for my first wedding; I didn't feel like I lost out on that experience, and this one was totally different. It is almost as if this was how it was supposed to happen. I'm not sure I would ever have gotten married otherwise. It is like John took all the stress out of it and just gave me a wedding without the planning.

On our drive to the hotel, there it was, the sign I was looking for—a giant rainbow across the sky. "Everyone, look outside, Daddy is right here with us." It confirmed what I already knew: John sent me Kevin, and he was all in for this ride.

We were greeted with leis, took in the sweet smell of the Hawaiian air, and were ready to collapse after a full day of travel. We were told at the Disney Aulani Resort that Kevin would have his own room until our wedding night, and then they would move us into the Honeymoon suite after the wedding.

Kevin and I had a packed itinerary that kept us busy. *Live with Kelly* took us out on a catamaran for whale-watching. We had surf lessons with Mark Consuelos, snorkeling, fish-feeding, couples' massages, a breakfast with all the Disney characters, and more dance lessons with Derek Hough, all while TV cameras followed our every move. We appeared on each show the week before the wedding.

On the show, we did cake tasting, picked out our wedding bands, and met famous people like Patricia Heaton, Carrie Ann Inaba, Daniel Dae Kim, and Matthew Morrison. And off-show, we had to do interviews for taped spots they would use in shows they filmed later that week. The whole experience was beyond surreal and exhausting. It didn't offer much time to spend with our kids or guests, but they seemed to have a blast sitting by the pool or at the beach. A world foreign to us, but I just held onto Kevin and let the magical world of television take over.

Our rehearsal dinner was a Luau with a pig roast, flame throwers, and dancers teaching us the hula. At times, I felt like I was an invited guest, and this all wasn't really happening to me. After the rehearsal dinner, I went back to our hotel room with my kids. I needed to check in with them, make sure they were okay, and, most importantly, reassure them.

"Nothing is going to change; you four will always be the most important people to me. I will never let anything happen to you. I'm sure some of this is a bit scary—all the cameras following us—but it will all be over by tomorrow. We will return home, and the only change in your life will be that Kevin will now live with us. You will have three parents to take care of you—me, Daddy, and Kevin. Daddy will not be going anywhere; he will always be right there helping us. He sent us Kevin to help him. I love you more than all the stars in the world. Is everyone OK?"

Kieran asked, "So nothing will change?"

I gave him the biggest hug. "Exactly, the love for all of you is only growing." My four loves snuggled under the covers, and I watched them drift off to sleep.

My sister was in the adjoining room and agreed to listen for them while I took a walk to clear my head, as a widow one last time. I strolled along the beach while John and I had another one of our conversations.

"So, I guess this is it. I have a feeling you are behind this. You made sure I found Kevin, so thank you. I still want you with me; nothing changes, right?"

It felt like I was Kieran, wanting reassurance that our relationship would not change. I still needed him just as much as before. Still feeling a sense of guilt, I had taken a vow to John, and I know I fulfilled "until death do us part," but your love does not just dissolve when that happens.

"I still love you, and you still love me till eternity do us part," I said softly in the darkness. Then I returned to my room, gave them all kisses, and whispered to Kieran, "I get it."

Our wedding day finally arrived, and all of the tapings and obligations were done. All of our guests had arrived. The difference is that we only knew thirty of the 600 guests who would be in the audience, and Kelly Ripa will be one of my bridesmaids. Mark Consuelos will be walking my mom down the aisle, and there's a good chance she doesn't even know who he is. A hairstylist will style my hair, and a makeup artist will do my face.

All along, Katreana was having a panic attack in the next room, and Colbie Caillat talked her off the ledge while she warmed up her voice to sing our entry song. My boys were getting dressed in custom suits with Kevin. I hoped the kids didn't think this was real life, because there will be a lot of disappointment if they think this is how all weddings are produced.

When I walked out to the lawn by the ocean towards the wedding stage, there were hundreds of people hanging off their balconies. I looked up and waved to them. "Congratulations!" they screamed, as I smiled, while my palms started sweating, and my bouquet was slipping out of my hand. *You can do this; just don't trip. Stop sweating, or your makeup will be dripping off your face. Smile, just keep smiling. Millions of people will be watching and judging you in a few minutes.* I approached my two handsome sons, who were waiting for me at the top of the white aisle runner, which was covered with yellow flower petals all the way down to Kevin.

I took my boys' arms and hoped my heels wouldn't stick in the grass. Hundreds of people stared at me. None of them were people I knew, but who cares? At the end of the day, I would be married to Kevin, and if not for all this chaos, I'm not sure it would have ever happened. As I held onto the boys tightly, it hit me that I was asking so much of them. Cameras, lights, and attention are being broadcast on all of us.

We reached the stage where it had just become real. I know Kevin is the right man for me, but there is a feeling of loss even in this happiest of moments. The loss of me being John's partner, his wife—and now becoming someone else's. My journey had been a crazy ride, one with so many bumps, pivots, turns, twists and was now smooth sailing off into a beautiful Hawaiian sunset.

Reverend Kimo performed a beautiful ceremony that was very different from the Catholic wedding I had with John. Our vows mentioned John and Liz, and they were included in video tributes. Little did I know that this was what I needed. Celebrating our love in such a different way. Yes, a surreal way, with famous people and over-the-top pageantry, but it was perfect.

The reception was terrific, and our dance was subpar, but at that point, I didn't care. I tried to be in the moment, but in the back of my mind, my kids were getting on a plane without me the next day. We also had one last obligation to perform for the show. The next morning, we had a photo shoot for Bride Guide Magazine promoting Dream Destination Weddings.

I showed up in tears since I had to say goodbye to my kids during the photo shoot. Hair and makeup were not very happy with me, plus wardrobe looked at me and said, "Oh, I hope we have a dress in your size?" *Didn't the show tell you my dimensions? They fitted me into my wedding dress. I'm forty-two years old, and these hips delivered four large kids, so give me the largest dress you've got.* They ended up asking the staff to get me a glass (or a bottle) of Pinot Grigio so I could calm down, and they put me in a pink wedding dress. We went out to the cliffs of the Aulani resort for an elaborate backdrop to our pretend wedding pictures.

My kids arrived right before the first photo snapped, and I had to say goodbye to them.

"Mommy, you look so pretty, but that isn't your wedding dress?"

"I know, it is just for this photo shoot. You know I'm going to miss you guys so much. Grandma is going to take good care of you, and I have lots of other moms and dads picking you up to bring you to all your sports and practices. I will be home so fast, you won't even know I was gone."

Their faces showed concerned looks. I prayed to John that they would be safe, that I would see them again. My anxiety was at a fever pitch, and all I could do was let go. I had a plan, though, if their plane went down, I would commit suicide. It was a full-fledged plan. It gave me control, which is what I felt like I had none of as they walked away from me.

I spent the next twenty-four hours tracking their plane and did not sleep all night. Kevin found me on the computer at 2 a.m., 3 a.m., 4 a.m., watching the flight pattern. I fell asleep at 5 a.m. after speaking to each one of them when they got off the plane, and then my anxiety turned toward the car ride home...

Hawaiian Wedding with our families

Hawaiian Wedding at our reception

CHAPTER 26

Civil Trial

Periodically, I would get a letter or a phone call updating me on various rulings or developments in the court case. For the most part, I put it out of my mind, and we never discussed it at home. After the heartbreaking verdicts from the criminal trial, I couldn't get myself to discuss anything with the kids related to the justice system. His life was so much more than a criminal or civil trial. At home, I focused on highlighting both their dad's great qualities and his funny ones. My kids needed me to focus on the positive aspects of John's life and joke about his flaws. We couldn't discuss the legal battle.

As the lawyers predicted, the civil court case finally came to trial in January of 2017, Brielle's senior year of high school, twelve years after it was filed. Once again, I went down to the Bronx and sat in the courthouse daily during the trial. The kids were so much older now and had more questions.

"Why do you have to go down there? Can't they do this without you?" They remembered the toll the first trial had on me.

"I need to represent Daddy; he has no voice, and even if it is just me sitting in the courthouse, I am Daddy's voice."

"Ok, but will you be home for dinner?"

"Yes, most days I will be home for dinner. This is the last trial, no more after this one, I promise."

This time, there were only two defendants—the building owner and the City of New York—and only one jury. Like déjà vu, each defendant's lawyer blamed the other defendant. The City of New York's lawyers blamed the building owner for the SROs, who in turn blamed the City for not providing the firefighters with proper safety equipment. I had seen this game before, and the results were not in our favor. So, as confident as I was with the criminal trial, I had no faith in the justice system this time around.

I had heard most of the evidence during the criminal trial, but there was some new information as well. A person from the medical examiner's office came to explain John's injuries in depth. They showed John's turnout coat.

"I would like to submit for evidence Mr. Bellew's turnout gear and helmet. As you can see with Firefighter Bellew's turnout gear, when the fabric turns the color reddish brown, it means that Mr. Bellew endured temperatures over 500 degrees Fahrenheit for approximately two to three minutes, which means members were exposed to heat levels consistent with flashovers. This evidence shows that Mr. Bellew was most likely on fire when he had no other choice but to jump. His helmet, which is made of leather, was melted and charred, indicating once again that Mr. Bellew endured a flashover. The unthinkable decision of burning to death or jumping would be Mr. Bellew's last thoughts."

It was beyond painful to see this. Even twelve years later, I had not seen the clothing that he was wearing, as it had been held as evidence for all these years. You could barely see his name on the turnout coat, as if the fire removed his name into vapor. No one should have to suffer such a brutal death. I imagine his broken body being removed from this coat in the Emergency Room, probably still too hot to touch. He had to jump to escape from the heat.

I broke out in a sweat almost as if I was in the room with John. My face grew flush, palms were sweating, and I was uncomfortable in my own skin. I listened intently, as the medical examiner sat on the stand and explained all of John's injuries. *How did he survive four and a half hours?* It seems almost impossible that he had the will to live even a minute after the jump. The examiner explained every bone that was broken. Unfortunately, besides those two references to John, that was it. I sat for six weeks without hearing his name mentioned. I had to rely on other accounts to give John's life meaning to the jury.

The New York City Fire Commissioner, Thomas von Essen, took the stand. "The fire department took the personal safety ropes out of commission because they had a lifespan of ten years. In 2000, firefighters were told to hand in their personal safety ropes. The fire department was to research a new system and reinstate the use of personal safety ropes after purchasing them. The fire department never researched another system and never replaced them, even after five years had passed."

He admitted that the intention was to replace the rope system, but it was not done. Von Essen explained that it had nothing to do with fiscal obligation, which ultimately helped our case. John was never given a replacement because they never got around to finding one. They had five years to find and purchase the rope system but never did. If someone had done their job, the firefighters would have been properly equipped with safety ropes and John, and the other firefighters, could have exited the building using them that fateful day.

The time was coming for me to take the stand. I had dreaded this day for twelve years, constantly thinking about what I would say when I had the opportunity. I wanted to represent John and give him a voice, but I knew I could never do him justice. How could I sum up how much he meant to his kids and me? It felt unsettling to have to prove to twelve total strangers how much we loved John, how much we missed him, and how much our lives changed because of the building owner's negligence and the FDNY's failure to provide safety equipment.

My lawyer came to my house to prep me, which was weird. While I certainly didn't feel the need to be prepped about my family life with the kids, I was concerned about being cross-examined and the questions they might ask. Especially questions about being remarried. I assumed I would be emotional, but you don't know how you will react in the heat of the moment after waiting twelve years for this.

"The jury wants to meet you, they want to hear about your life together, they want to know what type of dad he was. Explain how he was a stay-at-home dad on days he wasn't working. Explain how involved he was with the kids and how much his life is now missed."

Oh, that's it, you want that in two or three sentences? Talk about an impossible task ahead of me. Would I remember everything he meant to our family? It had been twelve years since he was in our lives. He has missed so much. It felt odd to mention that John missed out on being the parent helper in the kids' preschool when they are now in middle and high school. How could I truly represent those 4,380 days without him?

Brielle would have to go on the stand, too. My other three would stand up and be introduced to the jury. I was hesitant to put her through that, but they reassured me it would be quick and necessary in our case. At this point, she was seventeen, so I felt she could handle it. My kids never liked the press or any attention about Black Sunday. They were just regular kids who wanted no attention put upon them. You would think they would be excited to miss school, but they all wanted nothing to do with the trial or the press that followed.

When it was time for her to testify, Brielle was great. She was stoic and strong. Her siblings had to introduce themselves to the jury and tell them their names. I felt terrible that they even had to do that. They should have been in school, laughing with their friends instead of introducing themselves to a jury in a courtroom.

When I took the stand, I was a nervous wreck. You never think you will have to put your hand on a bible and swear to tell the truth, so help you God. The experience was surreal; the questioning was nothing as I had imagined for the last twelve years.

"Name, who were you married to, and how was he as a father?" I had rehearsed this in my head for so long. I was going to be spectacular. I would get our whole story out with just the right emotion. But I stammered, "Um, Eileen Bellew, my husband, John... He was a great husband, I mean father." All these emotions got the best of me, and I couldn't think clearly. I had so much to say, but it wasn't coming out how I wanted. I felt so unfulfilled with this being just a formality after having waited so long for the world to hear me.

Then, it was the defendant's lawyer's turn. I clenched my fists, sat tall, and was ready to take them on. They introduced themselves to me. "We are so sorry for your loss of your husband and loving father." They did not ask me any questions, and I was allowed to get down from the stand. *Wait, what?* Where was the confrontation, my day in court? John's day in court? There was no closure. There was no climax to our story. I felt no relief. I worried and rehearsed this day for years to feel nothing. And John was still gone.

Each firefighter gave their account of the horror they endured that day. These testimonies differed from those in the criminal trial. They were allowed to be more expressive about their experience and to explain the after effects of that day, rather than focusing on the technical side of the criminal trial. I realized, sitting there and listening to them, that they, too, were experiencing their own PTSD. They have direct trauma while I am experiencing it indirectly, but we all shared similar roads ahead of us.

Once the closing statements were completed, I felt strange. That was it. For over a decade, the court cases had been at the back of my mind. They didn't rule my life, but I knew they would be part of it. Now, they would be complete. It's strange to think of something for so long and then have to let it go. In some way, it was the closing chapter of John's story. It also worried me that I would lose Brendan as my friend. This one event connected us, and now we will not really need to see each other. He is such a good friend, and I didn't want to lose him too.

It only took a couple of days for the verdict to come back. This time, there were no court officers or press outside. The judge read the verdict for both defendants. "Guilty." The building owner's insurance company and the City of New York were guilty. The jury had to decide what percentage of the insurance company would be responsible for and what percentage of the City would be accountable for. The jury awarded each of us an amount based on our individual cases. They could award plaintiffs an astronomical amount, but in reality, they never actually pay it. In our case, the total combined for all six families was $183 million, but no one received close to that amount. After the verdict was handed down, a different judge would ultimately decide an amount for each individual family.

We had to meet with a judge, who had not been in the courtroom during the trial, to plead our case for the amount we should be awarded.

I walked into his chambers and I was ready. Finally I would have my day in court.

"Come on in Mrs. Bellew, I am sorry we have to meet under these circumstances, and I first want to express my deepest sympathies for your loss."

"Thank you, it has been a long process."

"Yes, I am aware the court system can be a frustrating process. We are here to discuss the verdict, and I would like for you to have the opportunity to speak on John's behalf before I make my judgement about your case. I am sure your lawyers have told you that New York State law has a formula for how much the loss of a mother or father is given in a civil trial. Then, they calculate the child's age, and a number emerges."

"Yes, I am aware of New York State law, but what New York State law does not know is that my children's father was not a "typical" father. He did not leave in the morning at 6 a.m. and returned from work at 7 p.m., five days a week. He was their primary caretaker as I worked as a teacher five days a week. He was the one who volunteered in their classrooms, drove them to school, brought them to library programs, and took them to AC Moore to buy supplies for school projects. I am not sure if you are a father."

He interrupted, "Yes, I am."

"Well, then I guess I don't have to explain to you how much my children have lost, all the celebrations, all the teacher parent conferences, all the missed coaching opportunities throughout their lives. No money can replace their broken hearts. Their father was their everything just like you are to your children. New York State has a formula, but that formula cannot replace all that is lost." The judge sat back in his chair and gave me his full attention. He was listening but I knew what he was thinking. *My hands are tied, the formula is in place and was predetermined even before she walked in here.*

"Thank you, Mrs. Bellew, I will take all of this under consideration."

I began to walk out of his office and turned around to say one last thing. "Thank you for listening to me and I'm sure this is going to come out wrong, but I'll tell you what I really want: one more cent than the survivors—for principle's sake. We lost everything, and they are still living."

The judge nodded his head. He seemed to understand my point but the judgement did not reflect my point of view. I must admit, I struggled with other people getting awarded more money than my family did. I made that clear to the judge. I understand it's not a competition, but we lost everything. I'm not being insensitive to the care that the others need moving forward, but I guess I wanted validation that a loss of life is the ultimate sacrifice.

The newspapers never report on what you are granted, only what the jury awards you. The headlines read: *Jury Awards $183* *million to NYC Firefighters in Deadly Blaze.* There was never any follow-up to report what we actually got because it wasn't sensationalized enough for print. Instead, I walk into my local supermarket, and people think I have $183 million. We were granted a small fraction of the jury's award, but my goal was achieved. The kids could pay for college. Whenever college tuition is due, I remind them, "Do not take this opportunity for granted; your father sacrificed a lot so he could pay for your education." My kids get it.

The reality is that I went from being "not the suing type"… to suing to ensure that my children could pay for college. My mom understood my motive, but it doesn't change the fact that John's death has changed me in so many ways.

While it was revealed during the trial that the FDNY could not find a suitable replacement for the personal safety ropes from the time they were removed in 2000 until the January 23rd fires in 2005, after John (and the five others) jumped, the FDNY Safety Team's firefighters worked tirelessly to develop a new prototype of the personal safety devices. I will give the FDNY credit for moving so quickly after Black Sunday, so no other family would have to endure what we have. A team of brilliant people built the PSS (Personal Safety System), a harness system that each firefighter can now carry and easily deploy if necessary.

As with many tragedies, action is taken after someone pays the ultimate price. It gives me some satisfaction that John's death brought about a positive change in the FDNY. I will never know how many lives were changed due to this new rope system, but lives will be saved thanks to the six men who had to jump.

Brielle's high school graduation, the year of the civil trial

CHAPTER 27

Second Marriage

Inevitably, after I talk to someone about my life, my trauma, and my PTSD, they get around to asking me, "So did you ever remarry?" I always hesitate to respond. If I tell you "no," do you continue to understand my story? I fell in love with my soulmate, we got married, we brought four amazing children into this world, and then he was tragically taken from us on a snowy day in January. I then raised them on my own, always trying to give them the guidance he would have provided, and to fill the role of both mother and father in their childhood.

Or I could tell you, "Yes, I met a widower, we fell in love and got married." The reason I hesitate to reveal my second marriage is because I watch people's body language change: they relax, their shoulders drop, they smile, the mood shifts, and they appear to lose interest. They have checked out of my story because they feel the sad part of my life is now over. "Oh, okay, she found another man. She is happy, and her trauma is complete." I see the disconnect as they tune out.

People are not being malicious; it is human nature. People do not want others to be unhappy or needy forever. But grief is not wrapped up after a specific time period, and though we may have found another to grow old with, it does not magically make the loss go away. I am not looking for a lifetime of sympathy, but more of understanding. Understand that though my vows said differently, my love for one man never ended, and it will not end for Kevin either.

John was my soulmate, the person I was supposed to live my whole life with. When he jumped, our relationship did not end. It changed. I still long to be with him, to touch him, to discuss our children's lives, and to bring them up together. Every day, I wish I could get his opinion about navigating the lives of four young adults. I still mourn the life I thought I would have had, but you must pivot when your journey takes a different path.

I was a fighter and survivor, and over time, I was willing to get back in the ring. If anyone could take the blows, it was me. It was worth the risk to find love again.

Choosing to put myself out there was scary and took vulnerability. I was opening up my heart for a chance that it might get stomped on or, even worse, for something tragic to happen to the other person. When I met Kevin, I came with baggage: trauma, PTSD, anxiety, four kids and a lifetime of tragedy. But I also brought more empathy, life experiences, and knowledge of the world, which made me unique. The "package deal" I brought with me included four remarkable young people who the right man would be lucky to fold into his life.

As I've said, I struggled with the idea of getting married again. I don't usually care about other people's perception of me, but when it comes to this, I do. It's one of the reasons I didn't change my last name for the second time. I still wanted that bond with John, and as my children's mom, I felt the name connected us. Marrying my second husband doesn't diminish my love and respect for my first husband. It doesn't diminish my love and respect for Kevin. I hold them both in the highest regard and cherish our lives together.

My second marriage is very different from my first. I am a different person than when I first met John. Kevin is a different person than when he met Liz. We met in a different time and space, and it clicked for who we wanted to be in that moment and in our future. I was dependent on John, and he was an extension of everything about me. Today, I am unapologetically independent and focused on living a happy life at all costs. I was never going to repeat my first marriage, and with maturity and life experience, I wouldn't want to. I am lucky to have a totally different experience with Kevin.

Second marriages often require us to face different life experiences than when we were young and in love. We navigate the loss of loved ones and our own health issues. When I was faced with a serious health scare after a colonoscopy, I was grateful to have Kevin by my side.

"Meet me in my office; I'm going to get your husband," my doctor said. I didn't think anything of it.

"I do hundreds of these, and 99% of them are routine, but not yours, Eileen. I am certain you have colon cancer. Do you have a surgeon? You will need to get a Pet Scan by the end of the week and consult with a surgeon." She was so matter of fact about this news. She had no emotion, no apology. I sat stunned. Thank God Kevin was there, I couldn't hear anything she was saying. My only thoughts were about setting up a proper will. Kevin stepped up and began asking the questions.

"Wait, shouldn't you take a biopsy? Why aren't we waiting for that information? It is five days before Christmas; can this wait til after the New Year?"

"No, it cannot wait. I am 100% sure she has colon cancer. She has a large mass in her colon, and it will have to be removed."

"Can they just remove the mass?"

"No, they will probably take fifteen inches of her colon along with many lymph nodes to figure out the stage we are talking about."

I sat stunned. They are having a conversation about me, and I'm not participating in it. I don't have a surgeon—or a lawyer, which I will also need because the Will has to be finished before my surgery.

The next three weeks were sheer hell, waiting for the surgery and figuring out where my future was heading. They performed major abdominal surgery on me at Sloan Kettering Hospital in NYC in early January of 2018. Thankfully, the doctor was wrong. The mass was 100% benign, and there was no need to read my Will.

I didn't think it was possible, but in Kevin I found a new best friend. One who only wants the best for me. We think of ways to make the other smile, and just spending time together brings me calm and happiness. He is the only person in this world who compliments me in the best way I know. Our marriages are very different from our first ones, but there is no single way to have a great marriage. We click, and it is not lost on me just how lucky I am to get to go through the rest of my life with Kevin. I think he is pretty damn lucky, too.

Kevin's the voice of reason, and his calm demeanor gave some serenity to the household. He has an easy way about him and rarely blows up (though I believe his kids might have a different opinion). He was a welcome male role model and a needed calming force.

"Thank God Kevin came into the picture because we could at least see what a parent without anxiety feels like," I overheard while my kids were talking in the backyard. Though I laughed at this, there was plenty of truth to it.

"At least he can talk her off the ledge and calm her nerves every once in a while."

"He also doesn't mind picking us up when we are out late so Mom can sleep."

"Who are you kidding? Mom hasn't slept in years." They all laughed and nodded their heads in agreement.

"I'm happy we can see what a normal parent acts like."

"Do you think he tells her that maybe she shouldn't send us so many warning texts?"

"No way, Kevin knows who he is dealing with. Mom is stubborn. He lets Mom be Mom. We lucked out. Someone who cares about us and supports her."

"I wish he had a say in our discipline. I have a feeling some of our sentencing might have been a little lighter."

"Mom certainly isn't easy."

Kevin somehow understands how my brain works and what I need. He understands my thought process, my anxiety, and panic attacks. Life events made me independent. It scares me to think of giving that up. Though we are a couple, he supports my independence.

What helped me the most was that Kevin never tried to replace John. He is a fantastic father; my kids are lucky to have his support and guidance. From coaching, helping with homework, taking them to ball games or fashion shows, and becoming a cheer dad and late-night pick-up driver, he is a great role model for the kids to see what a dad is. I am blessed that he came into our lives. He did all this while still parenting his own three kids. His children were older by the time we got married, so they did not move in with us after the wedding. Kevin's youngest daughter was a high school junior, so they stayed in their house until she went to college a year and a half later. We made our two households work for the sake of our kids.

It is not lost on me how difficult it must be to step into this role. First off, the magnitude of taking on four children is an amazing feat in itself. It must also be challenging to come into our spotlight with all of the notoriety at times surrounding the remembrance of my husband. There are anniversary Masses, golf outings, and Memorial 5K runs in John's name, which Kevin attends and helps out with. Kevin honors my husband as much as we do. He supports all that we do to create a legacy for John. It takes a remarkable man to have another man in his marriage. Most of all, Kevin knows how to step back and let me parent my kids. Once I figured out how to be both a mother and father, I was not going to relinquish that control to anyone.

I now make decisions thinking of three people (me, Kevin, and John) and pray that it is the right one. The three of us are a good team. I want to help him in the same way with his kids. We are sounding boards for each other, but we also respect the other parent who is not here. We have clear cut roles in our decision-making and responsibilities to our own children.

Second marriages have their challenges. We share seven kids between the two of us; both sets were dealt a tragic loss of a parent and then asked to accept a new parent. We asked a lot of our children to not only take on a stepparent but also accept other stepsiblings.

We've had many bumps in the road as we've blended our families. I'm not sure if you could call us blended. We are still working on it. The truth is, I am not who they want as their mom. They want their mom. I understand that, and never wanted to take the place of their mother. Time has been our most significant ally in respecting each other. Time has a way of helping resolve struggles. Grandchildren help with perspective and understanding. Our grandchildren help connect our families and bring us joy. I hope that as our children parent and experience the undying love for their own families, their understanding of our journey will become clearer.

I still yearn for John, especially at times of celebration and loss, as I'm sure Kevin does for Liz. Of course, we'd like to celebrate our children's successes and struggles with the person who created them. Yes, our hearts grew larger when Kevin and I met, but the hole for each other's first partner is still there. I love my husband, am proud to be his wife, and am thankful I found him. I wouldn't change a thing about marrying Kevin. When someone hesitates to say they remarried, it is not because they don't love their new spouse; it's because they still love their first one.

In Ireland with Kevin and the kids

CHAPTER 28

Eileen 2.0

Five minutes before our Zoom call, I imagine Claire staring at her phone, seeing a calendar reminder pop up: Next Appointment - Eileen. I wonder if there is dread running through her veins. *Nice lady, but it's the same appointment every time.*

Once on the call, I shared a recent epiphany. "I was doing what you told me, I was meditating by the ocean, watching the waves come in one after another, they never stopped crashing onto the shore."

I was not going to stop until I got this explanation out; I was on a roll.

"But then thoughts of my kids came rushing in. Brielle was taking the subway home from work; Jack was in Germany; Katreana was on a plane to India; and Kieran was driving home on major highways from his internship. I hate relying on the rest of the world to keep them safe. My mind began to race like the waves coming one after another, crashing, turning, and pulling the sand farther and farther away from me."

"What was your body feeling?" Claire asked.

"I could feel my heart pounding, a brick in my chest, and I broke out in a sweat."

Finally, the perfect way to explain to Claire how I was feeling. After twenty years of my rambling on and on, I finally explained my brain. My thoughts were the waves, one after another, violently rolling around in my head. The sand was my children; as hard as I tried to keep them close to me, life was pulling them farther away. This panic attack would manifest into another sleepless night, as the panic would stay with me until bedtime.

"Are you done?"

I did it! I finally put into words my broken mind, and now Claire will get me.

"Yes, that's it, I think I finally summed myself up to you."

"Well, this is an elaborate, grandiose imagery that took over your thought process, and you made it bigger than life. You couldn't let it go, so it took over your brain and body."

"Maybe you didn't hear me, my mind was racing, wave after wave…"

"That is a beautiful metaphor," she said, "But it is just a metaphor. Whether the waves came crashing in on the shore or not, your kids are doing what they are supposed to be doing—living their lives. And as much as you think you have control over this world, you have none when it comes to them traveling around."

And she was right. Just like that, I came back to my senses. My PTSD took over once again. I invented danger in my head so I could prepare for trauma. I need to be ready for future trauma. Claire understands this. Claire has saved me more times than I can count. She understands the trauma and helps me navigate it.

Claire and I don't always see eye to eye. One time, after telling her a crazy story I made up in my head, she hit me with,

"Did you ever think that your inner fears are actually fantasies you want to come true?"

"What!? Are you serious? Of course, I don't want anything to happen to my kids. I spend every minute of the day protecting them and keeping them safe from all evil in this world."

"Of course, but if something did happen to them, then you would be responsible for taking care of them for the rest of their lives."

Then it hit me. I would have a purpose, and they would need me forever. I feared that someday, my kids would no longer need me. After their dad died, I gave up my career and dedicated my life to being their mom. The day will come when they will no longer need me in the same capacity as when they were younger. So, my inner demons thought of all these fears that may be deep-rooted fantasies. I am well aware that it is a sick concept, but I understand what my mind was doing. Someday, they will not need me, my biggest fear.

In 2023, I went back to the leather couch without children jumping on top of me, and the doctor prescribed Lexapro. This drug helped turn ocean waves into river ripples. They create calmer waters, but my brain will always be my brain. My thoughts will always be here to fight with me. I also decided to stop drinking wine since some suggest it might help quell my anxiety. My kids ask me if I'll ever drink again, and my answer is maybe. I can't predict what life has planned for me. If I ever get diagnosed with a terminal illness or make it to eighty years old, I might just crack open a cold bottle of Dom Pérignon and drink from sunrise to sunset. If you say never, God comes back at you with that "funny" sense of humor and surprises you with a doozy.

I would love to tell you that I figured out how to extinguish inner demons, but unfortunately, I still have them. They are not as all-encompassing as they used to be, but that is because I have done work with Claire's therapy sessions, learned breathing techniques, taken medication, and know how my mind works, which have all helped me calm my thoughts. I don't think I will ever be able to eliminate my inner demons, but being open about my story has helped. I hope my story helps you understand that if you have inner demons, you are not alone. We may feel broken, but there are plenty of things out there to help us rebuild.

Me at FAO Schwartz

CHAPTER 29

Psychology Of Grief

I remember my first year teaching. I was twenty-three and believed I would be the best science teacher ever. I was tough but fair; I connected with my students and cared deeply about each one. Sometimes the parents didn't approve of my toughness, and I hated it when they asked, "Do you have kids?" I knew where they were going with it, and I would internally roll my eyes, thinking to myself that there was no way that when I pushed a baby out, I learned everything you need to know about parenting through the osmosis of a placenta. Fast forward, and bashfully, I admit there was some truth to those words. I didn't receive a diploma when I was getting stitched up after giving birth to Brielle, but the world suddenly became a very different place.

I tell that story because the only other event that taught me more about human nature than having kids was after John jumped. I walked through the emergency room towards John, passing by hundreds of firefighters, and my world of human psychology and grief blossomed into a whole new understanding of myself and people. Before that, I lived in a bubble where others' actions didn't affect me. After that, I learned how helpful, strange, compassionate, unaware, self-absorbed, empathetic, insightful, clueless, and bizarre other people could be. I quickly recognized people's true selves and either embraced them or distanced myself from them based on whether I trusted their intentions. But more importantly, I learned the value of empathy and open-mindedness in understanding others' experiences. It's easy to judge from a distance. Still, when we truly listen and try to understand, we can bridge the gap between us and others and foster a more compassionate and tolerant society.

Science has proven that humans don't use 100% of our brains. We can continue making neural connections daily if we choose to learn. The power is in our hands to continue learning and growing. Sometimes, you are given opportunities for this growth despite not seeking it out. The death of a spouse is one of them. I was given the opportunity to make trillions of neuron connections through the interpersonal and intrapersonal experiences thrust upon me. I had the choice to curl up in bed (which I wanted to do every day) or fight the good fight and begin to see the world with new eyes. I started new relationships with people from whom I needed help more than ever before. It was difficult to accept help because I was inherently a giver, not a taker. However, I soon realized the importance of offering and accepting help and how it can be a lifeline in times of grief. It's a two-way street, and by being open to both giving and receiving help, we can navigate the complexities of grief with more resilience and understanding.

When you lose your soulmate, the depth of sadness is like nothing you have ever felt before. The loss takes a toll on you both physically and mentally. You physically feel sick to your stomach for weeks, and your muscles ache and tire quickly. Science has shown that grief can be exhibited in many ways. The expression of heartache is physically accurate. There is evidence that the blow of the adrenal hormone from the shock of your trauma can affect the left ventricle of your heart. So, the saying "broken heart" has some validity. Your brain is also affected by hormones that can rattle your neurons and disrupt other systems, such as your immune system, and your desire to eat or overeat. The constant fight-or-flight response that your body and soul experiences is unsustainable, so you quickly become exhausted.

Between the sheer sadness and the incessant crying, my body couldn't maintain homeostasis, and all I wanted was for my mind to stop working. Little did I know that trauma tears have a chemical makeup different from your regular tear production and might help you release hormones that help bring calmness back to your body. If I had known that, I would have stopped trying to suppress them and let the tear ducts do their thing. All this chaos in your body wears you out. I woke up daily with headaches. I walked around with stomach pains. I believe it was because my brain would not stop thinking. My brain was working overtime, almost like a muscle, and the lactic acid buildup caused me to have headaches, stomach aches, and body aches. It's a wonder I didn't get physically ill during that time, but I think my body was running on fumes, and somehow, my deep inner cells took over so I could survive.

Mentally, my growth was enormous. I can compare it to my first visit to Europe. New architecture, food, language, cultures, and traditions surrounded me. All of a sudden, the world I once knew changed, and I became aware of a whole new Old World. The age of the buildings, the cobblestone roadways, the slowness of the culture, and the overall beauty of everything left me dumbfounded. I realized that my surroundings in America are young, and everyone is constantly rushing and hustling to find the next best thing. Once I saw Europe, I couldn't unsee it. I brought back a new perspective on the world. After John jumped, I felt similarly. My understanding of grief and sadness deepened, and now I see people through a new lens.

After John jumped, I didn't know what I didn't know. I didn't realize how little I knew about human behavior. But that's the beauty of our brain: whether we want to or not, we keep learning and growing based on our life experiences. I was in sensory overload right after John jumped, overly aware of my own emotions and body. I found myself in awkward situations and constantly meeting new people, which wasn't typical. My brain worked overtime to organize all the latest information and stimulation I absorbed. I might not have acknowledged all the new information I was synthesizing then, but slowly, I began to make connections about people, situations, and circumstances that blew my mind. We had to attend ceremony after ceremony, and often, we were the ones they were "celebrating." I was invited to fundraisers I would never have been asked to otherwise. I met famous people like Denis Leary and Mark Messier. I was expected to attend memorials in Maryland and Colorado, in which the trauma and sadness were always mentioned. I had to put on a brave face and be cordial and appreciative to all attending. Of course, I was grateful, but my body wanted to curl up on a couch and mindlessly relax. Instead, I had to be friendly, witty, and an enjoyable person to be around. These events all added to my physical and mental exhaustion.

I learned so much about people and myself. I discovered that two types of people show up right after a tragedy. There are trauma lovers, those who yearn to be around trauma and feed off the crazy environment. There are also trauma helpers who aid people experiencing trauma. The trauma lovers are those who show up at your house first and want to be with you at all times. They feed off your sadness, and it gives them purpose. They love telling people they have spoken to you and are helping you. They want credit for every chore they do around your house. They bathe in your sadness and then go home and tell people how distraught you are. They are short-lived helpers, and after two weeks or so, they move on to someone else, rarely check in with you, and are the first to tell people how much they helped you.

Then there are the trauma helpers. They give you time to grieve, slowly move into your life, and help you without you having to ask. They figure out what you need and just get it done. They keep your life private and are in for the long haul. They don't want credit for any help they give and do not go around bragging about it. These people are my true heroes. It doesn't take long for you to see who is who. The trauma lovers think they are helping, but they are using you to fulfill their purpose. They don't realize they are causing another hurtful loss when leaving you after two weeks. Always try to surround yourself with trauma helpers. They are loyal and real friends.

Another lesson I learned about people after a tragedy is the difference between energy suckers and energy givers. This one took me a lot longer to figure out, and ultimately, it becomes a sixth sense you develop about people. When you are a sad story, sad people will find you. Some people like to engage with your sadness by telling you about their tragedy, almost as if it's a competition. These people are what I call "toppers." They love to top your story to make themselves feel more important.

At first, you invite those people in because misery loves company, and you don't want to have the saddest story. It was not a competition I wanted to win, so I encouraged others to be more tragic than my story. It helped me feel less miserable. But after a while, I had to remove myself from their negative energy because it paralyzed me. The energy suckers have good intentions, but they want to stay in the sadness for life. Energy suckers take something from you and ultimately drain you of your energy. It's not a tangible thing they need from you, but your life helps fill their drama, loneliness, and sadness, and gives them a purpose for their existence. They wallow in your misery to feed their dysfunctional personality trait, all the while draining you. These types of people are cancer to your already damaged psyche. They do not help you. You help them. They are parasites that you need to cut off. Once I recognized this, I was able to distance myself from them.

Luckily, there are energy givers. These are the type of people who radiate a glow of sunshine around them when they enter a room. The tone is productive when they speak, and you feel freer when near them. They don't weigh you down, and the air seems lighter when they are in the room. They discuss your trauma, let you speak and give good advice. Whatever they put out into the universe, you want more of it. I felt it in my body language around them that they positively influenced my life. Their optimism is genuine. Surrounding myself with authentic people with positive energy helped me feel I could keep going. Their perception enables you to change yours. It's essential to find people who are energy givers. The world becomes calmer and gentler when you are around them, and your energy level is never depleted. Over the years, I have worked to become an energy giver because when I give to the world, I get back twofold.

After John jumped, I found it difficult to ask for help. I didn't need help before and could handle most situations independently. But after losing John, I was drowning, and I needed a life vest thrown to me. I had to learn how to ask for help, which was a new concept for me. So when I began to sink, I just started paddling harder, but sometimes the waves were too strong. I began looking around and became resentful that no one was helping me. *Can't they see that I am struggling and need help?* Even though my vibe said, *stay away.* But I discovered that very few people just step in and help. You have to ask. People do want to help you, but only if you ask. They respect your privacy and independence. I shouldn't have been annoyed with people if I didn't tell them what I needed, but still, I was. What I took from this life lesson is that I should try to help people before they sink.

During my tumultuous rebirth into society, I learned that we must look within to figure out how best to help this world. I was numb after John jumped. I did this as a protective coat, an armor, so I could not feel my trauma. Many people are doing the same. We need to be courageous and open up our brains to feeling. Most of the time, it sucks to sit in sadness, anger, resentment, or bitterness. I did it for many years. And maybe those emotions were more manageable than the sadness, loneliness, and misery I was truly feeling. If we can acknowledge and dissect our true feelings and get to the root of them, then we can shift. My journey of understanding my feelings and the people around me has given me a fuller life. It allows me to be an energy giver and a trauma helper. By looking at the world through this lens, we can throw more life jackets out and save our souls. SOS.

People have been good to me, and I want to repay the universe. My growth mentally through this trauma has given me a gift of empathy. When I see a need, it is my job to pay kindness forward without expecting praise. If you need a pat on the back and recognition, then don't do it. I will not list what I have done, but I will mention that my mindset has changed. I think of what others might need and drop it off or send it to them.

I don't pretend to understand everyone and every kind of grief, but I have learned a lot. The journey of both physical and mental anguish is exhausting, but getting to the other side is rewarding. I wish I had been more open to professional help from the beginning, and to people in general. My new knowledge of human psychology has helped me in every aspect of my life. Generally speaking, most people are good; some don't realize how their actions affect others. Keep your mind open and protected from all types of people. We control who is allowed in and who is not. We have the power to dictate our journey.

Family on vacation 2023

CHAPTER 30

Positivity Of Tragedy

"At least the kids are young."

"You have so much to be still thankful for."

"At least you have the kids to remind you of John."

And the kicker that I hate most of all, "Everything happens for a reason." *Really. What reason can you give me that would justify John having to jump and him losing out on his kids' lives?*

Do people actually hear what is coming out of their mouths? Do they give any thought into what their words mean? I understand people want me to feel better, but their toxic positivity and lack of empathy invalidated my pain. I wanted to sit in the pain; I did not want to find gratitude in the situation. Don't dismiss my suffering; that is more painful.

Time is a gift in many ways, but it is most evident in grief. The magic of time helps heal. It may take a month—for me, it took years—but at some point, I began to come around to the idea that my tragedy could yield something positive.

During a particularly intense session with Claire, I found my-self engulfed in a whirlwind of despair, venting and complaining about the overwhelming sense of loss that had consumed my life and my children's lives. It was a full-fledged woe-is-me fest, a symphony of sorrow for my children, John, and the life I once knew. I couldn't believe this was my reality.

In her wisdom, Claire asked me a question that would change my perspective forever: "Do you ever think something positive could come out of your tragedy?"

At first, seeing positivity amid the raw emotions that slammed into me daily was challenging. I didn't want to believe that anything good could come from my children losing their father. But as time passed, I began to see a glimmer of positivity. If you look past the obvious and dissect what this experience did to us, you can find real-life lessons and reframe the trauma that could serve us well. Amid the chaos and struggle, I found a strength I never knew I had, a resilience that kept me going, and a hope that things would improve. It's a testament to the human spirit's ability to overcome adversity and thrive.

I underestimated myself before John jumped. I happily as-sumed a traditional female role at home and in society. After John jumped, I didn't have to choose between "male" and "fe-male" roles. I had to learn how to wrestle with my boys to help them release their pent-up energy. I had to care for the lawn, trying to seed it and cut it (that never happened; we still have the worst lawn on the block). I had to shovel the driveway after it snowed, dressing four kids so they could play outside while I did the heavy lifting. I had to learn the difference between W40-C and W60-C oil, so I didn't blow up my engine. I built all the Christmas presents and pitched wiffle balls to the boys while I was supposed to be making dinner (though they will tell you I never did). I had to remember to call my in-laws, who didn't feel like they heard from me often enough, to update them on the kids' lives and check in on them.

I learned how to balance a checkbook, but worse, I realized how much we owed on our credit card bills. I had never paid the credit card bills, so I didn't know how much debt we had.

Once foreign to me, these tasks are now a part of my daily life. My resilience in taking on new tasks and responsibilities was impressive. I had no desire to learn these new tasks, and yet they were essential to keep my house running smoothly. I had to adapt to my new role. It wasn't so much an adaptation but more a doubling of my identity.

My abilities expanded well beyond what I thought I could do. The stereotypical role I once embraced was acceptable, and if John had never jumped, I might never have known that we held a balance on our credit cards. But the point is that I now have new skills in my arsenal.

The term is post-traumatic growth, and my resume shot up ten pages. My old reality ended, and the new world became full of discoveries I needed to make to survive. When life gives you lemons, you make lemonade and learn how to mow, shovel, throw a wiffle ball, assemble furniture, and develop a new relationship with your in-laws. I expanded my brainpower and discovered more about who I am. By redefining myself, I grew far beyond my expectations. The more significant change in me was not the physical tasks I could now accomplish, but the mental awareness and growth I gained.

Post-traumatic growth is a positive change that was brought on by the experience of tragedy. Even with positive growth, it does not diminish the sadness that can lie deep inside. Two things can be true at the same time. My trauma will always be with me, but if I only allow it to define me in a negative capacity, then it will have more power over me than I want it to. As time passes, I can see the positive effects without dismissing my sadness.

Tragedy tends to give you a quick doctorate in human psychology when you are thrown into survival mode. But it also allows you to grow, learn, and become more than you ever thought possible. I learned how to read people and relate to them more positively. As I struggled with my inner feelings and raw emotions, I began to understand that others might be experiencing similar struggles. The world is filled with humans coping with their own trauma and feelings of despair and sadness. My journey has given me deeper empathy for people and an understanding that we are all doing our best with the cards we are dealt. So when my local barista snaps at me and rolls her eyes, I understand it is not because of my iced Grande Mocha order. It is all of the people and experiences that got her to this moment. However, I would genuinely appreciate it if she didn't take it out on my drink. I am already overpaying for my coffee.

When the lesson that "life is short" is taught to you at a very young age, it gives you a great perspective. Our tragedy created a stronger family unit than we might have had. My children understand that life is precious and can be taken away in a split second. Because they learned this young, we have a sense of genuine connection and are truly bonded by unwavering love. Only four other people in this world truly understand what we went through. We will forever have each other to lean on and be connected by this. I thank God daily for having these loves in my life and knowing that part of John will always live on. His positive light will continue for generations to come. My job is to set a positive example moving forward and to help them gain a greater appreciation for the value of their lives and the lives of everyone they encounter.

I could come to terms with my own growth, but it was harder for me to see it in my children. I've spent my life protecting them from this tragedy, but it was inevitable that they would feel it. It took years for me to see how this could be positive for them. This is the true power of resilience and personal growth in the face of tragedy, a beacon of hope that we can find light and transformation even in the darkest times.

I spoke to my kids about my feelings, my heartache, my pain, my fears, and my sadness so they understood that it was okay for them to feel that way too. I encouraged conversation about just how much it "sucked"! And I think I used just those words. Because I was tired of people telling them, "It is going to be OK." What I told them instead was, "It isn't going to be okay for a while, and if you need to scream, yell, cry, or have a tantrum, I am right here and might even throw a bigger tantrum than you." Showing their feelings was not a sign of weakness; it shows the struggle that will only make them stronger. I believe it serves them well for the rest of their lives.

If my brain grew from this tragedy, my children's brains grew exponentially. Children usually learn empathy while caring for an animal or after a friend hurts their feelings, not typically after a parent dies. My children learned empathy through watching their mother grieve and navigate the struggles in her life. They gave me patience without having to be taught how. They watched me be vulnerable, outwardly crying in front of them while missing their dad. I didn't have to explain every tear that fell from my eyes or each breakdown I had to them; they knew. The intuition they developed was unparalleled by most other children's upbringings. They recognized my desperation for peace and would curtail their behavior so as not to push me over the edge. My kids read me and, in my darkest hours, gave up their needs to help me through mine.

Each of my kids has developed and flourished with high levels of emotional intelligence. They developed interpersonal and intrapersonal intelligence as they watched me be vulnerable yet brave enough to rise again. This allowed them to see human resilience firsthand, a perspective most children don't truly experience until much later in life. This enabled them to be truly authentic humans, which helped them be good friends. These intelligences will allow them to understand and empathize with the world.

There was only one of me. That meant my children often had to wait for things they wanted and display patience. They waited for their drink to be poured into a sippy cup, waited to be the next to get dressed, waited for help with their coat or shoes, waited for help with homework, waited to be read to before bed, waited to go outside until after I finished cleaning up or making dinner. The list could fill an entire book. It was a learned skill on how to struggle and be patient. Struggling teaches you how to handle adversity, and when you figure out what your struggle is, you come out stronger on the other side. I'm not saying my kids didn't demand things and show impatience, but for the most part, they learned to wait. They had no choice. Patience is a valuable trait that my kids had to learn while growing up with one parent.

Right along with patience was flexibility. I remember one Saturday at an all-star game day at the local Little League field. Three of my kids had made the all-star team, which meant all three games were going on simultaneously. I couldn't be in three places at the same time, even though the fields were in the same complex. I tried to figure out the batting order, watched one kid bat, cheered loudly so my all-star could hear their mom, and then ran a quarter-mile to the other field before the next child got their turn to bat. I loved watching my children play sports; it bothered me to miss even one play. However, I didn't see much of anything, and I should have picked one game to enjoy among the three. My kids understood. Maybe it was because they saw me running like a lunatic between ball fields with sweat running down my face after the games. They appreciated my efforts and were flexible regarding their need for personalized attention. All kids want attention, but mine understood I could not be everywhere, so they had to be happy with what they got.

I also believe I gained a more profound spirituality through my post-traumatic growth. When you lose as many family members as I have, you can either feel alone on Earth or develop a different type of relationship with your loved ones. I have more immediate family and loved ones in heaven than on Earth. If I didn't have my spirituality, I would have nothing. I believe in signs from heaven. They guide me through this life. Once I opened my mind to accepting and acknowledging these signs, I began using my angels' guidance.

John sends us rainbows, my sister sends red cardinals, and my mom sends me robins. When they appear, our connection to them feels very real. This, too, is a positive trait. We have a great understanding of the bigger picture. We are here on Earth to live, be happy, and make a difference. If we are good people, we go to heaven. When we get to heaven, we have an army of people waiting for us.

Our lives are a gift. They can be taken away in an instant or a single flashover, so we understand that life is precious. My kids don't take this life for granted or waste it on trivial things. They recognize every opportunity that comes their way as a gift and prioritize all the life opportunities they are blessed with. They feel obligated to do something good in this world, to make a difference. Just like their dad did. They understand this is not an easy task; they must work hard in whatever they choose, and it may take years to achieve it, but it is worth the ride. My kids learned that at a very young age. It only means they have more years than most to make a difference.

John's departure shaped them into who they have become, and I would not want to change who they are today at all.

Embracing gratitude has become an important part of our lives. I spend as much time with my family as I can. We travel and try to experience this beautiful world of unique people and places. We appreciate each other, prioritize our values, and see every opportunity as a blessing. We recognize how far we have come individually and as a family and realize we are not alone in our journey. We have many angels guiding us through this thing called life. Most of all, we celebrate even the most minor accomplishments, and when at all possible, as John taught us, don't skip the dessert.

Eat dessert!

Working in a booth to support Katreana's movie

Family photo summer 2025

When I Get To Heaven

First off, let's hope the Pearly Gates will be opening for me and not those gates entering fiery hell. I have not always been perfect, but I'm pretty sure my life warrants infinite bliss in the afterlife.

I'm worried about John's disappointment in my relationship with God. He has to understand that God and I didn't see eye to eye for a few years. My connection to God was through John. After John jumped, I prayed to John and my dad instead. As the years went on and I began to see the good in the world again, I added God to my list of those I pray to.

I will have some explaining to do about the missed church visits, but I should get some points for all four kids receiving their sacraments, and for the few years I taught CCD religion classes. Ultimately, I raised four morally sound human beings who treat everyone with respect and kindness. Their values are rooted in being good Catholics and in always thinking of others. They had many reasons to doubt God's goodness, but they continued to believe in being good people.

I have learned so much in this life that God has given me. I hope I have done enough to walk through those Pearly Gates. I tried to live my life as a good person, while cultivating four people to do the same.

I eagerly anticipate my arrival in heaven. I will reunite with John, my mom, my dad, my sisters Terry and Kathleen, and all the other loved ones and beloved pets I've lost along the way. The prospect of these reunions fills me with a sense of peace and comfort. John and I have so much to discuss, and we will have eternity to do so. Where will I begin?

I can only hope it turns out like this:

"Eileen, Eileen over here! Welcome to heaven, Hon!"

I will turn around and recognize his voice, even though it has been so long since I last heard it. John will be there with open arms, and once again, I will see the icy blue eyes I have yearned to see since January 23rd, 2005. All of his features will rush back to my memory: his rosy complexion, his cowlick in his wavy brown hair, the scar on his cheek, the dimple in his ear from an '80s earring. Will he recognize me? With all of my wrinkles, gray hair, and extra pounds since the last time he saw me in person? Of course, he will; he has been following me around since he had to leave.

I have waited so long to ask him so many questions. Let me start with the day that consumed most of my life. "What were you thinking when you chose to jump? Did you know others jumped with you? Were you ever in pain? Did you feel anything when you hit the ground? When did your soul leave your body? Did you get to choose whether you would leave or stay?"

"I thought of you and the kids," he'll say, "and how I wanted to get home to you. We were going to go sledding until the flashover happened. I didn't have time to really think; the wall of fire pushed me. I really didn't have a choice, you know, I would have always chosen you and the kids. I gave myself a chance, the only chance I had—I jumped."

And just like that, all the years of worrying, all my speculations will be confirmed. "Thank you, thank you for trying to get back to us, thank you for taking a chance, thank you for always giving me the best of you."

John will say, "Remember, for me it was a brief moment in eternity, but for you, I had to watch you live it over and over every day. I felt your anxiety, and I tried to relieve it, but you are stubborn; you would not give it up, you held on to your fear as if you were holding onto me."

"I told you this could happen, John. I never wanted to be a front-page widow, all I wanted to be was your wife and mom to our loves."

"I'm sorry, Hon, I made a promise I could not keep; my life's purpose was bigger than the "me" on Earth. I needed to be an extraordinary father and husband, and the only way I could do that was to be in five places at one time, twenty-four hours a day. I watched over you all, and if I stayed, I would not have been able to."

"Did you choose to leave?"

"Those hours in the hospital bed, the day of the fire, I laid there evaluating our lives. God gave me a gift and allowed me to see how my life would have affected yours and the kids if I stayed. I love you and the kids, and I gave up my life so you could all have a life. I never wanted my life to become your burden."

"But I would have taken care of you, I would have done anything for you, you were my life."

"I know, and that is why I had to leave, as difficult as it was for me to see you suffer, your life would have been even harder if I stayed. I know it seems like we lost so many years, but we now have eternity. I was still very much part of your life and the children's lives. I witnessed every minute of every day of their lives.

I was here guiding, loving you all, and protecting you. That does not mean you skated through life; it means you lived it."

I'll finally get the confirmation I was yearning for all these years. John left because he wanted to give us the best life possible. Oh, what a sacrifice, one life for five.

So many questions, so many debates, so many afterthoughts we were going to talk about, but it all melted away; it did not seem to matter anymore. He never left me in my journey, which is all I ever needed to know. We will now parent together in heaven just like it was supposed to be. Our love story has reached its final, never-ending chapter.

One last question, "How were you ever able to watch over all of us at one time?"

"It wasn't easy, so I sent you Kevin to help me."

"Thank you, my love."

John and I in the beginning

Afterword

I started writing this book as a memoir to my kids to explain the history behind my actions. So, when I set out to write this book, I aimed to have it read by four people. I hope they read it someday and gain a better understanding of what I was going through, which shaped me into who I am and ultimately shaped who they are. We can only do what we are equipped to do. There were plenty of times I was not equipped to do much, but I loved them. I have put them through a lot. I have been through a lot. I hope they can see the common thread through all of the stories. The thread is the endearing love I have for them. I have made some questionable decisions in their upbringing, but I have done many things right.

Somewhere along the way, I realized this memoir might help someone else. I hope this book gets into the hands of others struggling like me. Maybe you will feel comforted that you are not alone. Maybe my stories are similar to yours; hopefully, one of mine will make you laugh. Something I may have done might point you in a better direction. I may have pushed you to search out therapy, change your therapist, or start medication. You may open your mind to look for signs from the universe to show that you are not alone. You may allow yourself to be vulnerable and try again at love. You may cut yourself a break and forgive yourself. You may know someone going through something similar, and you'll now better understand their needs. You may now understand that grief has no clock, and people need more time than society gives. We are all living beings with pains and hurts, and we could be kinder to each other.

My memoir evolved from an opportunity to explain my actions to my children into a book about living with anxiety. Anxiety has shaped my life. It has shaped my children's lives. I shared my story to help others who suffer from anxiety, too. I am not a doctor, a psychiatrist, or a psychologist. I am just someone with a story; one that is filled with trauma and anxiety, but also lots of love and gratitude. I live a great life. You can choose to get out of bed or roll over and put the blankets over your head.

I chose to rise.

Gratitudes

I have always said it takes a village, and truer words have not been spoken when writing this book. So many people have come into my life and my kids' lives who have helped us on our journey.

First off, a huge thank you to the town of Pearl River, where I grew up and where our kids grew up, too. "The Town of Friendly People" has always had our back and supported our family. John and I chose Pearl River because of the people who are always willing to help and step up. I will always be grateful for the people who make up this town.

To all the Starbucks workers, especially Alex, who listened to all my stories that did not mean much to them but made me happy to be heard.

To the FDNY, firefighters who will drop everything if we ever need anything. Especially the members of Engine 46, Ladder 27, Cross Bronx Expressway, where John worked most of his career. We will be forever grateful for always honoring John and keeping us part of your firehouse family.

To Chief John Sullivan, Mike Smith, and Dan Coleman, who checked in on our family throughout the years. And to John for helping me with the Fire Vocabulary.

To Joe, thank you for being my boss when I was sixteen and for being my friend who has helped me with the famous plaque dedication video and any other media help I have needed through the years.

To Brendan Cawley, who got me through many tough moments by making me laugh.

To Claire, for putting up with me for all these years and not getting mad when I heard you but did not listen. You have saved me from myself.

To all the teachers who touched my children's lives. Thank you for caring about them as if they were your own and educating them to the best of your ability.

To my beta readers, Christy, Katie, Nancy, Stephanie, Laura, and Margaret, thank you for all of your feedback and for making my book better.

To Lisa Lucca, my editor, friend, and life coach. She took a chance on this book and, with a lot of patience, saw its value and importance. I will forever be grateful to you for making my dream of four people reading my story come true and for convincing me to bring it into the world. Also, thank you to her team, John Edger, for book design and Laurie Macomber, for proofreading.

To John's parents and family for shaping him into the man he became.

To Kevin's siblings and parents, thank you for welcoming our family into your family.

To Lauren, Luke, and Leanne, thank you for sharing your dad with me and for giving him so much joy.

To Kate, Kristen, Christina, Kelly, Blaithin, Sam, Tommy, and to all the sitters that made up our village. My life would have been totally different without the care and love you showed my kids. You gave the best of yourself, and my children benefited from all of your gifts.

To all my friends who were once my kids' moms but are now my friends. You are all truly amazing people. And to all my friends who have contributed to our journey and have given me many memories of laughter and joy.

To Marie, my best friend, I could always count on to have my back and make me laugh.

To Kathleen and Terry, my siblings who are now with the angels, thank you for loving my children as if they were your own.

To Pat, one of the kindest people I know, thanks for being a great aunt and sister-in-law.

To Bill, thanks for keeping John's legacy alive through your tireless efforts to raise money and create the John Bellew Memorial Fund. You remained one of his best friends long after he left the living world and thank you for being a very loyal brother-in-law.

To John, one of the best brothers and uncles made. Thank you for all the rides to the practices and games, and for being a fan in the stands.

To Patricia, with whom I shared a room for twenty-five years, the person who has witnessed every part of my journey. My best friend for many reasons, I am so thankful you were always there.

To my mom and dad, who are with the angels, thank you for all of your sacrifice and love. You gave all of yourself to give us a great life.

To Kevin, who puts up with my uniqueness, loves me, supported this book, and has always been my biggest fan and my best friend. I love you.

To Brielle, Jack, Katreana, and Kieran, you guys have always been and always will be my everything. Thank you for accepting all my flaws, for giving me all your love, empathy, and understanding of the life I could give you. I love you more.

To John, my soulmate, thanks for keeping watch over all of us. Thank you mostly for blessing me with our four loves, who have given me purpose. Until we meet again...

About the Author

Eileen Bellew lives in Pearl River, NY, in the same house she purchased with her firefighter husband, John, after they married in 1995. She raised her four children in the home along with their dad, who is doing his part from heaven. Her inspiration for this memoir came from her daughter Katreana's screenplay about the fire that took her father's life. Her film, *Black Sunday: Trial By Fire*, is currently in development.

Eileen now lives with her second husband, Kevin, and their dog, Blue. Eileen has returned to teaching and continues John's legacy through their foundation John Bellew Memorial Fund. She is learning to be an empty nester.

For interviews and speaking engagements contact Eileen at eileenbellew.com. To learn about Kat Bellew's film project, visit johnbellew.com.